This Errant Lady

This Errant Lady

JANE FRANKLIN'S OVERLAND JOURNEY
TO PORT PHILLIP AND SYDNEY, 1839

Edited, with introduction
and annotations by Penny Russell

NATIONAL LIBRARY OF AUSTRALIA

CANBERRA 2002

Published by the National Library of Australia
Canberra ACT 2600
Australia
© National Library of Australia 2002

National Library of Australia Cataloguing-in-Publication entry

Franklin, Jane, Lady, 1791–1875.
This errant lady : Jane Franklin's overland journey to Port
Phillip and Sydney, 1839.

Bibliography.
Includes index.
ISBN 0 642 10749 1.

1. Franklin, Jane, Lady, 1791–1875—Diaries. 2. Franklin,
Jane, Lady, 1791–1875—Journeys—Victoria. 3. Franklin,
Jane, Lady, 1791–1875—Journeys—New South Wales.
4. Governors' spouses—Tasmania—Diaries. 5. Victoria—
Description and travel—To 1850. 6. New South Wales—
Description and travel—To 1850. I. Russell, Penelope Ann.
II. National Library of Australia. III. Title.

994.02

Designer: Kathryn Wright
Editor: Francesca Rendle-Short
Printed by BPA Print Group

Cover:
Amélie Romilly
[Portrait of Jane Griffin, later Lady Franklin (1791–1875)] 1816
chalk sketch
Reproduced from Portrait of Jane: A Life of Lady Franklin by F.J. Woodward
(London: Hodder and Stoughton, 1951)

Background:
Jane, Lady Franklin (1791–1875)
Extract from Manuscript Diary of an Overland Tour to Sydney 1839
Manuscript Collection MS114

Unless otherwise indicated, all of the images that appear in this publication are held
in the Collections of the National Library of Australia.

Contents

for Joe and Sarah

Jane, Lady Franklin (1791–1875)
EXTRACT FROM MANUSCRIPT DIARY OF AN
OVERLAND TOUR TO SYDNEY 1839
Manuscript Collection MS114

Preface and Acknowledgements

IT IS ALWAYS DELIGHTFUL TO SHARE AN OBSESSION. I have been cultivating my own obsession with Jane Franklin since 1993. Throughout the intervening years—in the rare and fleeting spaces between other commitments—I have been working on a study of her life, wrestling with the ways her eclectic and voluminous writings became vehicles for expression of a shifting, fragile sense of self. This work, still in progress, was supported in its early stages by a large grant from the Australian Research Council, and has been sustained by periods of study leave from the University of Sydney. For research towards that larger project, which informs my introduction and editorial work in the present volume, I thank Melissa Harper, Claire Hooker, Maree Murray, Martha Sear and Paul White. I am grateful, too, to librarians and archivists for assistance they have provided to myself and to my research assistants at various times throughout the project, including those at the Scott Polar Research Institute, Cambridge; Mitchell Library, State Library of New South Wales; La Trobe Library, State Library of Victoria; Archives Office of Tasmania, University of Tasmania Archives and State Library of Tasmania; and National Library of Australia.

The challenge of writing about Jane Franklin lies in the breadth of her interests, the varieties of her cultural knowledge, and the multiplicity of nineteenth-century imperial narratives into which her own story must be inserted. It has been a welcome relief, as well as an important scholarly discipline, to turn from my endeavours to track and express all the complexity of her life story, and instead give close attention to a diary that covers less than five months of her life, but is, like all of her writing, so rich in specific references and descriptions, so revealing of an historical era and place, as to be worthy of a book in itself. So I am grateful to the National Library of Australia for inviting me to edit the diary of Jane Franklin's overland journey from Port Phillip to Sydney in 1839. I am the more grateful because it has encouraged me to attempt something I have long thought should be possible: to edit one of her bulky and formidably wordy diaries, to prune away the excess of detail but retain the ironic humour and passionate love of observation that enlivens all her writing, and thus to enable her voice to reach and, I hope, captivate new readers.

Jane Franklin has become something of a boom industry in recent years. In editing the present volume with a view to its accessibility and general interest, I have been glad to know that at the Centre for Tasmanian Historical Studies, University of Tasmania, the massive project is under way of preparing all of Jane Franklin's Tasmanian diaries for publication in a complete scholarly edition. I have enjoyed conversations with Alison Alexander in Hobart and Maria Pia Casarini in Cambridge about their own work on her life in different contexts.

In preparing the present edition I have been particularly grateful to the National Library of Australia for allowing me to work from Roger Milliss' typescript of the original diary. My debt to Roger Milliss himself for accomplishing that formidable task and making it available to other scholars is of course immeasurable. In writing my introduction I have benefited greatly from the perceptive reading and valuable commentary on various drafts by James Campbell, Salle-Ann Ehms and Martha Sear. I thank Francesca Rendle-Short for her careful work on the manuscript and her insistent attention to details I'd so much rather ignore.

My last and special thanks are for Joe and Sarah Campbell, who have grown up with the shades of Jane Franklin, and who have contributed to my ways of seeing, knowing and writing in countless ways, inexpressible but deeply felt. This book is for them.

Amélie Romilly
[*PORTRAIT OF JANE GRIFFIN,*
LATER LADY FRANKLIN (1791–1875)] 1816
chalk sketch
Reproduced from *Portrait of Jane: A Life of Lady Franklin* by F.J. Woodward
(London: Hodder and Stoughton, 1951)

Frederick Strange (1807–1874)
JANE, LADY FRANKLIN 1842
chalk sketch after Thomas Bock
Queen Victoria Museum and Art Gallery, Launceston, Tasmania

'Behold Another Sheba Comes'

ND WHEN THE QUEEN OF SHEBA HEARD *of the fame of Solomon*
Aconcerning the name of the LORD, she came to prove him with hard
questions.

And she came to Jerusalem with a very great train, with camels that bare
spices, and very much gold, and precious stones: and when she was come
to Solomon, she communed with him of all that was in her heart.

And Solomon told her all her questions: there was not any thing hid from
the king, which he told her not.

And when the queen of Sheba had seen all Solomon's wisdom, and the
house that he had built,

And the meat of his table, and the sitting of his servants, and the
attendance of his ministers, and their apparel, and his cupbearers, and his
ascent by which he went up unto the house of the LORD; there was no
more spirit in her.

And she said to the king, It was a true report that I heard in mine own
land of thy acts and of thy wisdom.

Howbeit I believed not the words, until I came, and mine eyes had seen it:
and, behold, the half was not told me: thy wisdom and prosperity exceedeth
the fame which I heard.

I Kings 10: 1–7

In May 1839, at a fancy-fair in Sydney, Lady Franklin was handed a note that compared her to the Queen of Sheba, visiting King Solomon. It was not a serious note—the delivery was part of a fundraising game—but the comparison was significant. Lady Franklin's very presence in Sydney was something unprecedented, something amazing, and the colonists of Sydney did not know what to think. She was visiting the Governor of New South Wales, Sir George Gipps. She was staying at Government House, being squired by Sir George about the town, meeting the principal residents at carefully planned dinner parties, inspecting schools and prisons, asking searching questions and making detailed notes of the answers. She was doing all this alone, having left her husband, the Lieutenant Governor of Van Diemen's Land, behind her. Sir John Franklin, whatever the temptation, could not leave the vexing administrative matters that crowded his days and disturbed his nights to pay a visit to his nominal superior in Sydney. Lady Franklin, with typical enthusiasm, had determined to pay this half-social, quasi-official visit, believing that to do so would be of 'use' to her husband. It seems to have been her own idea: Sir George made her welcome, but he had certainly not invited her. To make the thing even more astounding, she had chosen to travel not by sea, but overland from the four-year-old settlement at Port Phillip, along a road still unmade and little frequented. She had travelled slowly and—so far as tough colonial conditions permitted—in style, with a heavy baggage dray and a light cart, three gentlemen in attendance on horseback, her niece as a companion, two mounted police escorts, a number of coachmen and personal servants, and a mountain of baggage, including an iron bedstead she never travelled without. The image of the Queen of Sheba, with all that it implied of admiration and irony, must have been irresistible.

Lady Franklin mentioned the note in her diary without further comment, but the image lingered in her imagination. Two years later she still recalled her embarrassment at 'paying a visit to the Governor (Behold another Sheba comes) and not to his wife'.[1] Her discomfort was all the greater because Lady Gipps was ill and confined to her room for most of the visit. If Lady Franklin (as Sydney colonists must have murmured about her) 'thought she was the Queen of Sheba', the idea did not give her unmixed satisfaction.

By the time of her visit to Sydney, Jane Lady Franklin had already attracted more public attention than any governor's wife in Australia before or since. Yet had she acquired no greater fame, her diary of the visit might, like so many of the private writings of women, have been lost to history. She lacked the aristocratic lineage of later colonial governors' wives, whose private papers are carefully preserved among family muniments. She had no children of her own to cherish her written words.

And as a characteristically modest nineteenth-century woman, she lacked the confidence in her own powers of observation that might have encouraged her to secure her words lasting significance by publishing them. That her diaries have survived is due to the refracted fame she later acquired through the heroic endeavours, and the single monumental failure, of her husband.

Sir John Franklin was not a natural-born administrator. After his ignominious recall from Van Diemen's Land, he was keener than ever to resume his earlier life as an Arctic explorer. In 1845 he commanded a major Arctic expedition which was expected to complete the navigation of the long-sought North West Passage. He never returned. For many years, Lady Franklin lobbied governments and raised private subscriptions to support searches for the lost expedition. When she could no longer hope for her husband's rescue, she was still determined to discover his fate and to secure his reputation as the first discoverer of the North West Passage. Her efforts won her a popular and sentimental celebrity as great as that of her contemporary, Florence Nightingale. The celebrity was sufficient to ensure that Sir John's niece, Sophia Cracroft, would devotedly organise and preserve her aunt's voluminous papers, intending (until her eyesight failed her) to write a commemorative biography.[2] In the early twentieth century, Jane Franklin's papers were deposited in various archives in Australia and England. Their placement was determined by her husband's public activities and his involvement in what is generally acknowledged as 'history', and her diaries were valued almost exclusively for what they told of his enterprises.[3] 'Take out whatever is of Arctic interest, and burn the rest', the woman who deposited the bulk of the material at the Scott Polar Research Institute in Cambridge told the archivist.[4] Fortunately he did not follow her instructions—but the scattered and fortuitous survival of the archive is a suitable emblem of the place Jane Franklin has generally held in history.[5]

Jane Franklin's diary of her visit to Sydney is a uniquely detailed account of rural and urban life in New South Wales in 1839. It has been plundered by many historians for its comments on individuals, organisations, education, science, architecture or art. It is, indeed, difficult to think of an aspect of colonial life to which Lady Franklin did not make some reference in the course of her travels. But it has rarely been examined for what it might reveal about its author. For this, Jane Franklin's own style of writing is largely responsible. She wrote relentlessly of the external world, with a cramped brevity that is hard to decipher, and harder to understand. There is little in her diary that appears to display or reflect upon an inner self, or to illuminate a unique personality. As autobiography, the diary is, on the face of it, disappointing.

But as feminist scholars in recent years have increasingly argued, 'autobiography' is not to be found only in polished published narratives. Such coherent 'lives' are indeed rarely the most appropriate form for narrating the fractured, cyclical, subjected lives of women. Diaries, in contrast, record the minutiae of lives otherwise effaced from the pages of history. They do so not in 'authentic' scraps of the raw material of a life, or transparent records of experience, but as carefully crafted texts in which men and women give order and meaning to their lives, and clothe their sense of self in language. A woman's diary can thus offer glimpses of the subtle shifts and infinite variety in her imaginings of a female subjectivity. Jane Franklin's descriptions of colonial life, precise, vibrant and exhaustive as they are, gain new significance if they are read also as evidence of her own fragile but tenacious sense of self. Viewed in this way, they become a remarkable display of the paradoxes of nineteenth-century femininity: a sustained testament to the enormous contradiction of being, at that time, both a lady and a clever, energetic woman.[6]

x　x　x　x

Lady Franklin's origins were wealthy, though not distinguished. Born in 1791, she was the second of three daughters of John Griffin, a silk weaver of Spitalfields, and his wife Mary, née Guillemard. Her mother died when she was three years old, and John Griffin brought up his daughters to study and appreciate the art and literature revered by their generation, to develop an informed understanding of the world through reading and travel, to espouse a fervent English nationalism and a Tory ideology, and to regard marriage and domesticity as the 'supremest bliss' of women. Educated at a boarding school for young ladies in Chelsea, Jane found her formal education inadequate, and struggled in the years that followed to extend her awareness of the world around her. Her life became an enthusiastic quest for knowledge, understanding and 'Truth'.

Her thirst for life and learning gave her in turn a deep love of travel. From the age of seventeen, Jane was able, in the company of her family and with their full encouragement, to indulge this love. Early excursions through England and Wales in search of the fashionable 'picturesque' were followed by a more ambitious tour of France, Italy and Switzerland that lasted over two years, from 1814 to 1816. Thereafter she made annual summer excursions with her family to the Continent, visiting Germany, Holland and Denmark. By the time she married Captain John Franklin in 1828, when she was nearly thirty-seven years old, she was a veteran of all the fashionable tourist sites of Europe. She had shuddered with ecstasy at the sublime splendour of the Alps, she had made the popular Romantic pilgrimage through the Rhône valley, she had measured out the classical proportions of the ruins of Rome. More recently, her steps had strayed as far as Russia. Marriage, far from confining her to a more domestic world, liberated her still further. At the end of 1829 her husband, now Sir John Franklin, was posted to the British naval station in the Mediterranean. Lady Franklin followed him and, when she could not be with him, travelled ever more adventurously and independently through Greece, Egypt, Palestine and Turkey—culminating her adventures with a boat trip to the Second Cataract of the Nile, which she undertook in the company of a handsome German missionary.

She recorded each excursion in minute detail. At the age of nineteen, she had drawn up an ambitious 'Plan' for the improvement of her mind, hoping to restrain the 'looseness' of her imagination by dedicating three hours each day to a rigorous course of reading and note taking. The Plan was designed not only to extend her knowledge, but to discipline her habits, harness her curiosity, and hone a cultivated intelligence—to what end is less clear. She had not fulfilled her program of study. But she retained a strong desire to 'fix' things in her mind, to convert knowledge into a tangible acquisition, and this desire is apparent in all her travel writing. Though in her younger years she dabbled in a Romantic style, with occasional exclamatory passages describing her own sentiments of dazzled ecstasy, she was always conscientious in her record of facts and impressions. In her diaries, data on crop yields and manufacturing methods jostled with the dimensions of ruined churches, records of distances travelled, and pen portraits of tranquil agricultural landscapes, ancient ruins, sublime wilderness or crowded city streets. Her descriptive pen was ever ready to pin the outlines and rudimentary qualities of each scene to her page, as though to render it ever afterwards capable of retrieval, and thus an addition to her stock of worldly knowledge. As years passed, the collection of 'facts' became more important to her, and she gave less and less space to her own subjective impressions.

Travel gave Jane some sense of mastery over her world. But it was not complete. She was, perhaps, too conscious of the deficiencies of her own education, too bounded by the limits laid down for female knowledge, too aware of her own temerity in venturing into the masculine preserves of culture and learning. She was afraid to be laughed at for 'frivolous scribbling', and vehemently denied any desire to publish her travel writing. She enjoyed the comforting solidity of a growing mountain of volumes containing the accumulated travels and wisdom of years, but she had no desire to assume the authority of a writer or teacher. Her love of new experiences never gave way to a wish to interpret or communicate: she remained an eager sponge, thirsting for knowledge, and determined to learn, to know, to see with her own eyes.

This intense desire often drew her beyond the boundaries of conventional femininity. She herself declared that her activity and adventurous spirit were nothing out of the ordinary, that she did nothing that was not perfectly possible for a woman to achieve, that she had, above all things, a horror of 'notoriety'. But her intense, unconquerable curiosity, her passionate desire to see and to know for herself, and her understandable desire to share that knowledge with others—not through public writing and education, certainly, but by offering helpful advice in a private capacity— led her to embody transgression almost in spite of herself. With staggering self-deceit, she downplayed her travel across five continents and her persistent 'meddling' with public affairs as proof only of her domestic attachment to her husband. But if she persuaded herself, she rarely persuaded others. By the time she was in her forties, her insistence that she was not in the least remarkable was becoming less convincing.

For a woman who shunned notoriety, Jane Franklin certainly attracted and held attention. She gained some public stature from her marriage to an Arctic hero—the man who was forced to 'eat his boots' to avoid starvation on his first, disastrous attempt to explore the north coast of Arctic America, but was lionised by London society on his return from a second, more successful expedition. Her independent travels in the Mediterranean had certainly raised some eyebrows. But until she reached Van Diemen's Land, as the wife of the new lieutenant governor of the colony, she lacked the status which would make her behaviour a matter of public interest rather than mere private curiosity. Only then did she encounter directly the consequences of being a 'public person'. It proved to be a less than happy experience.

×   ×   ×   ×

Sir John Franklin's period of naval command in the Mediterranean came to an end in 1834 and for two years he kicked his heels in London, waiting for the Admiralty to offer him a new post. There was little prospect at that time of employment in the area of his first love, polar exploration, particularly for a man of 50. An administrative post seemed a desirable, and more likely, alternative, though he had no experience of administration. In 1836, having rejected the offer of Antigua, he agreed to replace Colonel George Arthur as Governor of the penal colony of Van Diemen's Land.

Sir John and Lady Franklin sailed for Van Diemen's Land in 1836, and reached Hobart late in December, a few weeks after Jane's 45th birthday. They were accompanied by Eleanor, Sir John's 12-year-old daughter by a previous marriage, her governess, and two of his nieces, Mary Franklin and Sophia Cracroft (always called Sophy), who were both in their late teens. Included in the party were Sir John's aide-de-camp, Henry Elliot, and his private secretary, an old naval friend, Captain Alexander Maconochie, who was accompanied by his wife and their six children. All these people took up residence in the rambling, much extended, but still very cramped quarters of Government House, where an initial appearance of domestic harmony began to fray. Though never openly hostile during these years, the relationship between Lady Franklin and her stepdaughter was always tense. Sophy Cracroft, too, was increasingly at odds with Eleanor. After Mary Franklin's marriage in Hobart to the colourful John Price,[7] Sophy came to assume many of the privileges of an older daughter. Eleanor, already locked in growing rivalry with her stepmother, evidently resented the preference the latter showed for Sophy.[8] The Maconochies also caused problems: Lady Franklin, although initially very attached to them, considered that they showed moral laxity in the way they brought up their children.

If there was tension within the walls of Government House, there was more open hostility outside. Jane Franklin had never previously given Australia much thought, except to imagine it as a fantasy region of tranquillity and peace, 'where to breathe the very air is happiness'.[9] The reality, for the Franklins, proved otherwise. Innocent of political experience, Sir John found the muddy waters of colonial politics impossible to navigate. He entered a world firmly divided into two hostile camps. On one side were those who, from positions well entrenched in government, had implemented Arthur's policies, and had no intention of giving ground to a new and inexperienced governor. On the other were colonists who, after years of hostility to Arthur, hoped for new direction under Franklin. Franklin was unable, even if he had been willing, to upset the existing power structure. The Colonial Secretary, John Montagu, the Attorney-General and the Police Magistrate were all Arthur's cronies. Sir John never won their trust or loyal support, but the influence which, through their entrenched power, experience and skill, they exerted over his decisions ensured that he would swiftly become as unpopular as his predecessor with Arthur's enemies. Within a year of his arrival he found himself isolated between two camps, uncertain whose judgment or integrity he could trust. The looming depression of the 1840s, which hit Van Diemen's Land particularly hard, made matters still more difficult.

The behaviour of his private secretary did not help. Though Maconochie's liberal views quickly won him the support of the more radical sector of the community and the press, they contributed to conservative distrust of Franklin's policies. The assignment of convicts as servants and labourers to free settlers, Maconochie argued, was a form of slavery: arbitrary, unpredictable, and damaging to the character of masters and convicts alike. In 1838 he despatched a report on these lines to England. There it was published in full, and used extensively by the Molesworth Committee, which in that year critically reviewed transportation as a form of punishment and proposed the abolition of assignment. This outcome appalled the 'Arthur faction' who, like their patron, had looked forward to the continued prosperity of Van Diemen's Land as the 'gaol of the empire', with all the benefits of cheap convict labour for the landholding gentry of the colony. The affair caused great embarrassment to Franklin. The furore, and particularly Maconochie's irregularity in sending a condensed version of his report to a British cabinet minister under Franklin's official seal, when Franklin himself was unaware of its contents, left the governor with no choice but to dismiss his private secretary in September 1838.

Maconochie's friends leapt to his defence, and major newspapers for some time afterwards attributed the failings in Franklin's regime to the loss of his only intelligent adviser. Maconochie himself, unemployed but now committed to promoting his plans for a 'marks system' aimed at the more effective reformation of prisoners, actively sought support, patronage and employment by writing to friends in high places in England and elsewhere in Australia. His innovative ideas and his interest in reform struck a chord in England, where ideas on punishment had changed significantly since Australia had been founded as a penal colony. Franklin's position, vis-à-vis the colonial office and his own colonial administration, was awkward indeed. In a climate of rapid change, he found himself isolated, blamed or reviled on all sides, bearing the brunt of responsibility for matters far beyond his control.

By the end of 1838, Sir John was left with only one trusted adviser and ally—his wife. From the beginning, she had involved herself in his administration. This was partly because a woman of her temperament could not help but throw herself, wholeheartedly and precipitously, into the project of the moment. But she was also putting into effect her own views on marriage and the proper ideal of complete wifely devotion.[10] Aware of the enormous pressure he suffered, she did her best to alleviate it by any means in her power. He hated letter writing; she helped him compose and write difficult despatches. He needed to discuss problems of administration and policy; she made her own contribution to the discussion more valuable by reading all available material on the subjects at issue. He was unskilled in detecting his enemies; she tried to smooth the fraught relationships of colonial administration through the exercise of drawing-room diplomacy— and somewhat naively assumed, when Franklin's enemies paid flattering court to her and praised her intelligent understanding of their affairs, that she had in truth won them over. He was oppressed and vexed by the weight of administrative business and petty politics; she eagerly promoted causes she knew were much dearer to his heart. Certainly she valued these projects in themselves. But she valued them still more, and promoted them the more heartily, for the relief and refreshment they gave to Sir John, by placing him among like-minded individuals who shared his interests, appreciated his goodwill, applauded his energy, and lampooned neither his geniality nor his appetite.[11]

The Franklins had come to the colony full of enthusiasm for the governor's role of presiding over an 'infant Society',[12] and promoting education, science and culture. By the time she embarked on her overland voyage in 1839, Lady Franklin had lent her enthusiastic support to the fledgling Tasmanian Society of Natural History, and was drawing on all the networks at her command to drum up correspondents and subscribers to its proposed journal.[13] She was full of plans for a natural history museum, to be funded out of her own private means. She had bought land in the Huon Valley, where she hoped to encourage small-scale agricultural settlement by allowing respectable families to purchase blocks on easy terms. She had welcomed the ornithologist John Gould and his wife Elizabeth to Government House, and was vocal in schemes for new schools and colleges, and a horticultural garden. She had even tried to rid the island of poisonous black snakes, by offering a shilling a head for every snake killed. She was persuaded to abandon her scheme, however, when it became clear that convicts were neglecting their labours in order to pursue this lucrative pastime.

Whether she was making copious notes on prison discipline or interviewing candidates for her Huon Valley scheme, Lady Franklin strained every nerve for the good of her husband and the colony he governed. In her own eyes, the two were integrally connected, and therefore her work for the colony was the proper and innocent activity of a loyal wife. But the colonists howled their indignation. They already distrusted Sir John's efforts towards civilisation, science, learning and culture, which, they believed, distracted his attention from more serious matters of colonial policy, and were a waste of time, expensive, and perhaps patronising. Their distrust was compounded a hundredfold when they observed a lady taking enthusiastic interest. In this misogynist society, there was no place for a woman in public life. It was bad enough to have a youthful queen on the throne, far away in England. To witness the 'queen's representative' so actively interfering in all aspects of colonial life was infinitely more alarming.

Every transgression—and in colonial eyes Lady Franklin was transgression incarnate—was punished by ridicule. Her snake scheme was a running joke—with an unpleasant edge, made explicit when someone sent her an anonymous and obscene valentine, with a decaying snake's head protruding suggestively from the card.[14] Her intelligence, her education, her desire to promote salons and *conversaziones*, and her collection of fossils, specimens and curiosities caused many to regard her, with boredom or hostility, as a curiosity herself.[15] As an educated woman, a 'bluestocking', she became a stock figure of fun. Her interest in colonial affairs, her passion for taking notes and her love of travel attracted increasing attention. By 1839, it was an established fiction that she was 'writing a book' about the colonies. The idea was guaranteed to increase distrust. For a woman to contemplate authorship at all was suspect, but colonists' fears were also raised by the question of what she might actually say about them.

What most surprised the colonists was her mobility. At that time, parodies abounded of the intellectual, the domineering or the meddlesome woman. But there were fewer clichés available to satirise the traveller. What was to be made of a woman who so persistently left Hobart, with or without her husband, to tour the island and neighbouring colonies, simply in the name of curiosity? She had already visited the Tasman Peninsula, and gained considerable notoriety by 'scrambling up Mount Wellington', as one newspaper scoffed, 'and being in some way accessory to the sticking up of a pair of ladies' boots on a pole of one of the barren rocks of that region of storms'.[16] It might be thought a harmless diversion for a lady, less dangerous than taking an interest in colonial policy—less dangerous, even, than reading, thinking, or writing. But it was also less comprehensible.

In March 1839, startled colonists reeled under the announcement that she was to sail to the infant settlement at Port Phillip and thence travel overland to Sydney. The venture defied description, though the *True Colonist* did its best, labelling it after the event as 'her last wild expedition in the Australian wilderness', casting her venturesome spirit and intense curiosity as vagaries, eccentricities and the 'perversion of ordinary female qualities'. Seizing on a less hostile description of Lady Franklin as the 'Lady-Errant' from a Sydney paper, the *True Colonist* gleefully headed its article with a reference to 'this errant lady'.[17]

At the heart of condemnation lay bafflement. The press of the day could not understand why a lady should wish to travel overland to Sydney. Though the road was becoming more frequented, as land-hungry squatters seeking the rich pastures of the Port Phillip district drove their cattle and sheep southward, the country through which it lay was wild indeed. Outside the towns, a rough station hut was the most the party could expect by way of accommodation and, for several nights at least, Lady Franklin would have no choice but to sleep in a tent. No lady before her had completed that overland voyage. Dangers of every kind lurked in the wild country through which they would pass—threats to a lady's dignity, her modesty, her comfort and perhaps even, in the most fearsome imaginings, her life. Not a year had passed since a party of shepherds had been killed by Aborigines near the Broken River. In response, a series of police stations had been established along the route, but white intruders still trod warily as they passed. To the fear of reprisals from the dispossessed were added fears of attacks from disaffected whites: at the fringes of white settlement roamed parties of bushrangers, whose depredations formed a chronic focus for press indignation. Even if Lady Franklin could evade these shadowy menaces, and overlook the snakes and native dogs, she could not hope to avoid sights and encounters from which a true lady should properly shrink. She must meet with—even accept hospitality from—the proprietors of rough grog shanties; she would inevitably see scantily-clad Aborigines living in conditions of wretched poverty on pastoral stations; she must share her camp with men of all classes and conditions; she must, in short, brush against modes of living far removed from those expected of a lady.

Everything possible, of course, was done to protect her. In 1839, Queen Victoria had been almost two years on the throne. Even in the colonies, women were feeling the effect of a growing emphasis on domesticity and passive, modest womanhood, however impossible it might be to put these ideals into effect in rough convict society or the raw pioneering world. As the home came to be imagined as the one secure refuge for virtuous femininity, travel in all its forms assumed new dangers for women, and required vigilant protection. This was particularly true for ladies, and never more so than when the governor's own wife decided to travel, and to travel without the governor. So Lady Franklin was escorted by three gentlemen: Henry Elliot—once Sir John's aide-de-camp and now his private secretary; a former military officer, Captain Moriarty; and an aspiring young doctor, Edmund Charles Hobson. She had a retinue of servants, including her personal maid, and the maid's husband, who was Sir John's own personal servant. (She referred to both, confusingly, by their surname, Snachall.) She had her niece, Sophy Cracroft, for female companionship, and an escort of two mounted policemen to ensure her safety. Wherever they stopped on their journey, settlers and officials did all they could to ensure her safety and comfort, and minimise hardship: moving out of their own homes or giving up their own beds to her, inviting her to their dining tables or making her gifts of eggs or flour they could ill spare.

If a lady insisted on travelling through the bush, such efforts were taken for granted as absolute necessities. Lady Franklin could not be allowed to take her chances, as would any male overlander of the time, with danger and discomfort. She herself thought that one mounted policeman would have provided sufficient protection, but found in Melbourne that, as she wrote to Sir John, 'we were not to be excused from having two'. She was thankful, indeed, that some hindrance had saved them from being inflicted with a third.[18] But the colonists who insisted on thus supporting her also groaned at the cost. The *Australian* in Sydney (which wrongly reported that she had *four* policemen in her escort) was probably not alone in thinking that the police force 'might have been much better employed in suppressing the outrages of the blacks, or in hunting out the white vagabonds, who are infesting the country to the southward'. Who, the paper demanded, 'is going to pay the expense of this freak of Lady Franklin?'[19]

Though Lady Franklin herself did not explicitly demand this effort and expenditure, there was some excuse for colonial resentment. Certainly she knew that her travels placed a burden on others, but, powerless even if she had wished to change the conventions of the day, she accepted this as one of the many disadvantages that she must cheerfully ignore if she was to accomplish her aims. With courage and insouçiance she disregarded inconvenience, discomfort or danger to herself, and defied the growing conventions against female travel. With parallel insouçiance she accepted the knowledge that her enterprises forced her contemporaries to endure trouble and expense on her behalf. Her selfishness is, in this respect, almost indistinguishable from her heroism.

What remains unexpressed throughout her account is her own motive for undergoing all this exertion. The Van Diemen's Land press condemned it as a selfish whim, offensive, because it was unnatural, in a lady. In response to this opposition, Sir John and Lady Franklin maintained the fiction that her trip would be 'of use' to him, because she would be able to take notes on the churches, schools and reform institutions, on wool, cattle and agriculture and the management of convicts in New South Wales—to 'collect whatever information or suggestions may present themselves and strike her as likely to be useful in this colony'.[20] Even if true, it is not to be supposed that such a motive would satisfy colonists who believed that the governor's wife already took far too great an interest in colonial affairs. But for Lady Franklin it was a buffer against the accusation so often levelled against her, that she was acting only from motives of curiosity. Curiosity was undoubtedly the driving force behind her travels, but one she found increasingly difficult to acknowledge. A rare, glowing commendation in a Sydney paper ultimately declared that 'Lady Franklin had in view those objects possessed in common by every enlightened traveller—to make herself thoroughly acquainted with the capabilities and resources of this colony'.[21] But few would give the 'enlightened' curiosity of a woman such legitimacy.

There were other motives, however. Sir John wrote to his wife's sister, Mary Simpkinson, that the trip would also prove 'a delightful recreation to herself', one that she both deserved and needed after the stresses and strains of the preceding year.[22] During that year she had found herself exposed to the relentless ridicule of the press, and witnessed the first catastrophic upheaval of her husband's administration. The dismissal of Maconochie had had its personal as well as official cost. The whole Maconochie family had to move from Government House, abruptly terminating a relationship of friendship and confidence. Jane Franklin expended many tears and much ink in lamenting this misfortune, filling pages of her own letters to her sister with regret and anxious self-justification. Burning with the desire to solve at once every problem that beset her husband, frustrated at every turn by the powerlessness of her own position and the illegitimacy of her efforts, she was nervous, anxious, ill and depressed.

The novelty of travel offered physical and mental escape. Constant movement and a succession of new acquaintance, new scenes and new impressions offered some respite from the gnawing cares, political backbiting, sameness and insularity of Van Diemen's Land society, giving fresh subjects to her mind and pen. The rattling discomfort of the cart might cause her head to ache, but still throughout her travels she was remarkably free of the illnesses that usually beset her. The mosquitoes and fleas might irritate her and prevent her from sleeping, but their effect was more temporary than the real and imagined slights she suffered in Hobart.

Yet her old worries were not left entirely behind. Still smarting at the treatment she had received over her snake eradication scheme, she recorded with careful satisfaction any approving reference to it made during her trip. Conversely, she was wary of the attention she received in the Melbourne and Sydney press, since any report would certainly be relayed by the Hobart papers, which would not hesitate to add their own savage twist. She writhed when the gentlemen of Melbourne presented her with a ponderous, complimentary 'address', knowing what scope it would give to the wit of Van Diemen's Land editors. With similar feelings, she repeatedly denied to her husband an exaggerated press report that she had attended a session at the police court in Sydney. The Maconochie affair, too, remained close to the surface of her mind, and references to him haunted her diary and letters home. Impressions of all sorts—of people, places, pursuits and policies—were filtered through Lady Franklin's continued implicit preoccupation with the interests of Van Diemen's Land. A visit to a colony at once so different and so similar in its social, political, economic and administrative concerns could never offer complete escape or distraction—and yet the possibility of both continued to enliven her trip throughout. Anxious and weary though she frequently was, she was not unhappy.

✕   ✕   ✕   ✕

Jane Franklin's desires, anxieties and preoccupations run like broken threads through the diary of her overland journey to Sydney. The whole venture was recorded in a small, blue unbound notebook, approximately three by five inches. Her cramped, spidery handwriting filled page after page, her daily entries often dispersed and interrupted by pages of undated notes and jottings containing stray scraps of information. When this happened, she would helpfully head a new page 'from 17 pages back' and continue her train of thought unchecked. The pages are yellowed and frayed at the edges; the stitching that confines them in a single package is aged and frail. It is extraordinarily difficult to decipher her words, still more difficult to recover her narrative in the form and order in which she wrote it.[23]

That task was not mine. In preparing this edition I have worked from a typescript prepared for the National Library of Australia by Roger Milliss.[24] His careful and scholarly efforts stitched the broken loops and hanging threads, the patchwork of unmatched segments which was Jane Franklin's original ragged tapestry, onto a formed, secure and legible canvas. In his typescript Jane Franklin's original words can be read in the order in which she wrote them, as far as this can be ascertained, and with all their original detail, expansiveness, and random association.[25]

The present volume is a much pared down version of Milliss' typescript. Despite the brevity of her style, Jane Franklin's comprehensive coverage of all the details of her trip made her diary a bulky manuscript indeed. In preparing this edition I have tried to take the brightest and strongest threads and weave them into a more compact design. I have also created chapters to emphasise the natural divisions of the diary according to place. Overall, I have tried to preserve the character of the original diary as a day-to-day chronicle of travel through particular locations, complete with descriptions of topography, agriculture and commerce, local societies and their religious or political rivalries, individual citizens and their houses. On these terms alone, it is of considerable historical interest.

Lady Franklin's record of her trip has survived as a unique and fascinating social document of a colonising culture. Nothing escaped her notice. No detail was too small, too mundane, to be recorded. The diary contains a complex portrait of the inhabitants of the remote districts of New South Wales in 1839: the squatters and their wives, the workers and servants they employed, the publicans and storekeepers, the police magistrates, bushrangers and clergy, and the Aborigines, some accepting dependence and cultural dislocation as the price of survival on pastoral stations, others still fighting to protect their traditional livelihood by courage, stealth and skill. Accounts of minute alterations in the passing landscape jostle with details of crops sown, harvested and sold, of mails exchanged and delivered, of travellers seeking new lands and opportunities, of stories of the 'blacks' told in hushed tones over the campfire, of houses and whole towns built and rebuilt, of building materials and business ventures, of poverty, drink and crime. Captured amongst these descriptions are the hopes and fears, the anxieties and drudgeries of men and women who dwelt in makeshift huts and rudimentary settlements, far from home, friends and all the imagined bliss and evil of civilisation.

Upon her arrival at Sydney, Lady Franklin was installed at Government House, and the tone of the diary changes abruptly. But Sydney, too, is chronicled with an observant pen. Again, the preponderant theme is physical description, and the diary brings to life the bustle of building and planning in this still sparsely settled town: the churches, shops, hospitals and schools, the lighthouse at South Head, the grand houses of Tempe and Elizabeth Bay—and, at the other extreme, the bleak façade of the Benevolent Institution, or the grim Female Factory at Parramatta, where the women ate food straight from the table, 'exactly like brutes'.[26] Portraits of individuals are, in Sydney, limited to the elite of the small colonial society. Among these, few escaped the candour of Lady Franklin's lightning sketches, from the New South Wales Governor, Sir George Gipps, 'short, self confident manner, grizzled hair—small, sparkling dark eyes—does not look you in face', to young Captain O'Connell, 'covered with orders, & a ridiculous & offensive sight in the eyes of other military men, who, however, all think him remarkably handsome'.[27]

Lady Franklin had not intended to stay long in New South Wales, but various factors tempted her to extend her visit. At first, the ships on which she might have embarked were leaving all too soon after her arrival in Sydney, and she determined to take her chances on a later passage. At the end of May, her desire to visit Captain King at Port Stephens gave her an additional motive for visiting the established settlements on the Hunter River, and she spent over a week examining in her usual minute style the towns of Newcastle, Maitland and Raymond Terrace, and observing the efforts towards industrial development being made by landholders in the region. Finally, she was invited to accompany the Anglican bishop, William Broughton, on an inspection of schools and churches along the Hawkesbury River, near Richmond and Windsor. She could not resist the attractions or the flattery implied by such an invitation, and hastened back from the Hunter to be in readiness, only to find that Bishop Broughton was delayed in Sydney and unable to set out until some weeks later. The excursion, when it took place in mid-June, extended to a fortnight of venturesome travel in a picturesque region, on roads so rutted or boggy that once her maid was thrown from the box of the carriage, and once they had to take to the fields to get past a team of bullocks drowning in the mud. She even wanted to cross the Blue

Mountains, but abandoned the plan in the face of complaints from an exhausted Sophy and Mr Elliot. Back in Sydney, she fumed at a series of delays in obtaining a passage, and finally endured a horrific sea voyage of over a month, battling against prevailing gales and drifting far off course towards New Zealand.

In recording this epic adventure, Jane Franklin treated her diary essentially as a notebook, producing a compendium of often unrelated scraps of information. This was in keeping with her general habit in travel writing. Despite her enthusiasm for knowledge, Jane Franklin rarely ventured to express her opinions, speculations, or interpretations in writing. The judgments offered in this, as in all her diaries, are generally borrowed from guidebooks, histories or local inhabitants. Whether she agreed with them or not, she did not see her diary as a space for formulating her own opinions. She confined her attention to the external, the observable—to what could be 'fixed' on the page.

The original diary, consequently, contains much that would capture the interest of a specialist. A local historian would find a wealth of material in Lady Franklin's descriptions of the layout, inhabitants and early buildings of Yass, Goulburn or Maitland; an enthusiast of early postal services would find in her diary the names of those who managed the mails, the points of exchange and the frequency of deliveries; an economic historian might delight in her conscientious notes on the price per bushel for wheat and maize all along the road, on early experiments in agriculture and industry, and on the impact of the drought which in 1839 had gripped the country for three years. On the building materials and methods employed for early station huts she is richly informative; on the appearance of the bush, the density of trees, the variety of geological formations, and the different species of wildlife along the road she is incomparably specific; on the purchase, sale and exchange of horses *en route* she is an unrivalled authority.

Too much of such detail can become oppressive, and a proportion had to be omitted from the present edition. To omit all would be to destroy at a blow much of the charm—and almost all the content—of the diary. I have tried to preserve the rich texture of Jane Franklin's portrayal of a colony arrested at a particular moment of development: a moment of optimism for the future, in a society still built on convict labour and pastoral expansion, in which progress rested upon the sufferings of the chain gangs and the brutally dispossessed Aborigines. Those sufferings hovered, almost out of sight, on the margins of the well-regulated society Jane Franklin wished to see. More intrusive were the troubles caused by a three-year drought, and the anxieties of pastoralists over their insecure tenure of the land. But the catastrophic pastoral depression that would destroy the hopes of so many in the early 1840s had not yet made its mark, and the grandeur of half-built churches and suburban villas, the growing concern over education, and the diversity of experiments in agriculture and industry all suggest an overall confidence.

In choosing what to retain and what to omit, I have emphasised particular stories, bringing into bolder relief images that are blurred, tangled or broken in Jane Franklin's original. I have preserved the social vignettes with which, almost in spite of herself, she relieves her earnest chronicle. These bring to life faces, voices and personalities which would otherwise be forever lost to history: disagreeable Mrs Smith, her temper frayed by the incessant demands made upon her hospitality by passing drovers, but starved for human companionship and mollified when Lady Franklin takes notice of her little daughter; Mr and Mrs Hardy of Yass, with their absurd devotion to their flea-ridden cats; old Mrs Ready, with her sprained ankle and her fourteen grown children living nearby, 'dangling' a half-naked grandchild in her arms; and the nameless woman from the Isle of Mall with 'fine features & animated countenance', who has 'married to come out' and now looks as though she might be confined on the road as she follows her blacksmith to Port Phillip.

I have also preserved those entries which throw light on Jane Franklin herself. In a diary so firmly focused on the external world, such entries are rare. Her opinions, her thoughts, her own personality must be deduced as much from what is *un*written as from what is written—her character sketched in the space left vacant in her accounts. And yet her 'self' emerges from these pages: fragmented, elusive but surprisingly tangible amidst the preoccupation with what lay before her eyes. The sheer volume of her writing reveals the breadth and eclecticism of her interests; its minute detail displays her enormous enthusiasm; the voluble communications she elicited from experts in all fields is testament to the flattering force of her curiosity. More particularly, she reveals herself in accounts of her exchanges with individuals—her sense of affront when presented with an extortionate bill, her high-handed disposition of her servants, her profound sense of social obligation and responsibility, her frequent agonies of self-consciousness in a fraught social world. Such vignettes, whether self-righteous or self-deprecating, humorous or indignant, fleetingly centre her *self* at the heart of her own dramatic existence. And they become more frequent as the diary progresses. As the trip extended itself indefinitely, the diary, while never losing its character as a notebook of information, took on rather more of the role of confidant. Just occasionally, Jane Franklin found space for personal anecdote and the expression of personal feeling.

Amongst the jumble of impressions and observations there develops, for example, a fascinating account of the awkward pleasure of her relationship with the Gippses, on whom she three times descended at a moment when she was not quite expected and, for various reasons, not quite welcome. Lady Gipps paid her every attention possible, but for the greater part of the visit was confined to her bed, seriously ill. Sir George carried the burden of hospitality single-handed, and delighted Jane with his gruff humour—but she never got over her awe of his brusque manner, and wrote to her husband that though she could 'quiz' him she could not 'make speeches' expressing her sympathetic appreciation of his efforts.[28] The relationship seemed to encapsulate the ambiguity of Lady Franklin's reception in New South Wales. She was a governor's wife, visiting from a neighbouring colony, and on the whole the colonists of New South Wales vied to show her hospitality and do her honour. But all, from Sir George down, were baffled by her presence. Extravagant praise was underpinned by a subdued mockery; hospitality was generous, but not ungrudging. Jane Franklin, accustomed to ignoring all difficulties that might discourage her from travelling, would not be deterred by the recognition that she was causing others inconvenience, but her diary is marked with moments of profound realisation, accompanied by distress and awkwardness. The crisis of her visit came when she borrowed Sir George Gipps' carriage and then kept it waiting in the rain, to the ruin of its upholstery. His understandable anger, palpable and prolonged, caused her days of mortification.

Such moments of revealed sensitivity bring Jane Franklin alive, as a personality with her full share of human weakness. Other passages, conversely, betray a shocking insensibility. Her indifference to the discomfort and occasional distress of her maid, Snachall, is striking, and mirrors a wider indifference. Jane Franklin was acutely attuned to the trials of property holders, investors, educators and employers of labour. She was considerably less sympathetic to the needs and difficulties of the labourers, the convicts, the poor. Such interest as she took was patronising at best, at worst indifferent to the point of cruelty. She was at her most patronising, ignorant, and indifferent when she wrote of Indigenous Australians.

By nature, education and position an ardent supporter of colonisation, Lady Franklin had but little sympathy for Aborigines, whose efforts to defend their land and livelihood from destruction aroused the fear and hatred of the white colonisers. With mingled compassion and curiosity, she regarded them as miserable primitives, objects of scientific interest and sentimental regret. But she seemed blind to the material and cultural imperatives of their situation, and to their efforts to preserve their lives and culture with dignity. Her combination of curiosity and insensitivity was frequently displayed. At the close of his dazzling display of skill with the boomerang, she peremptorily demanded of 'Dabtoe, Chief of the Hoombiango' that he give her the weapon for her collection. Her diary records that he 'did not like giving it'; the telegraphic style leaves it unclear whether or not she overrode his reluctance.[29] But on other occasions her attitude was less highhanded. She was pleased when '2 Wollondilly natives' praised her courteous interest in their language and culture. '"You speak very well to me," said Ounong to me', she wrote complacently.[30] In this instance, scientific curiosity was combined with a profound sense of the obligations of ladylike courtesy to propel her towards the edge of conversation. As a white observer of Aboriginal dance, hunting methods and skills, and of their working conditions, poverty and dependence when 'brought in' to the pastoralists' runs, Jane Franklin provides an account which is revealing in spite of, or rather precisely because of, its wilful ignorance and prejudice.

But when she was herself suffering from fear, she was all too ready to record story after story that either denoted the savagery and primitivism of the 'blacks', or offered some reassurance that they would ultimately be civilised or 'tamed'. While her expedition wound its way from the Goulburn River to the Murray—a part of the road little frequented by white settlers and noted for its dangers—Jane Franklin filled her diary with such anecdotes. As statements of fact they are thoroughly questionable; as expressions of racism they are deeply disturbing. But as an illustration of what white colonisers assumed they knew, and of the ways they thought fit to behave in consequence, they are a necessary part of the historical record. Jane Franklin did not openly endorse the brutal murders of Aboriginal people that occurred so frequently during that period of colonisation. Rather, she turned a blind eye. She shared to the full the white fears that underlay the brutality, and had nothing but praise for the mounted police who provided her escort—a body noted even by contemporaries for their cruel treatment of Aborigines. To her they seemed 'a choice body of men ... intelligent, well behaved, active and efficient. They must be a blessing to the country which they not only protect but serve to humanize.'[31]

In this, as in so many other respects, Jane Franklin's diary not only describes colonial society, but represents a colonial *mentalité*, in which she was simultaneously an awkward anomaly and a typical participant. The very fact that she was thoroughly steeped in the culture she described sometimes limited her description. During her visit she generally employed the pen of a stranger, and thus recorded for posterity moments and objects that passed unnoticed by those who lived amongst them. But with the familiarity of a near neighbour, there was much she took for granted, and therefore omitted to mention. Individuals are casually named but not identified; stirring contemporary events are assumed but not mentioned; pressing concerns are given little emphasis compared with the detailed attention to the apparently trivial. As a result, many of her remarks float free of context and significance. In preparing this edition I have followed, therefore, two countervailing principles: on the one hand to remove the excess detail that detracts from the historical interest of this source, and on the other hand to recreate the wider canvas of history against which the blurred, fragmented images of Jane Franklin's tapestry can be restored to something of their earlier significance. The contextual material threaded through the text of the diary and endnotes is intended to help her writing to live again with something of its original freshness, immediacy and resonance.

Throughout her journey from Port Phillip to Sydney and beyond, Jane Franklin seized on words and glimpses, facts and opinions, conversations and experiences, and wove them into a tapestry of colonial life. On a canvas of imperial conquest and colonisation, anchored to a frame of nineteenth-century ideology, she wove her textured image, peopled with the figures so well known and so familiarly imagined in her world—ladies and gentlemen, clergymen and squatters, prisoners and 'primitives'— against a shaded background of distant plains and wooded ridges, creeks and mountains, sheep and bullock drays, crowded city streets and suburban villas, makeshift huts built for the day and sandstone churches built for the future. Other colonists perhaps thought that the centre of the picture should be occupied by a vibrant image of Lady Franklin herself, sweeping like the Queen of Sheba with a grand retinue to visit Solomon in the person of Sir George Gipps. But as Lady Franklin wove her tapestry, she was not the central spectacle, rather the seeing eye and listening ear, and the clever indefatigable hand which set all in place. She resembled the Queen of Sheba only in believing not what she had heard until she came, and her eyes had seen it.

×   ×   ×   ×

Note on the Text

The task of editing Jane Franklin's diary requires minute, subjective judgment. There is no core narrative here, no central concern that might be seen as the pith of the diary, to be revealed by paring back irrelevant or unnecessary detail. There can only be a careful selection amongst details of perhaps equivalent interest, keeping enough to preserve the texture and fragmented illuminations of the diary, shedding enough to allow those fleeting lights to gleam more brightly. Since most omissions and emendations are not shown in the text of this edition, I offer here a brief account of the principles I have followed in selecting material. Scholars who seek to use parts of the diary for detailed analysis and interpretation may wish to refer to the typescript of the original manuscript, held at the National Library of Australia.

I have tended to favour people over trees or buildings. Jane Franklin's writing and powers of observation are at their best when describing chance encounters on the road, and her vignettes of domestic and social life are probably the greatest aesthetic strength of the journal. These I have retained almost in full, while trying to keep enough of the physical, topographical, botanical, and architectural detail to show the breadth and diversity of her interests—and indeed of the colonial life she describes. I have kept many descriptions of landscape, buildings and street layouts, which convey the tone and preoccupations of her writing and give a sense of the particular localities at the time, but I have not reproduced the exhaustive and inexhaustible coverage of the original. In Sydney, where the round of calls became repetitive, I have retained all references to introductions and social events that are accompanied by pithy sketches of character, situation or appearance, but have omitted passages that merely enumerate calls or the guests at a dinner party.

In general, information based on hearsay has been omitted. For example, Sir Gordon Bremer's arrival in Sydney soon after her own, following his second attempt to establish a naval post at Port Essington, triggered Lady Franklin's interest. A significant proportion of the last weeks of her Sydney diary is devoted to elaborate detail on the vegetation, inhabitants and conditions at Port Essington, but as she never saw them herself they have been omitted from this edition. Conversations about mutual acquaintance who otherwise do not enter into this narrative have generally been excised. So too, for purely pragmatic reasons, have sections where the notes are so brief, scrappy or indecipherable as to defy interpretation. For reasons of space, two substantial sections of the diary—those covering a visit to the Illawarra district and the sea voyage home—have been omitted and replaced by a detailed summary account.

Throughout the remaining text, I have trimmed excess wordiness and detail from descriptions, to give them greater narrative cohesion and more dramatic immediacy. For the same reason, I have silently inserted pronouns, articles, and verbs where these are implied by the text. My guiding principle has been to improve the clarity of the account, while preserving something of the telegraphic flavour of the original. I have amended obvious spelling errors or slips—the repetition of words, or substitution of names. Particular spellings characteristic of the period— 'shewed' for 'showed', 'headach' for 'headache', 'lanthern' for 'lantern'— have been retained. At the time Jane Franklin wrote, few efforts had been made to standardise the transliteration of Aboriginal words and names, and her own attempts at spelling, inconsistent as they are, have been retained. Where the conventional spelling of proper names has changed over time—or when Lady Franklin herself was perhaps uncertain of the correct spelling—I have used, for the sake of clarity, the modern accepted spelling. Conversely, place names that were in use in 1839 are in themselves a matter of considerable historical interest, and I have retained the names and spelling Lady Franklin used, giving the modern equivalent name, if known, in a note. Spelling has not been altered at all in quotations drawn from Lady Franklin's letters or other manuscript material, so some inconsistencies do occur.

I have tried to improve the readability of the text without significantly altering its meanings. In general I have avoided using editorial marks to draw attention to changes within the text of the diary itself. There are, however, some exceptions to this principle. Where considerable passages have been excised that may be of interest to particular readers, I have made some reference to the omitted material in the notes. Where omitted material is essential to the sense of what follows, I have inserted a brief summary in italics. Square brackets are used to show editorial changes or additions only where the interpretation of a particular sentence was open to doubt. Where no interpretation could be made with certainty, I have retained Jane Franklin's own words and added '[sic]'. Punctuation has been silently amended throughout.

In the notes I have included explanatory or supplementary information that provides layers of context or alternative accounts of particular episodes. Several times during her trip, Jane Franklin wrote long, informative letters to her husband, and passages from these are included as they often add clarity or more vivid imagery to her bald diary account. For the first part of the journey, as far as the Murrumbidgee River crossing, Dr Hobson kept his own journal, and some passages from this, alluding to Lady Franklin, have been included.[32] Also included are a number of disconnected and undated notes, which formed a part of the original diary. Jane Franklin was in the habit of using pages of her diary to record unrelated scraps of information that she found of interest. Many have been omitted from this edition, but some have been retained because they expand upon persons or places mentioned elsewhere in the diary. Some of this additional material has been threaded through the text of the diary because of its particular relevance and the way it illuminates her sometimes spare narrative.

In addition, I have tried to give sufficient detail on individuals to identify them and explain circumstances that are referred to only obliquely in the diary itself. This has not been possible in all cases. But the bulk of the task was made almost absurdly simple by the scope, quality and comprehensive coverage of the early volumes of *Australian Dictionary of Biography*, to which I here acknowledge my debt.[33] Biographical information that is not otherwise referenced is drawn from these volumes. Other valuable works of reference that I have consulted throughout the preparation of this volume include *The Dictionary of Australian Artists* and *The Oxford Companion to Australian History*.[34]

Jane Franklin did not write for publication, and would be astonished to see her words now in print. When she did write for an audience, she vividly communicated her feelings and impressions. In her letters, we can often see the raw material of her diaries reworked with style and humour into entertaining narrative accounts. In preparing her diary for publication, I cannot write the stories she would have written. But I have tried to ignite the dormant power of her words, to captivate a new audience she never imagined.

William W. Knight (fl. 1839)
COLLINS STREET, TOWN OF MELBOURNE,
NEW SOUTH WALES, 1839 1839
watercolour; 49.2 x 39.3 cm
Rex Nan Kivell Collection NK142

I

Melbourne
1-5 April 1839

*E*arly in the morning of 1 April 1839, Jane Lady Franklin sailed from Launceston in the government brig Tamar. She was bound for Port Phillip, and intended to travel overland to Sydney and then return to Hobart by ship. She expected to be absent for perhaps two months, but in fact it would be August before the Van Diemen's Land newspapers could announce her safe return. She had three gentlemen in attendance. One was the Hon. Henry Elliot, whose father Gilbert Elliot, the second Earl of Minto, had entrusted his son when fresh from Oxford to the care of 'Sir John Franklin, one of the finest characters that ever lived'.[35] He had travelled to Van Diemen's Land with Sir John as his aide-de-camp, and had later succeeded to Maconochie's position as his private secretary. A natural history enthusiast, he possessed by the time he left the colonies a collection of specimens that filled Lady Franklin's soul with envy. The second, Dr Edmund Charles Hobson, shared his passion. Hobson was colonial-born, and had recently returned from university in Europe. Newly married, he was now seeking to establish himself in Hobart. The third gentleman, Captain William Moriarty, was considerably older and more experienced than either of the others. Emigrating to Van Diemen's Land with his wife and two of his children in 1829, he had lost all his possessions in a shipwreck. He received extensive land grants from the then governor, Colonel George Arthur, in recognition of his naval rank, and in 1832 was appointed port officer, first at Launceston and then at Hobart. Though he had since retired from this position and assumed others—as assistant police magistrate at Westbury and a coroner for Van Diemen's Land—his expertise was still much in demand.

Hobart's Colonial Times, *a stern critic of Lady Franklin's venture, condescended to approve her choice of escort, and to acknowledge in particular that Captain Moriarty was 'in every respect, second to no man in the colony, for such an expedition, and to discharge such a trust'. Sir John Franklin was equally pleased, describing Captain Moriarty as 'a most excellent person and skilful Bush traveller' and Dr Hobson as 'a young medical officer of great ability'.[36] Lady Franklin herself seemed especially to value the company of Dr Hobson, and from the outset of her journey quotes him as an authority on the geological formations and vegetation of the areas they traversed.*

Included in the party were Sir John's niece, Sophia Cracroft, and the two servants, Mr and Mrs Snachall. Mr Snachall, Sir John's personal servant, did service during the trip as an alternative coachman and general factotum. Mrs Snachall was Jane's own maid. The relationship between the Snachalls and Lady Franklin seemed on both sides tolerant rather than warm, and even tolerance wore thin as the miles passed. Also on board the Tamar *were the horses for the proposed journey, their odour permeating the small cabins of the ladies and accentuating their sufferings from seasickness during what Lady Franklin nevertheless described as a 'very fine passage' across the Bass Strait.[37]*

Her initial destination was Melbourne, the four-year-old settlement at Port Phillip. The town had been settled illegitimately in 1835 by separate parties of pastoralists and traders led by John Batman and John Pascoe Fawkner, who jostled thereafter for the right to be considered the founder of the town. Its official existence was of still more recent date. Police Magistrate, Captain William Lonsdale, had been the official administrator of the region since November 1836, and the streets of the city had been laid out in their famous grid pattern only since 1837. Though the township was still so rough and new, the discontent of its principal residents with the Sydney administration was already in evidence, and would lead to continued political pressure over the next decade for the creation of a separate colony. During Lady Franklin's visit she heard discontent expressed over such issues as expenditure on public works, the provision of convict labour, and the role and effectiveness of the Aboriginal Protectors recently appointed to the region.

The most interesting news was of the recent appointment of a new superintendent to the Port Phillip District. The hopes of several colonists that they might be chosen for the position were disappointed by the selection of Charles Joseph La Trobe, a young man who had never visited the colonies, and who would arrive to take up his appointment later in 1839. At the time of Lady Franklin's visit, news of this appointment was very fresh indeed, and she would later suggest in a letter to Sir John, unlikely as it seems, that she was the first to convey information about it to Sir George Gipps. Among the disappointed was Captain Maconochie, who appears to have hoped much from his friends in the Whig government in Britain. In Lady Franklin's eyes, his interest gave the appointment a peculiar significance.

The Tasmanian press had unanimously condemned Lady Franklin's departure, but the Melbourne papers offered her a heroine's welcome. John Pascoe Fawkner's newspaper, the Port Phillip Patriot, was particularly effusive. Lady Franklin stayed at Fawkner's Hotel, which—so the paper claimed—was the aesthetic and social centre of the illuminations and celebrations that greeted her arrival. Announcing on 3 April that Lady Franklin intended to 'honour Melbourne with a visit', and might be 'hourly expected', the Patriot added: 'This distinguished Lady should be received with all due respect by the loyal Melbournians, formerly Vandemonians.' Fawkner, indeed, sought every opportunity to build his own reputation by his flattering attentions to the governor's wife. Lady Franklin, unimpressed, showed more interest in the scenery.

Wednesday 3 April

Entrance of Port Phillip.

In these countries, said Dr Hobson, basalt by some convulsion has risen above the sandstone—the outer sand ridges on the coast of Port Phillip were, he said, basalt, crystallised and covered with sand—Point Lonsdale does not immediately answer to Point Nepean as it appears at first to do— Dr Hobson's brother is settled between Point Nepean & Arthur's Seat.

Enter heads at 11, having been 50 hours from leaving heads of George town—might have entered except for dark at 10 the night before. As advance towards Cape Shortland, look behind on Cape Lonsdale—on— down to dinner at 2—up again, were passing wide entrance bay of Geelong to West—to North of it over plain, see 3 or more peaked hills.[38] A grey sunless day—on right rising coastline is marked & red cliffs. Smoke ahead shows Williamstown, 9 miles from Melbourne.

Saw the *Vansittart*, which brought in [George Augustus] Robinson's family, went along side of her & spoke to the Blacks[39]—10 on board—all knew me by name 'John Franklin'—1 woman among them—Lalla Rookh was on shore.[40]

Today has been mild, and sunless, the sky and the water of the same leaden hue. This may have had something to do with the somewhat unfavourable impression we received of this harbour, otherwise a most noble sheet of water. The entrance is between sand hills partially covered with vegetation, and within, the shores are tame and monotonous.

Letter, Jane Franklin to
John Franklin, 3 April 1839

The Protector's hut was on other side of river, on elevation opposite Captain Lonsdale's. Everybody laughs at them & thinks it humbug. They wrote to Sir George Gipps to know what they were to do & he can't tell them—2 of them are vulgar illiterate men, of mean appearance & figure—Mr Parker declares that he has only to present himself among them, his bible in his hand, and be sufficient—Mr Sievwright is the only one who is a gentleman. They suppose he will not stop to be under Robinson. Latterly the natives have had a feast given them at Melbourne—the tribes from the Goulburn [River] have come up there—Somebody is said to have told the blacks the Protectors were going to poison them at the feast—a few were afraid to eat.

Jane Franklin, Diary, undated note

Thursday 4 April

1st day at Melbourne.

Calls of people—lunch—out in carriage—see Aborigines—end at Captain Lonsdale's[41]—not asked to dinner—none ready on return—wished for mutton chops.[42]

In the evening Captain Lonsdale called to take us to Corroboree. Mr Robinson said he would get together 3 or 400—but it was over when we went—seven tribes—crown band, opossum skins, ancle ruffs—They are great beggars—they like white money better than black—buy bread with it—very fond of bread. We saw the old Flinders people by the fire—Lalla Rookh is infirm—she did not like to speak of dead—liked Port Phillip better than Flinders—Did they like sleeping in house or bush?—in house—are in house here. Mr Robinson was very shy on ground—he did not bring up the protectors.[43] There were illuminations—squibs and crackers.

Lady Franklin offered rather more detail in a letter which she wrote to her husband over the following two days.

Friday 5 and Saturday 6 April

My dearest love,

Yesterday morning the luggage and horses were disembarked; and about eleven we left the 'Brig' in the Tide Surveyor's Boat, having previously sent up a message to Captain Lonsdale and Mr Simpson, and received a visit from all the Captains in the Port, (5 of them I believe) who came all in one boat ... About half way in our passage, we met ... [two more boats, one] containing Captain Lonsdale and Mr Simpson. Each of these boats fell behind and when we came to the confluence of two waters coming from different directions, and entered that to the East, called the Yarra Yarra, we held a short parley and proceeded as before.

The river is deep and narrow, the banks flat, in some places open and marshy, in others covered with the tree scrub ... We landed in a mud bank on our left, (ascending the river) and found ready to receive us the same gentlemen we thought we had left behind but who had taken a shorter cut by land; and many others collected there. Amongst these were Mr Robinson (whose family had arrived a day or two before in the *Vansittart*) and Mr Hawkey (of the *Fairlie*)[44] dressed like a wild German youth, with flowing locks, moustachios &c. A smart little carriage having three seats for six people placed one behind the other, with a pair of horses was waiting. The carriage bore on its panels 'From Melbourne to Geelong' with a Fox's head for a crest, and the motto 'Tally Ho'. It is the property of Mr Tulip Wright and is to start shortly as a regular stage coach also carrying the mail, for Geelong, a distance now of 50 miles, but which will shortly when the punt is ready to cross an intervening salt water creek be only 40. Captain Lonsdale informed me he had one room in his house at my service; but having learnt in my way that there was an Hotel with respectable accommodation I begged to prefer the latter as we could then all be together, a proposition which met with no opposition, and we accordingly drove to Mr Fawkner's Hotel where we were expected.[45] Mr Fawkner formerly kept the Cornwall Hotel at Launceston, and is the son of a man who came out on the first Convict ship 36 years ago. They are not people of the first respectability but are doing well in this money-making place. He is the Editor of a Newspaper, the 'Patriot', and his printing press is in the room adjoining my bed room.[46]

On arriving at the Inn, Captain Lonsdale asked me when I would like to receive visitors, and I told him at three, expecting thus to have an hour of quietness. Mrs Lonsdale however immediately arrived and sat with me about an hour before any one else came in. Then they came in, one after another for an hour and half, when finding myself and poor Sophy too, quite ill and absolutely unable to go through any more of it, I procured first some luncheon and then the same Mr Tulip Wright's carriage to be brought to the door in which we escaped from the rest.

We were driven round about and through the Town and outskirts and ended with Captain Lonsdale's residence where we left them and returned home as it was getting dark. No one had ordered dinner and it was a long time before we could get some mutton chops …

About eight or nine o'clock we went out to see Corroberry of the natives who are encamped in the outskirts and who, consisting of the tribes usually frequenting this port and of several more distant ones, are supposed to amount just now to about four or five hundred.

The Coroberry of one of the stranger tribes was over before we arrived on the ground. After a long delay during which the men were painting themselves the home tribes began their dances. For this purpose they had thrown aside their skins or blankets and were perfectly naked (except bundles of heavy fringes hanging round their loins like aprons), their breasts, arms and thighs, and legs were marked with broad white belts of pipe clay and borders of the same were traced round their eyes. Round their ancles [sic] they wore large ruffs of the gum tree branches and in each hand they held a piece of hardwood which they were constantly employed in striking against each other. The leader of the band was an elderly man, dressed in a blanket who stood with his face towards a group of women squatted on the grass, and who beat time with their hands on some folded opossum skins, thus producing a dull, hollow accompaniment. They sang also the whole time, in the style of the Flinders Island people, led by the old man.

Lady Franklin's late arrival caused some annoyance to George Robinson, who had hastily organised the corroboree for her entertainment. As he wrote in his journal:

Her ladyship having expressed a wish to see the Port Phillip natives' corrobbery, I attended to the natives camp and succeeded in getting up a corroberry, among the Waverong natives … It was the best corrobbery I have seen, but Lady Franklin did not come … Very late in the evening her ladyship and suite arrived … Her ladyship much pleased with her reception. Said to me it was very interesting.

George Augustus Robinson, *The Journals of George Augustus Robinson*, 4 April 1839[47]

With the exception of these songs there was little else which reminded us of the exhibition at Flinders.[48] The principal feat performed by these savages was quite indescribable. It was performed by stretching out their legs as wide as possible, and making them quiver with great rapidity, and as if they didn't touch the ground, a deception aided by the boughs round their ancles. One would have thought the trunk of the body a prop on which to rest, while the lower limbs were thus shaking, apparently without touching the ground. They did not all commence simultaneously, but rapidly advanced one before the other, never clashing and constantly coming forward—and reminded me in this and in the manner in which they addressed themselves in face to the spectators, of the kickers and jumpers and spinners of the opera boards. At last they formed a line close to our faces, changed their postures and measures, kicked up the dust with tremendous vehemence, turned half round and with bent bodies and with extreme rapidity slunk away. Mr Robinson and his family have not called on me, and he seems a little shy when I meet him, tho' always respectful ...

Mr Wright's carriage was again put in requisition yesterday (Friday), and we drove a few miles out of the town towards Mount Macedon on fine open grassy grounds of beautiful verdure in many places and very scantily wooded. These grounds fell down towards the South West in low shelving banks, towards a dried lagoon whitened with salt and which is skirted on the further side by what they call the South Yarra, the embouchure of which we had passed in our passage up to Melbourne. The scenery on the whole is somewhat novel to our eyes, long accustomed to our own mountainous country, dense woods, and bush-encumbered ground-surfaces. It is however less picturesque and much tamer.[49]

The weather yesterday was extremely hot, and Mr Wright's horses stopped short at every hillock ...

Captain Lonsdale received only yesterday a letter from Sir George Gipps begging him to do every thing for me. It seemed to give him increased zeal in my cause, but he said it was impossible for him to obey his instructions since I wanted nothing. He had received the first intimation of our intended arrival from Mr Forster a very short time ago.

Our first enquiries were of course as to the practicability of the road, and the fitness of the season, and as usual all difficulties vanished on a near approach. We could not possibly have chosen a fitter season of the year, nor have hit upon a more lucky moment, for rain had fallen and forage and water were said to be in sufficient quantity, and 'the rains' were not likely to come on for a month to come. We have not heard a single dissenting voice upon these points. Two mounted policemen, one being a sergeant, were in readiness, and an additional one was intended but something prevented.—I thought one quite enough, but we were not to be excused from having two ...

The horse bought at Launceston for the spring cart is found to be not fit for the journey, and another has been purchased at a higher price of Mr Wright.

What do you think is the farce that is getting up for me here? I heard of it last night, and when convinced it was not a hoax, was obliged to write an answer to an address which I am now expecting every moment to be presented to me before my departure.

We heard of it first from the master of the inn, Mr Fawkner, and late last night Capt. Lonsdale told me of it. We neither of us were able to say in plain terms how ridiculous we thought it, and the consequence is that we are all going to play with serious faces our parts in the Drama. I was asked whether I would reply at once or have it forwarded to Sydney. I preferred anything to having the subject revived in Government House there. I enclose copies for your perusal and admiration.[50]

You will see by the style of the address that neither Mr Simpson nor Capt. Lonsdale nor this person nor the other can have had anything to do with the composition. Mr Simpson I hear has so far interfered however as to prevent their adding to their promise of a public entertainment that it should be on 'a scale of magnificence'. Mr Elliot is to read my reply, having first helped me a little to write or correct it. It is much too grand for the occasion. Mr Elliot was decidedly of opinion that I could not decline to accept it, and he is the more likely to be right because he must hate so much the part he has to perform in it. The author of the address is, I am told, a Mr Brown, a merchant here whom I have not seen.

We have had the greatest difficulty to make Mr Fawkner agree to take any payment for the accommodation, &c. he has afforded us. 'The honor was everything.' This would not do, and at last Capt. Moriarty has made him promise to make out his bill, but this is only on condition that I will honor his 'library' with a visit. I suppose I must subscribe to the good man's paper in return, but as the other one is said to be the best of the two, this is a pity, and perhaps should lead to a double subscription or not at all. It is not probable that both will last. We hope to get to-day as far as Mr Thornloe's station 20 miles off, he is expecting us ...

Believe me, most affectionately yours,
Jane Franklin[51]

Saturday 6 April

I finished my letter to Sir John, and sent it by *Henry*, as *Tamar* was painting—cart packing. Address Deputation—it was long before it came. Captain Lonsdale and Mr Simpson came in first, immediately [followed by] about 12 or 15—saw Captn Bacchus amongst them—Captain Lonsdale said the inhabitants were desirous of presenting me with an address—if I pleased he would read it. I stood near table with Sophy on right & Elliot on left, my answer lying on table—Captain Lonsdale read, instantly blundering to shew he did not write it—the Military were left out & clergy put in—while reading I glanced at the party & saw Mr Simpson trying to look serious—gave my paper to Mr Elliot who read it loud, but several times boggled & blundered—if his object had been to shew he was not the author, nor knew before what he was going to read, could not have done it better—gave the Paper to Captain Lonsdale & curtsied to the gents in reply to their bows—disappeared immediately.

Unknown artist
ON THE MERRI CREEK,
NEAR CRAIGIEBURN, VICTORIA 1880s
wood engraving; 16.1 x 22.5 cm
Pictorial Collection S2905

II

Melbourne to the Goulburn River
6-11 April 1839

*A*t last she was free to pursue her journey.[52] She was troubled only by the prolonged absence of Dr Hobson, who had left them earlier to visit his brother at Arthur's Seat, intending to return in time for their proposed departure on Friday. They had already lingered an extra day, to allow the horses to recover from their sea voyage. On Saturday 6 April they left, trusting that Dr Hobson would soon overtake them on their way.

Saturday 6 April continued

Off at past 11. Cheering led by Simpson *con amore*. Carts ready & 2 mounted police, we got in, Captain Lonsdale mounted his horse, also Mr James Smith, Mr Darke,[53] whom I had not seen before, Mr McArthur, Mr T. Wright in a gig & Mr & Mrs Fawkner in their gig. Mr Darke advanced to thank me for sister &c. He is rather well behaved, his long nose tipped with sun. He offered his horse to Mr Elliot for journey, it was accepted as one might fail, & he went back with Mr Wright. Spoke to Wright to get specimens sent—bought a boomerang or curved flat stick of John Ball, a native dressed in European clothes—Mr James Smith came forward to thank me in name of Episcopalian committee for subscription to church (£10) asked for some time back by Archdeacon & secured now.[54]

The gents accompanied us 6 or 7 miles through choicest part of country, fine park-like pasturages, quite green, or more or less so—passed several water holes, saw some natives ascending up back of one—the greenness of the country proceeds from its having been recently burnt & some heavy rains falling since. The trees were gum, wattle and she oak—road perfectly smooth of colour of soil, natural.

We diverged a few minutes from the road to pass a small flock of sheep with one shepherd, a stranger in country probably in search of land— afterwards a tent & sheep fold of Mrs Kiddle? [sic] going up the country with sheep—country became more bare of wood—hills flat topped & bare—looked like cultivation. The local gents left us, & the carriages— Passed a large tent & brush yard on left & water holes or pond on right & beyond met 2 mounted shepherds & herd of cattle on opening banks of dell. We left the main road at entrance of this park-like dell & drove on higher ground to right, this being the nearer road to Mr Thornloe's where we were to put up, being 20 miles from Sydney road.[55] Road led over forest & plains, thinly wooded, with surface generally green & free from underwood, but thin & in small tufts—much she oak. We had views of Mt Macedon—the wood here green & rather thicker—crooked old gums, ground very rocky & road bad over it—The heat & hot handles in cart & the jolting made us very uncomfortable—Sophy got out & mounted Kitty. We heard the beautiful note of the Bell Bird which always denotes the vicinity of water—here it was a creek or suite of water holes, where we had to cross by a bridge to Mr Thornloe's hut. Saw in way a hawk, under tailed red—Mr Elliot shot a honey sucker different from those in VDL.[56]

Mr Thornloe's station just sold at 7sh 3d & 7sh 9d per acre. 13 or 14 men—7 shepherds at £38 each—2 hut keepers—1 bullock driver—16 bullocks—4 men & a boy besides who out of shearing & wash times have little to do—all VDL people—estimated costs £1500 a year—each man costs about £50 per year—one has a wife, who cooks for Mr Thornloe & washes &c—a young free emigrant by Princess Royal 7 years ago to Hobart, was brought here by Mr Thornloe. VDL shepherds & men are not so well liked as Sydney—they do not like hardships & moving—accustomed to comfortable hut &c—& seldom to count sheep—here they must be folded every night—2lb flour, 1lb. meat a day if rationed—some people here make men grind their own corn.

Sunday 7 April

Felt very unwell—great flies humming about my head prevented sleep after the sun had risen—got up & had breakfast in tent while Sophy went into hut & breakfasted with gents—at 11 or 12 went with notebook & Sturt[57] out of tent & found Sophy under small shade of cherry tree seated on opossum rugs—gents lolled there too. Mr Elliot skinned & stuffed the little honey sucker he had killed the day before & made mixture of arsenic, pepper, tobacco & burnt alum—I endeavoured to watch him but his large hands hid the bird—talk of sheep. Dine at 2—boiled fowl & haunch of mutton—gooseberry pudding of Mr Mundy. Soon after dinner delighted to see Dr Hobson arrive at house accompanied by his brother.

After visiting his brother Edward, who held a station at Arthur's Seat, and whom he had not seen for four years, Hobson returned to Melbourne. Crossing the Yarra on the punt he learned from a passenger that:

Lady Franklin had sent her carts on and would reach the Goulburn on the morrow. This I must say put me into a slight consternation for in the first place I had no conveyance to overtake her nor did I know anything about the Sydney road. This proved greatly to my comfort to be an exaggeration. Her Ladyship had started and got to Mr Thornloe's station on Saturday evening where she was to halt till Monday morning which enabled me to overtake her.

Hobson, Diary, 6 April 1839

Monday 8 April

It rained at ½ past 4, about 3 hours before were off. Dr Hobson put some of the lining fat of an Emu skin in a box, good for oiling & anything—is of bright yellow—a fat Emu will yield 3 quarts of fat—they are not very often to be seen—being very shy—way to approach them is the natives' way, covering themselves with boughs & moving very slowly. Dr Hobson said the natives' instincts & perceptions were remarkably quick—they knew all the habits of animals, their breeding &c—Dr Hobson's brother speaks their language well & has a very intelligent native—his brother is 22, has 700 or 1000 sheep & 150 cattle—is steady & active—has love of literature.

Killed Owl, Moorpork [sic] & Bell bird—latter yellowish green & bronze wings yellow beak & claws.[58]

Messrs Thornloe & Cobb accompanied us to Thom's in way to our day's station—over Mr Thornloe's open ground where Mr Cobb's heifers feeding, a dotted green hill in front, Malcolm's station & on. Fall into Sydney road at right angles & turn to right. Fell asleep, found myself on flat black soil, naked plains with small rocks in it extending to foot of pretty, lightly wooded hills, at foot of which is Mr Thom's station—The hut was leaning forward, the mud falling away. It is tidy inside— found Mrs Thom a broad Scotch woman, dark. Mr Thom is rather an ill-looking person, he is from VDL & retains property there. Mr Thom has 3000 sheep & a few cattle for home use—& raises corn for his own consumption. They have been here 18 months or nearly 2 years. When they landed at Melbourne in August 1837 there was not a single house built. They have 3 children, a boy at school at Hobart Town, & 2 little girls here, running wild. Being on Sydney road causes them much interruption & probably expense & they are going to move 2 miles back. A man has just received a licence to set up a public house here which adds to their determination as their men would be ruined by it. Had damper & butter & small biscuits mixed with mutton fat, light snack—I was offered cold meat & heard there was dinner cooking for me, but nothing said to me about it. He gave feed of oats and chaff to all the horses.

Mr Thornloe left us here—Mr Cobb went on with us. It was 14 miles hence to Green's outstation & 18 to the upper house where we were to sleep—country thin forest & a burned part not far from Thom's was very green and bare. I was on pony. About half way to Green's outstation, or at about 7 miles, we crossed a low part of the gentle ridge which divides the

> *[Before tea] we made a strong party to the Bell Birds. The two ladies accompanied by Messrs Moriarty, Elliot and Cobb sallied forth and in half an hour we arrived at the scene of action. I shot a very fine specimen of the bell bird ... A beautiful specimen of the podargus was shot by Mr Elliot and an owl by myself identical with the small one of VDL.*
>
> Hobson, Diary, 6 April 1839

waters. Being tired by the pony, I walked a little and then sat on front bench of cart driven by Snachall. Found I liked this seat much better than inside.[59]

Met Captain Smyth on horseback, gaily dressed in police costume, with a man dressed in green collar & front of native dog skin & straw broad brimmed hat—Captain Smyth came up in a very courtly manner to me who was ahead to pay his compliments. He had just heard of us—had been to Murrumbidgee about an unpleasant affair with cattle—and was going on to the settlement—he should join us on the Goulburn.[60]

The sun set behind a ridge of wooded hills as we approached Green's, where we disturbed the quails. He is building a new house of stones picked up nearby, the roof not yet shingled in—verandah along front—on entering see good room of 35 feet long—this is to be divided in 3. The house stands on the side of the bare hill whence can see over bare sloping foreground several ridges of hills, without being able to see into hollows. The situation is thought very pretty—it is decidedly best thought of as a run as any & the situation is admired—I should think it more fresh & airy than any other—the water is good but only in the waterholes. The sheep are taken to Plenty to be washed, 9 miles off.

Mr Green had slept the night before at Mr Thom's, where he is a frequent visitor & generally eats his Sunday dinner, going over on Saturday evening. Mr Thom sang his praises—also spoke of Mr Powlett as a gentleman—they were examples to the country—exemplary. Mr Green had been only 3 hours returned—he expected us, yet had nothing prepared— sheep however had been killed, but chops had to be cut from it for the purpose. After a long delay we sat down in his tiny hut on a floor of loose earth, with table fixed into it, carried off a bottle of his lemon syrup for our water—the tent was pitched for us.

Dr Hobson had no sooner supped than he began skinning. He said all birds that feed on insects are difficult to skin—those which feed on grain are easily skinned. He observed today a number of parasitic plants on trees which never exhibit them in VDL as Gum & Wattle—some trees exhibit several different sorts.

Tuesday 9 April

To Mundy's 9 miles, Hamilton's 5 miles.

Nothing interesting as we approach Mr Mundy's—saw Mr Mundy in blue jacket & plaid trousers—he had come in only 5 minutes before from his journey of 30 days to enquire into the affair of his cattle attacked by natives about 30 miles from the junction of the Goulburn with the Murray. Mr Mundy, with whom Captain Smyth is joined, was sending near 700 head of cattle overland to South Australia—12 shepherds under charge of

Mr Brock. The number of cattle was too large for the number of men, & the latter not carefully enough chosen. They had proceeded about 150 miles on their journey when they had an interview with natives—gave them a cow which had died. This seems to have whetted their appetites, for they afterwards speared 3 of their cattle, which frightened the others & they dispersed—266 were lost—Mr Brock went after them—had dreadful sufferings from hunger & thirst & obliged to kill his horse to preserve his life—was unsuccessful also. About 400 remain. Failing in supplies, Mr Brock could get no one of the men to go back & give information to Mr Mundy—they were afraid. At last one volunteered & told him—he is still going to send them. They cost him £4.10.0 per head, and he expects to sell them at South Australia for £10. He has left 170 here, where he never had more than 370—they feed on pasturages both sides of a creek extending about 8 miles.[61]

Mr Mundy formed a dairy excavated in a clay bank above water hole—the real clay forms the dressers, tables or ledges for milk pans—it is not now in operation—he used to send 100 lbs of butter a week to Melbourne where it was sold to a contractor for it at 2/3 a lb—showed us the wooden trays fitting into stout boxes in which they were carried—each pound wrapped in little napkin—contractor was obliged to send the napkins ahead. He is determined still to send same as before or to South Australia. He has been 6 months here only—repents having left the army—did not fear India—some of 21st [Regiment] were disposed to try doing the same—he had written to them to stick to their colours, or act first & repent after.

Mr Mundy lives like a gentleman in his hut—has 2 rooms—one a good sitting room—plastered inside with one small bed in a corner, a large table, easy chair by fire, shelves of books, writing table, slabs for sideboard & various ornaments—a square headed partition divides it from the inner room in which are a neat camp brass bed, dressing table, chest for washing &c. The roof is singular. On a framework of stakes or lathes in squares, are laid sheets of box bark, some as large as 14 feet in length—lapping over each other & lying like great sheets of lead. These are kept down outside by poles laid lengthways along sides & ends of roof both top & bottom—they are mortised in 3 places to receive slanting uprights & at place of junction a wooden peg or as it is called a rider is thrust through holes formed to receive it in the 2 crossing pieces of wood, locking them together—the upright poles from each sloping side of the roof rise above its top forming a cross & have a very pretty effect—a good chimney of stones in lower part, but upper or tunnel is not completed—is formed first by a barrel, over which is an old tea chest, & some moveable planks to shift according to wind. The erection of walls & roof of this building, including I believe the prowing & shaping the materials was the work of 2 hired travelling men for 21 days & cost £14 which was the price of the job. They found their own rations or rather bought them of Mr Mundy—which reduced their gain to £9. The bark is from the Box or Swamp Gum— Several trees as we passed on to Mr Hamilton's exhibited this appearance— they cut the outlines of the sheet of bark they want with a tomahawk or axe, & then with a mallet hammer over the whole surface which loosens & disengages it from the trunk. They then place the pieces of bark upright as if forming a hut & light a fire under to singe or heat them which removes their curve & flattens them. This barking operation can only be done in the spring. Mr Mundy's own men plastered the hut inside—this operation occupied a month before it was dry.

Mr Mundy has been here 6 months—he & Captain Smyth have not always quite agreed—latter is thought to be selfish—he was much absent, from his military duties, & would come back & find fault or give fresh directions—they do better now—Mr Mundy seemed to me quite an altered man—I used to think him a fine gentleman, fastidious &c—the stories, probably calumnies, I had heard of him were not in his favor. I now found him open, hearty, cordial, natural, with sweet expression of countenance. I knew that Elliot always liked him better than any of the 21st. He seemed cheerful & robust—he had taken 2 horses with him to his cattle company to their relief & in order to take them in fresh, walked the whole way & all the way back.

Mr Mundy accompanied us a little way on road to Mr Hamilton's to put us in the right way. Cobb staid behind—he did not take leave of us. He must have some practical talent, for Mr Mundy said he had tamed his cattle in no time—Cobb's hands are evidences of his works—black, blue, red, torn, pocked, scarred, broken. Beyond Mr Mundy's are pretty narrow gulleys & steep banks, bare at this season of grass & slightly timbered— no views scarcely, nor any extensive distances, owing to general level—& so few hills to ascend. We rose from this sort of up and down to a higher & flatter level—about 1 mile before came to Mr Hamilton's, got a view of long reach of water hole on left which looked like a river—a ridge of hills appeared over the level to East as we approached—sun was near setting as we arrived—but there was time enough to erect tent by daylight. Mr Hamilton is on the Sydney road, which we had left at Green's outer station & came upon again here. The main hut is boarded with bark roof, but not neat as Mr Mundy's. Inside, the rooms have canvas lining to keep out chinks.

Dr Hobson had time before dark to kill a couple of blue ducks, same as those in VDL, which were dressed at the house for our next day's dinner. He saw a wood duck also, one which nests in trees. I was surprised at the high flights of the black ducks—this is the case when they are disturbed. Dr Hobson shot today a snake in a water hole. They are not, as far as we could hear, common. Mr Hamilton had seen but one since he was first here.

According to his diary Hobson began by throwing a stick at the snake, but

contrary to my expectations he remained fixed and determined to dispute with me his right to the bath. I threw a second and third—he erects his head about a foot from the ground and as all the poisonous snakes do he expanded his head to double or more the original breadth. The evening was closing in and I had got off the road so that I had no time to watch more of this creature's habits. I therefore discharged my gun at him.

Hobson, Diary, 9 April 1839

Dr Hobson's geological observations are confined to the water holes, for the country presents so unbroken a surface that no section can be found. He found the water holes to consist of horizontal strata of basalt, except 2 which exhibited the anomalous appearance of upright or perpendicular strata of sandstone, evidently shifted thus. The loose stones on the soil, were always sandstone.

Mr Hamilton has been one year at his present station—He was previously 1 year at the Murrumbidgee and 4 in Argyll. They have 3000 sheep, 150 head of cattle, 11 horses. He grows grain sufficient for consumption—gave feed of oats & straw to all our horses. They have 1 boy of 4 years old. Paid £10 for licence—have paid £45 for licences having 2 stations—thought it hard for this not to be preserved from being intruded on & very pressed in by neighbours on all sides.[62] This run not sufficient & he was obliged to go away and seek for another. When first came a year ago, had only 2 neighbours—now they were on all sides—none good but Captain Smyth's or Mundy's—Mr Wills encroaches on their run—Colonel White has diseased sheep with catarrh. Found newly arrived Irish female servant who with her husband, a shepherd & 2 children (boy learning to be useful in field, girl of 10 washes up & waits) are paid £45 per annum— are engaged for 2 years. Mr Hamilton was an overseer in VDL and has married since he left. He bears a high character.

Wednesday 10 April

5th day 22 miles to the Goulburn.

Dr Hobson shot a beautiful crane before breakfast. Had mutton chops & eggs—took both mutton & eggs away with us as there will be none at night station on the Goulburn. Mr Hamilton would not let us pay for them. We joked Dr Hobson at breakfast. Rising up at one end of his wooden bench, he tipped Mr Elliot down on other—[I] said he was a theorist not a practical philosopher. However, he might be a practical joker. When a man had got Dr's degrees & a wife [he said], 'twas time to leave off practical jokes. Off at 8—distance today 22 miles divided in 10 & 12 by watering place at Stony Creek. Over scanty forest ground, about 4 miles bad hillocky road, dead men's graves— came to chain of fine water holes

I took my gun before breakfast intending to go in search of duck but I was delighted to see perched on a tree over a hole close to the house a beautiful crane. I succeeded in killing him without doing any injury.

Hobson, Diary, 10 April 1839

in bottom of gully. Mr Thomas Wills' station here—afterwards met a flock of his sheep with a shepherd, feeding in compact square in a place where something green coming up but which did not appear to be grass. Continued on, scanty forest not very interesting—Jack Iodine was not used & 3 horses put in the cart, so that 2 gents walked—generally Moriarty & Dr—both the latter & Elliot had shots. Mr Elliot shot a beautiful kingfisher—came to the water hole called Stony Creek, mostly dry—the first that had water we stopped at & encamped.

We arrived about 11—had tea, the cold duck killed & dressed last night, & the men had mutton cut off the half sheep given by Mr Hamilton. In our way thro' the monotonous forest beyond, in which the trees were thicker than usual, with some undergrowth, road running close between their trunks, we saw numerous parasitic plants which as Dr Hobson had observed before are peculiar to the trees here tho' not seen in similar trees in VDL. We observed notches or holes in several tall trees made with stone by natives for climbing—no branches till top—Dr hurt his foot with his boot & went in cart; Sophy & I divided pony.

Arrived about 5 or earlier at [John] Clarke's cattle station on left bank of Goulburn. His wife has 3 children—she has never been well since she had her first child. He keeps a public house, sells spirits, wines & salt meat, beef—he furnishes the police station adjoining with rations, under Mr Batman the contractor. He kills a bullock about once a month—they eat fresh what they can and salt the rest. In summer they are obliged to do this immediately, in winter the meat keeps a week. There are 5 policeman here, 4 men & sergeant. The latter is one of the most ridiculous dandies ever seen.

Clarke would not make his inn answer if he did not join it to other things—he said in answer to my question that on an average only one person, or not one person, passed to or fro in a day—till yesterday had not seen anybody for 4 or 5 weeks except the 2 postmen who meet here. The site of this place is laid out for a township, to be called Mitchell's town.

Later, from their halfway camp on the Murray, Lady Franklin wrote to her husband a cheerful account of their travels and the good condition of the horses to that point:

The horses are still fresh and are only galled a little by their collars, so as to require indulgent management. Mr Elliot's Belladonna has for several days borne the lady's saddle and the weight of one or other of us, generally Sophy. Except when the day's journey exceeds 12 or 15 miles, I prefer the cart, where I sit upon the narrow bench in front at the side of the driver, holding myself in in bad places as well as I may, and jumping off at many of the precipitous water dykes where a false step is more likely to happen.

You would be pleased to see the care with which the heavy cart is held back on the precipitous, tho' sometimes tortuous descents of these natural bridges, and of the skill and spirit with which the 3 and sometimes 4 horses one before the other are made to twist about up the steep sides, or if need be, breast them in a straight line with an impetus calculated for the occasion. Sheldrake (otherwise Sam) our excellent prisoner driver, declares that our appointments, carts, horses, and all are worthy of all admiration—nothing like them could have been had at Melbourne. We have perhaps however a horse or two too few. We could ill have spared Darke, tho' the possession of him is only a lucky accident—and had the gentlemen all required to ride the stud would not have been sufficient. Jack Iodine has an easy time of it; his good natured master leaves him day after day to be led by one of our military attendants.

Letter, Jane Franklin to John Franklin, 20 April 1839

A ford is above the house a little way for carts, & a little way below is a punt & dragging rope for passengers—descent of bank at both places very bad—banks are sand & steep.

Weighed our provisions at Clarke's as heard could perhaps not get more for 3 weeks till arrived at Murrumbidgee—thought they would suffice but bought 6 additional bushels of oats which with 3 already make 9.

We pitched our tent in mid distance from the huts as feared should be disturbed by noise of people—a man named Lawson from VDL was going with 1000 sheep to Melbourne. We were right—at night the 2 postmen became drunk & others also—fires were lighted on the bank of the river and guns fired (all it was said in my honour)—drinking & swearing went on in the house till a late hour.

The party halted for a day to rest and refresh the horses. Dr Hobson made his natural history notes, skinned his crane and wrote to his wife Margaret. Sophy and Lady Franklin wrote their letters, notes and journals.

Thursday 11 April

During the day we found no shade. We descended from the flat down a steep bank to a lower level on which is the nearest bank of the stream, and some fine gum trees. Among these trees Sophy & I sat with our writing, in the shade not of trees, but of boughs—for the sun is let in in a dozen places in every tree—we were obliged to be constantly shifting—In the evening we took a little walk on river as far as the ford. Very bad descent in bank.

Dined in open air—boiled fowl of the house & boiled leg of mutton of Mr Hamilton. After sunset was sultry, & not for 2 hours after did cool air come on—the fires made the trees look beautiful—we have heard every night the notes of the morepork, whistle of the bats, screeches of cockatoos. Mr Elliot told me the whisper of the bats was one of those sounds inaudible to certain ears on which Dr Hobson I think has written—his mother's were the certain ears he had to quote. Mr Elliot in the course of the morning chased & shot a black swan, one of a pair on the river. In doing so he found it necessary to swim across, but the heat of weather & his own exertions had so heated him that he was obliged to rest an hour before he could return.

Samuel Calvert (1828–1913)
MIDDAY HALT
[Melbourne: s.n. 1873?]
wood engraving; 21.5 x 35.4 cm
Pictorial Collection S5065

II

Goulburn River to
the Murray River

12–20 April 1839

*T*he next stage of the journey passed through the least settled regions of the
country, and the fears of all rose accordingly. Until they reached the Murray
River, their nerves were on the stretch, and at the sound of a distant shout or the
call of a dingo they would set an armed guard to watch through the night.

As they travelled through the day and sat around the campfire at night, their
conversation turned to the 'wild natives' of the region. It was just a year since,
on 11 April 1838, a group of men of the Pangerang people (reports placed the
number variously at anything from 20 to 300) had attacked shepherds camped
at Broken River (near the present site of Benalla), who were overlanding stock
for William and George Faithful to pastoral land in Port Phillip. Seven or eight
shepherds were killed and numerous sheep lost. Historical accounts of the motive
for the attack vary. Some suggest the Pangerang people were simply spearing
cattle for food and the violent conflict developed only when the shepherds tried
to fight them off. Some suggest the motive was retribution, as the Faithfuls'
party were said to have made a number of attacks upon the Pangerang people,
and sexually abused the women. An alternative version cites the evidence of
George Stewart, Police Magistrate of Goulburn, who was sent to investigate the
incident and found that there had been no provocation of the Aborigines by any

member of the white party and that no women had been molested. Stewart concluded that robbery had been the sole motive for the attack. But then, in the conflict with Aboriginal people, the police magistrates and pastoralists tended to side together.[63] In the version of the story that Jane Franklin heard, it was acknowledged that the shepherds had previously given 'some offence' and that the Faithfuls' station was the only one in the district to suffer repeated attacks.

The Faithfuls abandoned their intended settlement, selling out in September 1838, but soon afterwards George Faithful established his station, Wangaratta, on the Ovens River. The incident encouraged overlanding parties to travel together, and hastened the provision of police across the Port Phillip District—including the police establishment at Broken River, still unroofed when Jane Franklin dined there in drenching rain. For this stage, Lady Franklin's party was augmented by three travellers, who sought safety in numbers, and who contributed their own stories of the dangers to be encountered from 'blacks'. So too, did the 'intelligent Corporal' who took over their escort at Broken River.

Lady Franklin, as ever, recorded all the stories she was told, and offered little of her own opinion. But it is clear that she shared the fear, contempt, patronage and curiosity that characterised the attitude of white colonisers to the Aboriginal people. Her accounts of savagery, primitivism and experiments in 'civilisation' here have none of the authority of the eyewitness, and are matters of hearsay only— hearsay shot through with guilt and fear. Henry Reynolds has argued that the climate of fear that pertained on the white 'frontier' in the colonial period is evidence of whites' consciousness, at some level, that their settlement was unwelcome, illegitimate and resisted.[64] Jane Franklin's diary reveals some of the elements that comprised that consciousness, a consciousness thrown into relief by the fact that this was the only moment during her six-year stay in the colonies when she herself was not buffered from fear by a solid combination of white 'civilisation', distance and ignorance. The past decades had seen the near total devastation of the Aboriginal people of Van Diemen's Land, and she had only recently spoken with what appeared, at least, to be their last sad remnants at Port Phillip. Here, in the scarcely settled regions of New South Wales, the process of dispossession was not complete, and as a consequence her usual spirit of anthropological curiosity was shaken.

The stories recorded here are the products of a fearful imagination. They contain material that is potentially shocking in its violence and misleading in its allegations. They are retained in this volume as evidence of a particular stage of white Australia's black history. They suggest callousness and incomprehension on the part of white colonisers, and on the part of Lady Franklin herself. These were indeed important elements in her character and experience. But fear and contempt were edged in her case by a curiosity which, though often superficial, occasionally roused her to genuine interest, and to recognition of an alternative identity and culture to that laid down by white society.

Friday 12 April

Two men of Mr Hawdon's going to Manaroo, & another travelling back to Sydney, were glad to take advantage of our convoy, the distance between Goulburn & Murray rivers being the greatest resorts of natives.[65]

We paid here our last orderlies a sovereign & gave them letters for Melbourne—new orderlies from house in white straw hats—one told us that about 6 weeks ago, a servant of Mr Ebden's on foot on this road with a letter to his master was set upon by 8 blacks, stripped completely naked & robbed of his rations & clothes & whatever else, of any thing he had. The man sent back immediately to the Goulburn[66] & in half an hour afterwards the police were on the track of the blacks & saw the marks of their naked feet in the spot where the man had been seized, but all search for them was useless—they twist round trees—hide & very slowly move— stand motionless like a stump. The district in which we were now entering between the Goulburn & Murray is said to be most frequented by them.

The Goulburn to Seven Creeks is 30 miles, the direction at first North North East but as proceed more to East—road today most uninteresting— went a little way below Clarke's to the punt, a bad descent in sand bank— square or oblong punt—one of our late orderlies dragged us over by boat placed to other side—about 50 yards wide here & appears deep—on top of opposite banks found the carts, at bottom the luggage, which had been brought in the punts—latter dragged up bank, loaded on carts—when this was over & all ready, it was half-past 8.

They passed across a monotonous landscape of plains and thinly wooded forest, relieved only by one 'acceptable but rather transient view'.

At about 14 miles from the Goulburn Sheldrake, the driver of cart,[67] said that in spite of the length of the journey today we had better rest for an hour—miserable food, no water but what brought in our keg from the Goulburn. Thrown on our own resources—had cold salted pork & tea—no shade. How the natives hide themselves I can't conceive where there is no shade nor cover. On—tedious—no change—saw sun getting very low & thought it time we should arrive—day had not been so hot, owing to a breeze, but after sun set it became hot—asked orderly how far now; he said 2 miles (it was certainly 7)—on—the same—grew dark—Dr Hobson went in advance of the heavy cart with which was Moriarty—it was left behind as we pushed on—it grew dark—no moon—at last we were obliged to keep close to the police to see—we heard a shot—it was from Dr Hobson who wished to know if he was on the road. Mr Elliot answered his shot—saw fire ahead & heard shots from hence—it was Dr Hobson, answered by us—

nevertheless we did not arrive. Dr Hobson however who must have walked at a fast rate, overtook us—in one part we thought we had mistaken the road, lanthern was lighted, we soon got back & soon arrived.—had 2 or 3 flashes of lightning—encamped—lighted fires—afterwards a sudden rain came on—gents had the small cart with tarpaulin—the men took the great one—I invited Snachall to be in tent—she would not—got her to lie down on ground with cloaks &c—she was much out of sorts—went out in night & lay down on a wet stretcher. She did not however appear the worse for it next day.

The light cart having gone on considerably in advance of the baggage cart I followed on foot but on coming within a few miles of our halting place Lady F was fearful of being benighted so moved on at a rate so rapid that I found it impossible to keep up and as the natives were seen here yesterday in a very considerable body I felt myself in rather an unpleasant condition especially when I remembered that this tribe are the most sanguinary and cruel of any natives in New Holland. They also move at night which is a feature in their character marking at once their superior courage. I accordingly prepared for exigencies, loaded my gun with buck shot and put in new flints and made the best of my way on. It soon became pitch dark and as the track was very narrow I found it exceedingly difficult to keep it and on several occasions actually lost it but I found the darkness became so intense that I was actually obliged to feel for the track and in this uncertain condition I travelled several miles. At last as a dernier resource I fired my fowling piece and had the satisfaction to hear it answered by Mr Elliott. In a few minutes after I caught the glimpse of a distant fire which I knew to be that of the Postman. I soon came up with my friends and had the satisfaction of putting them on the road which they had strayed from. I was welcomed by my companions especially the ladies who were afraid I had lost myself and perhaps fallen into the hands of the Blacks.

Hobson, Diary, 12 April 1839

12 miles to Honeysuckle Creek.

We had an easy morning's journey & arrived about 1—forest thin all the way. We rested at a creek full of water-holes of pretty good water, slightly weeded—many parasites hung like drapery on pegs, being blown about by wind; they have not the stiffness of death in them as dead boughs have. Tent pitched—fires lighted, small tree or two cut down, for props & boughs. The gents with these, a prostrate truck & tarpaulin made themselves a shelter—carters had the great cart, 2 Snachalls ensconced themselves inside the little one. I watched the cooking of the black swan of Goulburn, which had been par boiled at Clarke's and was now stewed with curry. We have been obliged to fall, since we left Clarke's, on our own resource. The men had bacon or pork.

Preparations of birds were made in the evening by the light of common fires, in which some beautiful & gigantic moths one after the other sought their deaths. Dr Hobson prepared a parrot of a different species from VDL.[68] He thinks the country remarkably barren of interest—very different from the Port Phillip shores, where his brother lives, in which there is much.[69] The spare stretcher served as our dinner & tea table & the lanthern, for which we had brought a provision of waxes, was raised on a small measure in which Mrs Lonsdale's eggs had been packed in oats which now served to measure out their corn to the horses.

Rain during night. The light of lanthern on the ground in front of our tent was crossed by shadow—at same time we heard a little transient tread, too light for horse, which were near in front but hobbled. The barking of the dog given us by Tulip Wright convinced us that something was amiss. We heard next day it was a native dog that had come down, and was frightened away by ours barking.

Cloudy & rainy morning. 16 miles East North East to Broken River where is Police Station—thro' some eternal forests. We crossed, about one fourth perhaps of the way, a creek of dry water holes with some elevations of ground near them—rather pretty here as relieving the dead level. The water holes are divided by bridges of earth in which however there is always a depression more or less steep & awkward & sometimes exceedingly so, particularly as the width of the bridge is sometimes very narrow on the twist. We think these water holes are caused by overflowing in flooding of rivers & might be traced to them. Observed dwarf wattle by road side in flower. By state of road, observed that much rain had fallen in several places & partially it appeared also that the rains must have commenced at earlier period than now, as young green grass was beginning to appear.

Showers fell & thunder pealed, a black horizon—flights of white cockatoos and parrots chattering & collecting in trees. We approached thro' ponds, one of which was of great size & covered with pink or red weed, to the Police Station, begun 6 weeks ago—4 men here. There are police establishments over 4 districts besides Sydney: Jerry Plains, Bathurst, Yass & Port Phillip. Captain Smyth's jurisdiction extends from Geelong to here where it ends—then commences here Mr Waddy's to Yass. The policemen said they had 30 shillings a month—believed they were to be there for 5 years—for 6 weeks have been living on flour, tea & sugar—the Corporal[70] said only from 15th of last month, rather more than a month—their supplies in the drays not having yet come up—their only meat is salt beef. Policemen get 20 shillings for every runaway they take & 30 shillings for a man escaped from irons 30 hours after his missing.

Roofing of house was delayed by dryness of weather which would not permit the bark of box or stringy bark to peel off. The house consists of 4 rooms of which 2 are partially covered in, & the 2 outer rooms, with large & good fire places, have no roofs. There is very poor timber about station— they have had to go 8 miles for timber to build the house—in 9 or 10 days after this rain they will be able to get bark to roof it in.

We had scarcely arrived before it began to pour. Tent put up—tarpaulin for gents—potatoes, rice & tea prepared at soldiers' fire—& cold ham & tongue. We gave a hand of pork to the new orderlies here—waded thro' sea of water in outer intended room to inner place where soldiers berth—here water poured in in many places & contents of first room overflowed into it—Thunder, lightning & torrents—when the weather moderated a little after dinner, Captain Moriarty carried me, & Mr Elliot Sophy to our distant tent, from which we did not emerge again. It was placed on elevated ground near edge of pond filled with large bulrushes—a trench was dug round it to drain off water.[71]

Between 9 & 10 at night, when Snachall had retired and Sophy gone to sleep, & gents were also in their tarpaulin, I heard what appeared to me a distant shot. A few minutes after I heard another. I called Sophy, who was sound asleep & did not hear—a few minutes after I heard a short cry & then roused Sophy & consulted whether we should go to gents—set off to their tarpaulin with lanthern & called Captain Moriarty who is said to be a light sleeper. He aroused at my second call, I told him my story, & he said it was probably somebody adrift & would give them a shot. After this Sophy & I both heard distant sounds of a dog. They fired, after some delay, several shots, but no answer—& Captain Moriarty came to me & said we might go to bed—the Corporal & another would keep up on watch all night. The Corporal had often mistaken for shots the falling of trees—& as for dogs, he had some always about at night, they were probably in search of opossums.

Monday 15 April

Next morning Mr Elliot shot 2 ducks but lost them both—they fell into water where they dived & were lost in weeds. Some of the ponds here are full of bulrushes—these ducks have long flight sometimes after being wounded. Mr Elliot killed a third which we kept for tomorrow's dinner, also a slate coloured crane, prepared for same purpose, & a hawk which had such tenacity of life, it could with difficulty be made to die. Much rain in night— district had not seen such for 12 months before.

While drying the opossum rug at the fire with Captain Moriarty, one of the paddies[72] told us stories of the Blacks. He was sure they had seen us the whole way but would not venture to attack as we were too many. They will attack 2 or 3 but not 5 or 6. This man, belonging to Mr Hawdon, said that 3 weeks ago at the Murray, 3 men were left in charge there with a man of Mr Hawdon's. When 150 or more blacks came to the hut, the latter contrived to seize a horse & go off to police station—one corporal & 2 privates came down, remained all night & got them to disperse. The same man said he had known a black kill his gin (who had run away to another tribe) quarter her & eat her. He saw another man bleed his arm, pour it into a pot, mix it with siftings & drink it off, saying badgery (merigig is the word at Port Phillip).[73]

The intelligent Corporal at the Broken River said that many stories told of the blacks were false—but that they were cannibals there could be no doubt—he knew a servant of Mr Lipton's who was eaten all but one leg which was left in his boot. Mr Faithful had 7 men speared & killed—the men had been associated with blacks coming before and some offence given—next morning when sheep moved on & these seven went to look after cattle & horses, unarmed, they were attacked—The blacks' campaign is lasting—at last counting of Mr Faithful's sheep, 600 were missing—he is now at his 3rd station since his men were killed, & is going to shift again on account of the blacks. Mr Faithful's neighbours do not suffer in same way.

The Corporal told us the natives were in the tiers 7 or 8 miles off—he had lived a year at the Murray where he saw much of them—has never seen one since he came here. The police have the greatest influence over them. They would not think of attacking one. Corporal says the blacks care much more for Police than settlers—& like better to be at police stations than at settlers'. He thinks it very useful to have a black boy at each station & means to get one.

Corporal told me the Blacks ate great quantities of the Moths both in chrysalis & moth state, singed in fire. During 2 months in the year (the 2 last) they go up into a range of mountains 70 miles off—called the Boogong [sic], on account of the quantities of Boogong or moth to be found there. He has seen natives come in with moths or chrysalis in their nets—some of their nets are so fine, a pea would not pass thro'. The Corporal has eaten both moths & grubs.[74]

This Corporal told me (I having heard it before & questioned him) that he had saved the life of a little black girl. It was in an encounter with Blacks on the Big River, when this child who he thinks could not have been more than from 18 months to 2 years old (here he must have been mistaken) threw herself into river in alarm—he got her out & placed her on a bank—she got a bit of stick & threw it at him & then either jumped in again or attempted to do so. She now lives with a settler's wife in Manilla District? [sic] & is a remarkably intelligent child, learning to read, & will not look upon a black.

Corporal told us also of another Black a very wild man they took, so wild that they were obliged to tie him to a tree every night & drive him before them in day—he was at last quite subdued & so fond of whites that he will not quit them.

During the morning we looked for the grave of Mr Faithful's men murdered by natives about a mile from station, by the creek—we saw but one grave which was that of a man in Major Mitchell's expedition who was drowned here in a pond about 2 years ago, as driving thro' some drays—man's name was Wm Taylor which was cut in tree adjoining. Faithful's men were buried round about where they were found—one was unburied & his bones are to be seen near one of the ponds.

The corporal accompanied the party as far as their next stopping place, at Reedy Creek, presumably imparting his stories to Jane as they rode. The way took them through forest, across waterholes, and then up a gentle ascent. A hill by the road tempted them to divert, and they found themselves looking down on a 'forest sea of uniform hue except where a streak here & there was under shadow of cloud'. To the east they could see 'fine ridges, some are Snowy Alps' and altogether Jane found it a 'fine interesting view and more extensive than usual'. They resumed the road, and had almost reached their destination when an accident occurred.

Sophy & Mr Elliot were riding behind together, she on Duke, for Belladonna had taken his place in cart. Soon afterwards the orderly spoke to Dr Hobson & me on the cart, & said the lady was thrown from her horse. Duke had suddenly bolted & thrown her. Dr ran back instantly, I followed. She had fallen on her face & her nose received the blow—it was much bruised but it saved her head, and she had no other injury except a headach which existed before. Her nose bled & we applied cold water. She was removed at length into cart, thence on stretcher to our encampment, from which we were not 1 mile when the accident happened. This station is Reedy Creek, near the edge of a small yellow plain.

Tuesday 16 April

67° at 8. Started near 11, 15 miles to the Ovens—We determined to cross the Ovens at once—we were told we would find only water holes, but it had risen by rains—encamped on other side—trees were fewer here & thicker & there was a little feed. We were now 170 miles from Melbourne—it was thought advisable to push on at once for Murray, a 3 day journey, as the waters might have risen by rain & punt there is destroyed.

When we retired to our tents for the evening were startled by the horses galloping past as if alarmed—Mr Elliot who was a little beyond the encamping ground, looking for birds, was nearly run over by them. The Corporal instantly said they were the blacks, whom the horses had scented. They could not endure the smell of the blacks, he had known them break from their tether to get away. Thus it could be difficult to run down the blacks, as the horses would in all probability turn—would not follow them. It was judged advisable as they had no fires & looked likely to steal the approach to keep watch & 2 gents & 2 orderlies did so alternately, 2 at a time during the night—The Corporal thought they were probably on the other side of the river, close to us. There was no alarm during night—In morning some cooees were said to be heard—the tribe in this neighbourhood is said to be not friendly.

The comfort of our journey had well nigh been marred by a serious accident. The horse on which Miss Cracroft was riding suddenly took fright, dashed into the woods and threw her violently upon her face. Fortunately her nose sustained the brunt of the fall. The concussion notwithstanding was severe. The sufferess bore the misfortune with more courage and resignation than most men and contrary to my expectation did not appear to be anxious about its effect on her beauty.

Hobson, Diary, 15 April 1839

×   ×   ×   ×

About 8 our horses suddenly came rushing in as if frightened. This was said by some of our men to be a sure indication of the approach of the natives. We accordingly took up our guns and went to reconnoitre the direction from which the horses came from [sic]—but no symptom of them was visible. As a precautionary measure watches were placed for the remainder of the night. The last or morning watch heard the cooey distinctly.[75]

Hobson, Diary, 16 April 1839

Off near 9 to Rocky Water holes 19 miles North East.

In dryest season there is not always water in these holes & [travellers are] obliged to go to Black Dog Creek 2 miles farther. Pretty scenery on bank of Ovens—this river has sometimes risen 12 feet in one night—trees, particularly near river, larger & greener—some destined to death by being ringbarked. In about 1 mile pass near a mound, flat-topped, with only very few scattered trees on it, but a few of these as large as those in plain, otherwise its appearance could be artificial—below it is a hut of split boards with chimney but unfinished roof, built by Mr Docker when he sent his diseased sheep out here. He thought of making a shepherds' station, but finding the grazing to fail, abandoned it. The stockyard by which the herd of sheep is confined when anointed for disease stands near. Revd Joseph Docker, who is said to have been deprived of his gown, lives about 5 miles from the crossing place of the Murray. The ground here is parklike & rather uneven.[76]

On, towards ½ way felt air cooling owing to our gradual ascent, from head of it see ranges of hills at back & on right over trees—a succession of descents & ascents follows these, being a continued range with depressions. The 3d ascent had a headland stretching off to right & ending in a pile of rocks which seemed to overhang valley—I was not able to walk it tho' it seemed as if it should command a fine view. The Corporal went to the spot near it—said it shewed nothing particular, but saw the Blue Mountains[77] better than we did when we saw them before from the hill we ascended the day Duke threw Sophy.

I suppose we on the whole descended towards close of [the day's] stage as we came to small creek or water holes where water was expected in consequence of the rains, but not found tho' the sides to a considerable depth were black & wet—by digging we should probably still have got some. Met postman & put in 2 letters, one for Sir John to say we had crossed the Ovens.[78] The post left the crossing place at the Murray today and gets to the Goulburn on Saturday. Obliged to go on near a mile farther & stopped at first water we came to in a rocky hollow. This creek or station is known by name of Rocky Waterhole.

Dr Hobson went out in search of opossums, & was cooeed for by Captain Moriarty who declares he is such a naturalist & philosopher as to be quite unfit to take care of himself & that he would not be alive now, if he, Captain Moriarty, had not looked sharp after him.[79] He found a bag of honey bees formed on a gum tree, the bag being formed of a gossamer web strengthened by ribs of firmer texture—see Mitchell & Sturt. Temperature today was 75° about 1 pm. It was excessively cold in the night & at sunrise was about 47°. Many native dogs were about & their howling disturbed the sleep of some of the party—a watch was kept as the night before. There was good feed for the animals on the other side of the creek.[80]

Thursday 18 April

Set off at ¼ to 9. 20 miles to Joe Slack's station at some ponds within a mile of the Hume or Murray.[81] At Indigo Creek, passed a barked tree, on which was marked with red paint 'From Port Phillip 174 miles'. Sheldrake, or Sam as he is also called, said one of his companions in a journey had done this—we were glad to hear it was not the surveyors as it made our journeying come much short of our reckonings. Proceeded very slowly, & told Mr Elliot who drove that he was going to sleep—arrived notwithstanding between 2 & 3 at the station of Joe Slack, which he has lately quitted—he sold the good will to a person of name of Hume[82] who has been here only a month. A hut of gaping boards, divided in 4 chambers without doors, covered with slabs of bark—an open shed for stable besides—to west is a wet lagoon or flat valley, between low banks containing 4 neat pretty sparkling ponds. It is a pretty spot & the trees are better than usual. We found a native in European clothes with a pipe in his mouth hanging about the hut—he is employed there.

We had for dinner a white cockatoo, killed yesterday, & a magpye. This evening more white cockatoos were killed, and a large laughing jackass, much larger than found in VDL. We were told they were not killed in this country, because they were so useful in killing the snakes—the bird is called the Squatter's Clock. Today, Mr Hawdon's man told us he had been bitten in the leg by a snake in the grass—he tied it above & below, fell down sick—natives were brought, who applied herbs & burnt it, & it was afterwards cut out. Dr Hobson has a great dread of snakes—he found one once in his waistcoat or coat on taking it off; another time at Norfolk Plains, one coiled round his leg—he dreamt of this & leaped out of bed on ground to the astonishment of his companion—a second time, another night, he gave such a leap in his sleep from dreaming of snakes that he overturned his bed, which was a cedar one, with him. He told me he had heard I had done great good by it.[83]

Friday 19 April

Went up to speak to Mr Hume before we went—& thanked him for papers & milk. He has been here only a month—came from Yass—has some cattle—more coming & some sheep. This is not a good sheep run—it wants

The only [snake] I have seen since we landed was a dead one on the road, and from all I can observe or learn, they are much less numerous than in our highly favoured isle, and are not as supposed to be with us, all alike venomous. The natives eat them in some part of the country, but avoid the poisonous ones. Do you know that short as was the time the Doctor spent in Hobarton, he had heard of the war 'à l'outrance', which I had been waging against the snakes and moreover that it had greatly diminished their numbers. This is the third or fourth testimony, unbought and unbribed, I have received to the utility of that much ridiculed warfare. The Doctor however is the only person who thoroughly sympathises with the view I took of the enormity of this evil, and of the extraordinary apathy which exists respecting it. He thinks he has even a morbid sensitiveness on the subject, and no wonder, for once on taking off his coat, he found a snake in the sleeve of it, and at another a snake coiled itself all the way up his leg. I do not know whether it was immediately after these fearful warnings, that he leaped out of his bed in his sleep, upon the floor under the influence of a snake attack, and to the great discomfiture of his sleeping companion in the same room, and the next night took another similar leap but with such vehemence that bedstead and all were overturned with him.

Letter, Jane Franklin to John Franklin, 20 April 1839

back water. The Murray is good for sheep washing only ½ a mile off. There were also here a herd of Mr Stuckey's going down to Portland Bay, & a flock of sheep of Mr Shepherd—he is going to look for land at the Ovens. Hume said he would not refuse him feed as he went—he promised to stay but 2 nights, but going away, came back again saying there was no water (he meant no feed so good as Mr Hume's, for delay would make water worse, & would make feed better). Joe Slack, the late proprietor, was once a prisoner, but being diligent & sober & industrious had got on & is said to have £3000.

The Corporal told me of another suffered outrage of Blacks—Mr Snodgrass was sending about 2 months ago 1184 head of cattle with 22 men. 4 of them went down to bathe—afterwards they divided to see which would get home first by different paths—2 arrived at station, & a man & a boy have never since been heard of—it is believed they were seized by natives, whose tracks were all about.

Returned to road from Hume's station under a line of small undulating hills, on the nearest slope of which the road passes. Through forest land, with dried flats subject to inundation & lagoons, several awkward banks to ascend & descend. Came to Murray bank on right, being on its left bank—saw field of maize edging banks other side below it. Mr Brown's hut[84]—here river makes great bend—descend bank & over bit of pebbly beach. The ford was up to horses' bellies—beach very steep on bank opposite. We encamped within fenced paddock of mounted police between river on one side & the embanking hills other. Their station is on side of hill—begun in October when they arrived—finished in 17 days—4 men & a serjeant—The 4 rooms are neat—Joe & Mary are blacks, buy wood & water—jabber English.

Lady Franklin wrote at length to Sir John about the Aborigines at the Murray River.

Saturday 20 April

My dearest love ..

The river here makes a deep bow the bight of which is towards the East and a little below it is the crossing-place or ford. The banks were not lofty but were rather steep. They descended however in the present state of the river not into the water but upon a flat beach of shingles which was a great advantage to us in crossing. The water in the deepest part did not come above the horses girths, and the current was not sufficiently strong to render it a matter of any difficulty to stem it. The water here may be about 80 yards across, and the stream tho' thus easy of passage, was much more rapid than any other we had hitherto seen. In times of flood it is dangerous on account of this rapidity—as well as on account of the steepness of its banks. We were told that parson Docker's drays had been overturned in it, and one bullock drowned on the occasion. Accidents to human life have also occurred at this passage since it has become the highway between the old colony and the El Dorado of Port Phillip. On the right bank of the Murray are two inhabited dwellings, and a smaller unfinished one, the latter belongs to a Mr Lewis whose cattle station we had passed 2 miles on the other side of a river. Of the former, one is the spacious hut of a Mr Brown erected for a store, and standing on the forest plain near the water, and the other is the station of the mounted Police perched upon the steep declivity … of the lofty and undulating bank. On a flat enclosed paddock between these two dwellings and meant as a reserve pasture for the horses of the mounted police we pitched our encampment rejoicing to have passed that formidable river which had hitherto been represented to us as the greatest obstacle we had to fear and at the same time to have accomplished the half of our journey to Yass or 200 miles exactly in a fortnight …

A native black, named Jem, dressed in a jacket and trousers, with his gun by his side and a pipe in his mouth was squatting on the ground by the size of [Mr Brown's] maize field and on the river banks to frighten away the crows. He had a heap of burning ashes before him and had placed a plank between him and the ground, all which signs of civilization were curiously contrasted by the loss of two front teeth in his upper jaw (one of the distinguishing marks of his tribe) and by a pendant ornament to his shock-head consisting of two kangaroo teeth fastened by strings to the twisted hairs.

I heard a good account of the useful and amiable properties of this man, as well as of another named Joe who is particularly attached to the police station, where he with his wife and young daughter perform the drudgery of bringing wood and water for the house, all being paid to their entire satisfaction for their services by such refuse victuals as may be given them. They eagerly seized upon the potatoes' parings and raw outside stalks of our culinary fare, and were ready to make themselves useful in any way they could for the sake of anything left upon the plates, and which would otherwise have been thrown to the dogs. We were told that Joe used his gin, (wife) very kindly. They were all including another woman, who was probably Jem's wife, and an old man and boy whom I did not see, uglier than the people we saw at Melbourne but the women's figures were better. One was dressed in a thin cotton shift, the other in an opossum skin, and the child held a small blanket about her with which she at times concealed her figure completely from observation, as if intent on doing so, while at another, after seating herself with great care upon the ground she would let her dingy mantle drop, and display her juvenile proportions with childish insouciance. This young girl, who appeared to be about 12 years of age, was not yet arrived at the age when the scarifications with which these poor savages, female as well as male, disfigure their skins, are performed. The operation however was soon to be performed on her. The gashes are made with broken glass, they are not allowed to close, but I believe are kept open by some stringent bark, granulations formed at each edge—these come together, and the skin forms over them and makes ridges. The hair of some of these blacks was extremely curly, and that of others nearly straight. The women wore it short, as well as the men, but extremely thick. One of the women's heads was a perfect mop, impeding her sight.

As we have spent a whole day on the banks of the Murray in order to rest the horses, we had time to amuse ourselves a little with these people. One of them has been out to search for opossums and flying squirrels in the trunks of the trees. Their acute sense can detect by the scratches which these animals will make on the bark in climbing, as well as by holes in the trunks, such trees as they have rested in, and however lofty or branchless the trunk, they will by the help of their tomahawk (taw-win) soon notch, and toe their way to the spot. If the trunk is at all bent, they always, as may be supposed, choose the sloping or convex side. Joe was not successful in his first search, and indeed did not appear to me to be very ardent in the pursuit: either he was too lazy or thought he had little to gain by it, or he had no great hopes of finding what he sought for, and rather humoured his employers than followed his own behests. To an unpractised eye the most obvious sign that a tree was or had been occupied by the flying squirrel was the young twigs which strewed the ground beneath, bitten sharp off by the teeth of that beautiful little animal.

Jem was invited on the evening of our arrival to dance at the fire but he seemed to have little inclination for it, whenever he began to attempt it the dogs barked at him, and he seemed as much afraid of the dogs as our horses at the Ovens were of his own black fellows in scent and complexion.

The blacks in general in this neighbourhood are said to be quite quiet, but at Mr Brown's sheep station 18 miles off, they had been spearing someone's cattle, and between this and the Murrumbidgee, had attacked several men in a similar manner …

Your affectionate wife,

Jane Franklin [85]

Saturday 20 April

Noisy morning with screeching of cockatoos & women frightened at dogs which bark at them—grey cloudy morning & a little rain fell early. River had increased, not by rain here, but by increase of a stream joining it 1½ miles above, coming from 18 miles up in Snowy Mountains, where there has been a considerable fall of snow. It is a very dangerous river when high—current strong—a man at Mr Brown's had known many accidents in it. Parson Docker's drays had been overturned in river—only one bullock lost—they turned over & over, could not resist strength of current.

Mr Brown from Stone Quarry, 50 miles from Sydney, has been here about a year—his house has been built about the same length of time—gaping boards, bark roof—has 5 rooms in it—he is going to keep a store—has some cattle here, keeps his sheep at station 18 miles off where stream comes from—has 4 acres of land [in maize?] & more in wheat— 4 quarts of [maize] seed are sufficient for the acre—in favourable season he produces 200 bushels per acre—ground requires no preparation but ploughing & harrowing—seed is sown in November; requires rain when cobbing or fruiting at end of December or beginning of January. Had only one rain this year—soon after put in, 5 months before harvest which is about this season—requires rich soil & is often used as preparation for wheat in soils of over richness—sometimes a soil will require 5 or 6 crops of maize before fit for wheat. It was the tallest maize I ever saw, much of it 12 feet high—but cobs not well filled. Sophy had never seen it before—she admired its rich glowing ear, the careful manner in which this is sheathed & enveloped in dry leaves, the bunch of hairy filament-like tassels or tufts at top emerging—the bunches of dried flowers so fit for plume of straw bonnet at apex of plant.

Mr Brown's store has been erected about a twelve month; it consists of 5 rooms and closets built in the same way as the barrack but is not yet furnished with its supplies. We should not have found it easy to make any purchases here either for ourselves or our horses had we required to do so. Mr Brown has some cattle here, and 4 acres of ground on the brink of the river planted with maize the finest looking I think I ever saw in any country. Many of the stems were over 12 feet high, '3 times as tall' as Sophy observed, as Mr Elliot, who was measuring himself by them, and who seemed by no means to understand why he had fallen so immeasurably low in her estimation. Sophy had never seen a field of maize before, and was struck as well she might be with the noble dimensions and brilliant colouring of the cob, the beautiful provision of enveloping leaves, which preserve it from injury until it is ripe for the harvest nor least with the bending plume of dessicated and straw coloured flowers, which crown the summit of each tall and graceful stem, and which if they could be transported safely to the straw bonnet shops of Regent and Oxford Street would, fragile as they are, make the fortunes of the owners.

Letter, Jane Franklin to John Franklin, 20 April 1839

The police station here was formed in October of last year, and the house completed in 17 days. The walls are of split boards of stringy bark, and the roof is covered with sheets of bark. It contains four rooms for a sergeant and 4 men, and is probably sufficiently weather tight for so fine a climate, though the light and air enter through the gaping boards, and the windows are unglazed. A small shed at a little distance is the poultry house giving shelter to about half a dozen fowls, one of which the sergeant said he would immediately knock down for us if we were pleased to have it for our dinner.

Letter, Jane Franklin to John Franklin, 20 April 1839

Dined in Police hut owing to rain.—after dinner went up hill—saw little more of river, but more of hill ranges. Mr Elliot had cotton rope for tinder—struck light with flint & steel—got dry grass & tried to flame—Sophy could not. Drank tea in open air—but driven into tent by rain—interrupted writing to Sir John by moth diving in & putting out lanthern—much rain during night but temperature milder—parted from our 2 mounted police here & had 2 new ones—rained all night but not so cold—cloudy & slightly showery in early morning but sun came out & dispersed them—became a pleasant day with equable & by no means hot temperature. Mr Brown gave gents a nankeen crane half stuffed, before they left.

Alexander D. Lang
AN EXPLORING PARTY LOOKING FOR A SHEEP RUN
[London]: McLean & Co., [1847]
hand-coloured lithograph; 22 x 27.4 cm
Rex Nan Kivell Collection NK1643/A

IV

Murray River to the Murrumbidgee River

20-27 April 1839

Major Nunn, Commandant-in-chief of the Mounted Police, had written to the sergeant at the Murray River asking that 'every accommodation as to horses &c should be afforded' to Lady Franklin if she passed that way. Accordingly she was able to borrow a packhorse to relieve the labour of their own horses. On the whole she was well pleased with the condition of all the animals, and with their stocks of provisions, and could face the next stage of their journey, to the Murrumbidgee River, with confidence. She could complacently compare herself with the less happy fortunes of Mr Oak, a traveller they had encountered at Seven Creeks and who had beaten them to the Murray by three days. They found him still there, waiting in vain for his exhausted horse's recovery, and on the day before their own departure he set off once more, this time on foot—'thus realizing the proverb,' wrote Jane sententiously, 'the more haste &c, which so many of the bustlers of human life have occasion to verify'.

The sergeant himself and one of his men now replaced the 'intelligent corporal' and the private who had escorted them from the Broken River. Lady Franklin, grateful for the protection she had at first decried as unnecessary, was moved to comment in her letter to her husband: 'They seem a choice body of men, these mounted police, intelligent, well behaved, active and efficient. They must be a blessing to the country which they not only protect but serve to humanize.'

To express her sense of obligation she sowed white clover seed in the trench that had been dug around her tent: 'which if it succeeds as I expect on this rich alluvial soil, just freshly prepared, by the moisture, and for the first time turned up by the spade, will not only leave the flowery outline of our principal encampment thus imprinted on the soil as an enigma for the inquisitive traveller next spring, but will in all probability spread itself from this point all along the banks of the Murray. I gave the returning corporal some seed also which seemed highly to delight him, this being the first occasion on which I have recollected at the right moment that my packet of clover seed was brought for the express purpose of thus disseminating pasture along the travellers' track.'[86]

At the Murray, Lady Franklin and her train said farewell to 'our two humble travelling companions Paddy and Mick', who quitted them to make their way to Mr Hawdon's station further down the river. Paddy, who then had to travel to Yass on his way to Twofold Bay, hoped to rejoin the party as soon as possible. He had been, wrote Jane: 'right glad of our protection and companionship on the road and does not at all relish the idea of making his way alone when he parts from Mick. He is equally afraid of natives and snakes having seen something of the mischief perpetrated by both. Being asked which he would rather have the most of? The snakes or the black fellows, he replied, "six of one, half a dozen of the other."'[87]

For Lady Franklin and her companions, however, there seemed from this point to be a diminution of fear. They had by no means reached the settled districts, but from now on the density of the scattered white population noticeably increased. From the time of their camp on the Murray River, Lady Franklin was once again able to observe the Aboriginal people as objects, not of terror, but of anthropological curiosity. She could take an interest—often an acquisitive interest—in their artefacts, and mourn the degraded state she now believed them to inhabit as a result of their contact with white society. But as the road became more frequented, new fears arose: particularly of the 'bushmen', or bushrangers, who as the Sydney press frequently noted were 'infesting the country to the southward'.[88] Other problems beset the travellers. Their supplies were running down, and they could rarely obtain wheat or flour at any of the stations where they halted. They were reduced to hard biscuit and rice, and Jane began to yearn for the taste of fresh bread.

Her descriptions of what she acknowledged was 'monotonous' scenery were unflagging but uninspired. Many passages of somewhat repetitious description of roads, forest and hills have been omitted from the following section for this volume. But perhaps precisely because the landscape offered little to inspire her pen, Lady Franklin's descriptions of the people encountered on her way became an increasingly important part of her diary, and her colourful glimpses of rural life in 1839 enshrine her as a chronicler of social history—of sulky Mrs Smith's unexpected gift of precious eggs, or Dabtoe's dazzling display of skill with a boomerang. Her account makes it clear that the novelty of her presence caused a flutter in the houses and districts she visited. Men and women who heard in advance of her coming tidied themselves and their parlours, and hurried into clean *shirts and fresh caps, to show that their standards of respectability had not been diminished in their makeshift surroundings.*

Sunday 21 April

Off at 9—leaving Murray behind.[89] Encamped in gully by water holes under small hills to left, 22 miles North East—this day brown sugar was found to fail—sent back to Clark's to know if he had any—had heard 2 shillings charged in these parts for 4d of sugar—Clark however said his price was usually 1/6 but to me would charge less—bought 10 lbs brown sugar—if I had been a poor person, he would have charged a great deal more, he said.[90] Cold night—Moorpork's melancholy note.

[At the Mullingandra] a person by the name of Clark keeps what he designates a store!!! which is nothing more than a piece of canvas stretched over a ridge pole. The most cruel thing of all was—the perfect emptiness of this store! All we could get was a little dark sugar—which this scamp charges poor people 1/6 per lb but Lady F only 1/!!!

Hobson, Diary, 21 April 1839

Monday 22 April

17 miles—so called, but as we thought 20—to Tagoon Moonil Bingar—also called 10 Mile Creek, being 10 from the next where is permanent water. A spur winged plover shot on road here & soldier bird shot here—the latter has no feathers on its head—but black silk night cap & bump on upper part of beak—or nose—white silky feathers on breast—rest grey.

Snachall tipsy. The night before the Sergeant, unsolicited, had brought him 2 glasses of rum from Clark's. In the morning instead of getting breakfast he was under the cart & his wife did all. In setting off he generally drives & of course, tho' much recovered he was made to walk—he lagged & we all got on slowly perhaps in consequence. I went halfway on Kitty.

The ground was pretty about Mullingandery & continued so in the valley—road undulating & hilly, but nothing steep except water hole banks—saw water in many holes, but none permanent till we reached the station. A good hut here—walls & roof of stringy bark—owned by man & wife of name of Mitten, natives of Campbelltown in NSW. At their door we saw Mr Oaks—he arrived yesterday & soon after we saw him he walked on to a station 6 or 8 miles on. We passed by Mittens' as they had no feed there, and went on up creek—this was one of the least favourable places we had been at. We established ourselves above half a mile up the creek. After dinner we walked back to the house. Mitten was away—I spoke to her. She told us the native name of the creek. They have been here a year—have a few cattle, about 50 head & intend keeping a house of accommodation. They have 6 rooms, such as they are—no glass in windows, but the little curtains look neat—no butter now, but she gave us new milk & offered us as a present a couple of fowls which we declined. They have a half underground room for future dairy—now keep meat there—a fenced stockyard & a paddock or enclosed field of 9 or 10 acres where they hope to raise 2 crops of wheat. There are 2 young children—& other people of household—they have no sheep. She gave us milk & we took some away next day.

Dingo tails nailed against tree—horses got good feed some little distance from encampment. Father Therry had a station here—now removed. We had met the postman going to Melbourne in the early part of our stage—a horseman with bag—he looked & lingered, but we did not learn till after that he was the postman.[91]

Tuesday 23 April

Off between 8 & 9—repass Mitten's hut & on—10 miles north east to Billabong Creek. About 2 miles before we came to Billabong Creek the Sergeant went off on left to the station of Lieutenant Stapleton of the 50th—his overseer was here with sheep. He asked to purchase one—the man would not let us pay for it—he drove his flock down of about 1000 sheep, & one was chosen & killed by Sam [Sheldrake]. We enquired of shepherd if water to be found 6 miles farther on, as was supposed probable on account of the rains. He said no—till the late rain here, they had not had any for 18 months. We took up our encampment on a pleasant position, as usual considering not only vicinity of water but of loose faggots on ground for fuel, the closeness of latter, on account of carriage, being even of more importance than closeness of water—as one can scarcely find any not undermined by ants & holes in small raised hills—and other larger ones. Water is good here—we arrived before 12—being 10 short miles. Dined at 2—& tried to nap on stretcher in tent before hand, but great humming flies prevented.

After dinner we went to see native grave found by Dr Hobson in secluded spot by the creek—it was an oval of about 12 feet by 9—of white sandy soil distinguished by this from greener & darker earth around—a rim slightly raised formed an outer border as of a dish, & in centre of the flat space inclosed, was a mound between 2 & 3 feet high which appeared to be formed of burnt wood covered with sand. It seemed to have been partially disturbed & marks of cattle feet within ring—but Dr who would have liked to see the contents would not disturb it, lest vengeance should be exercised on the shepherd near or on the first European they could find, instances of their revenge thus provoked having occurred.

Mr Elliot's gun, while he was shewing us the construction of the percussion lock, accidentally went off & passed thro' edge of adjoining stretcher into ground, igniting canvass & taking off some of wood. Dr shot a flying squirrel—thought he heard opossums. The gents placed their tent under an unusually spreading Eucalyptus, with low & ample branches; & calm as was the evening, when blazing fire, or air agitated by fire, went up into them, they were in rapid & restless motion. The night was milder.

Wednesday 24 April

18 miles to Kyamba or 20. Off soon after 8—a close, nearly sunless & cloudy day, eventful as to objects met. We returned into the high road, about 2 miles on left passed field cleared of wheat, off which Father Therry, now Vicar General [in VDL] had crop of wheat 2 months ago—his station is 3 or 4 miles from the last place.[92] Soon after, we met the wonderful sight of a cart, with one horse & 2 men, carting some bags, belonging to & going to Mr Faithful's, from Goulburn to other side of Murray—we stopped, & spoke of feed & water—the man said some places were as bad as hard beaten road.

On—at about ½ way, we were astonished at the sight of a smart tandem or carriage, with one horse in shafts & one outer—3 persons, apparently gentlemen, in it, who looked, stared—one very slightly bowed as we had nearly passed & then drew up & pulled a letter out of his pocket for Mr Elliot from his cousin. They had set off from Parramatta on 6th of April; had thus done rather more distance than ourselves in the same length of time—but they seemed to think we had done well & that our horses were in good condition. They looked much sprucer than ourselves. They were followed at a little distance by a light cart with 2 horses, tandem fashion, & 2 men, one on horseback—mutual questions as to feed, & on their side also as to state of roads—they had travelled on an average 15 miles a day, would have got on faster had it not been for the cart—on leaving we found by the note that the one who got off & spoke to us was Mr Verner, 'a very good fellow'. He said he had not been above a year in the colony—and told us of some of the arrangements made for our travels. Mr O'Brien would receive us at Yass & forward us to Dr Gibson's—the latter to Goulburn—there, if we chose to pay so much, Mr Crisp, an innkeeper, could furnish us with carriage & horses to Sydney. They were in want of flour & could get none at Smith's. They had seen no natives, but 2 bushmen had robbed 2 men of whom Verner had earlier asked the road—soon after he first encountered them, having occasion to turn back, he was told that during the short interval 2 men with policemen's muskets had presented them & taken all they had, viz 6 shillings—this near Yass. All these signs of outskirts of civilization were rather unseasonable[93] to me.

We got engaged in pretty defiles in the hills & had pretty continued ascent of about a mile to highest part when began to descend—defiles bare & much burnt—others were pretty. Country grew less pretty as we advanced, & quite bare of vegetation. We came to a station of Smith's on the border of Kyamba Creek, which had water holes, dirty black water, & apparently no feed—we passed one hut & encamped beyond, before we came to the 2d of Smith's stations. Horses were taken over the water holes and up bank on opposite side to feed, & found something. They do not, except Tulip, seem to care for oats, which are given only to the draft horses—they prefer the grass. Our position was not very pretty. Bareness of ground & want of colouring from sun burning it made it one of the least attractive places. A large herd of cattle were advancing as we approached—they looked rather lean having been long on road & belonged to Mr Chisholm & were going to his station beyond the Murray. We expected to be much annoyed by their noise, but they passed on—they were followed by drays with 6 or 8 bullocks to each. A female was trudging with this party.

After dinner, tho' we had heard a very bad account of the manners of the people at Smith's hut both from Mr Verner & our own gents, Sophy & I thought we would go there. Smith was absent, but his wife, a disagreeable-looking woman seated in her hut, suffered us to come into the doorway & then rose & begged us to sit down which we did for few minutes. We learnt they had been there a year. 'What part of the colony did they come from?'—'She was not a native,' spoken as if with great contempt for natives.[94] They had been a mile & a half farther back, whence road then ran. They had removed here, where the water was worse, to avoid passengers, & now the road ran this way, & herds & flocks encamped, & the feed was eaten up—hence no doubt one cause of Mrs Smith's sulkiness. They were now going to move 3 miles farther away where they would have better water and be out of the road. These holes in great droughts were sometimes dry—till the late rains they had to go one mile for water. They have several flocks, amounting to between 2 & 3000 sheep—have cleared a piece of land here & tried wheat & potatoes—don't do—about 9 miles off, however, had got 100 bushels from 3 acres of wheat. Her husband had been buying 200 head of cattle & was bringing them up—had given £3 a head for them great & small—price of steers £6 a head—or 1 guinea the cwt.[95] I noticed the woman's 2 or 3 young children, and gave the little girl bits of biscuits. Whether or not in return for this, the mother came out with 3 eggs—told me she had no more—they were a great rarity—we should get none on road. I estimated them as she desired & accepted them—the gents considered this quite a triumph over her ill humour.

Talked for some time to a carrier seated near her door by the side of a dray loaded with Smith's bales of wool which he is engaged to take to Sydney at 20 shillings the cwt—the dray contained 26 cwt drawn by 8 bullocks. It would take 10 days there & back—he could not dispense with a second man if another dray were not going also, & they could travel in company. This carrier keeps 20 bullocks & hires out their services as required—he ploughs with them at 16 shillings the acre old land, & 1 guinea the new—or 10 shillings by the day for any work, ploughing, dragging trees, &c. He said the ground till lately could not be ploughed—too hard crust. Speaking of 'up' & 'down', I found 'down' meant to Sydney, differing from the London expression 'up to London'—'Yes,' said the man, 'It is so in London—the only place for happiness with plenty of money.' He had left it, & has been here, 13 yrs. He appeared to be above 30—said a wife was very useful to a person in his line—she could relieve him driving the team, and they could sleep alternately—in sun & heat he could not sleep. He would generally set off as soon as he could after catching the cattle, packing drays & breakfast—went on to 10—rested till about 2— went on till evening—travel average of 10 miles a day—sometimes 15, sometimes 8, according to water.

Thursday 25 April

Stage today 21 measured miles from Kyamba to Tarcutta Creek. The horses had wandered several miles off to better feed which came above their fetlock, the best since leaving Melbourne—we supposed they had had enough, since they had wandered beyond & playing pranks. It was 10 before they were found & we off. Dr killed new flying squirrel, larger, different in claws, feet & tail & skin different hair not soft Chinchilla but long & hairy—their flying is rather a leap.

We encamped in a very pretty spot, trees larger & bare—very little fuel. A tree is regularly cut down every evening for the forked sticks of the gents' tarpaulin. The horizontal roofing pole is rested on one end on the poles of a tree, on other on 2 poles with formed ends fitting into each other at the top—Carter & Neale, & 2 mounted police sleep under cover of a tarpaulin stretched from the last.

We arrived only a little before sunset. As evening came on, we saw lights in the 2 huts, & several fires of natives, who to a number of 8 or 10 were lying round them. We went up to see them. One man, who wore a shirt & a crescent-shaped flat piece of copper by a chain round his neck, was presented to us as the Chief of his tribe—his copper had been given him by Mr Manton[96] and a neighbouring squatter who had also presented him with a suit of armour, made also of copper, & which they keep for him. On his copper were engraved 2 emus, 2 kangaroos & a native in the midst of them hurling his spear—over this was engraved 'Dabtoe, chief of the Hoombiango'. A poor woman was lying flat on ground, moaning, being ill, her bosom uncovered, but a skin thrown over her below. Her husband felt & rubbed her stomach & seemed to pity her—she rose at last from ground, with bent body & leaning on stick & walked away a little, the man looking after her but not following her. I sent the Dr to her afterwards—he ascertained they were spasmodic pains & gave her a little morphine, which produced instant effect on her, so as to make them cry out 'budgery coradje' meaning 'good physician'. She was not disposed to take the medicine till her husband in an authoritative tone insisted on it—he seemed anxious & tender of her. One or 2 men about were entirely naked, so were the children. Captain Moriarty took hold of one little boy, lifted him up, slapped him behind & put him down. The boy did not like it, the mother tittered. They present themselves occasionally when can find no opossums or kangaroos—they are content with the offal of the animals killed, & for this they will bring wood & water. They do not pilfer—one person we asked would sooner trust them than white men. They make very small fires & sit close into them—sometimes fronting them, at others thrusting their scarified backs into them.

Mr Smith of Kyamba, whom we found here, said he had lost a great many sheep by them. He said he had had 2 sheep stolen by a black boy—he took him & desired them to flog him—they told him he might—he said they should do it themselves—if one of his people had stolen from them he would flog him—upon which they all gave him a few strokes each.

Mr Smith had his cattle here in stockyard, travelling down—Mr Mates was absent. I told Mr Smith his wife had been very kind to us—he laughed as if wondering. We found a little girl in a hut who said her grandmother was in the next hut eating her supper—her name was Hightman. Presently came in a young man—who answered our questions as if the plain belonged to him[97]—& the grandmother of the little girl. This youth was sensible & well behaved & intelligent. He said the native name of this place was Umumby. The natives have name[s] for every creek & every hill. Mr Mates has been 3 years here—is too much surrounded—thinks the land will sell well when put up to sale, but no fear of it at present—is both a sheep & cattle station. Fine soil here & excellent water—keeps supplies for sale & expects a licence to keep public house. They will sell any quantity of their own wheat. They don't sell it in flour. Mr Verner & Campbell yesterday would have given anything for flour, but had not got. We are here 300 miles from Sydney, 300 from Port Phillip & 200 from sea from which divided by blue mountains.

Friday 26 April

Dabtoe & 2 others, all in cotton shirts, came to throw Bommerengs. Dabtoe was chosen chief as he has the most clever action. [They throw the boomerang in] 3 ways—1st, along the ground to a great distance—2nd, along ground & make it return to man by coming up in air—3rd, throw it in air— it goes level some way & then rises above trees, flutters like bird in the air, skims or floats & returns, dropping at the man's feet. [I] asked Dabtoe afterwards for his—he did not like giving it—'Bel (no) good'. [Dabtoe] had his front teeth out. He spoke pretty well. He had lost one of his gins, who had gone away with another man—he was very philosophical about it—'Let him keep him' said he—he was told his other gin would go—'I believe not' (he had always in his mouth, 'I believe so', & 'I believe not'). When speaking of the head chief at the Ovens who had speared white fellows—'You'd fight him, Dabtoe, would not you?'—'I believe so'. When pressed about losing his last gin, he said, 'Let do—plenty whitefellow—all mess-mate together.'

24 miles to Jenkin's Upper Dairy station—off at 8 am. [The way at first was so] monotonous in scenery, with cart & horsemen picturesque[ly] wheeling round jutting points, I felt as if the past were repeated—the picture again & again presented to the eye. Where steep ascent really begins, trees are cut down & lying prostrate by road, lining it—they are to be used as drags to carriages going down the hill to Port Phillip. The steep ascent at top & past is on a bad slope, rendering it dangerous—we descend again on fine plain, ground more verdant, trees large, & feathered down trunks—some gracefully thus draping—proceed about 5 miles then come to second ascent, larger than other as far as steepest part of such is concerned, but less bad—had 4 horses to heavy cart throughout day—descend again on plain of imperfect verdure & prettier trees than we are accustomed to see.

Bell bird heralds river—& so it proved—in 2 miles arrive at steep banks of creek or backwater parallel with river, now dry, over this a close line of dark handsome fine-looking trees, new to us with spreading branches (the swamp-oak?) marked course of river right to left. Coming up to this dark line of trees, find them to be on the edge of the bank of the Murrumbidgee, exposing a dark sluggish surface, with here & there banks of shingles—in some places the water is covered with some floating weed of pink hue (a linferoca) which we had first observed at Broken River (Violet Creek). We drank of the water & lingered 10 minutes on these first banks of the Murrumbidgee—then proceeded up its banks—several times today, crossing places bad & cart forcibly held back, in our light cart Tinker (the policemen's horse) was disposed to gib. At close of evening came again on border of the Murrumbidgee where island is formed by a branch of it— junction of this with large stream is just below Mrs Jenkins' hut or station. Mrs Jenkins is a rich person living at Campbelltown—the widow of an officer in Commissariat.

Mr Elliot measured a Swamp Oak, about 20 feet in girth—[the timber] is fit for shingles—Larry told us of the mountain ash in the mountain ranges above—not the same as our ash—is fine wood for doors &c—the bark is astonishing—rolls up like floor cloth—will cover a rod[98] in extent— is rolled down the mountain—is like whalebone—axe sticks in it like glue.[99]

Saturday 27 April

Baggebury to Gundagai 12 miles—off at 9. Proceeded along immediate banks of river, which had beautiful reaches. When at a little distance, its existence beneath the general level of the plain might be known by the upper half, trunk high, of the swamp oak, their roots & lower trunk being below in bed of stream. The first part of this stage is prettiest as commanding reaches of river—I could not cease to admire swamp oak from unusual contrast—gum trees also handsome & graceful, the prettiest if not the largest I have seen—noticed some firs along the margin of river, the first I have observed, not large enough to be of that size which always indicates rich soil in VDL. Soil here however is good. Cross a steep creek & come to another hut & station of Hardy's. At the door of the hut saw little boy in Scotch cap & fillibag. Captain Moriarty spoke to him—his mother replied he spoke scarce any English. 'Is he Irish?' 'No—from Isle of Skye.' They had been there 14 months. Her husband's time was up with Mr Stuckey and they were going away. She had not been well there—would rather be in Isle of Skye. Somewhat more than a mile from hence to a bank falling down to the ford of the Murrumbidgee. The river is very shallow—current sufficiently rapid—and opposite bank very bad. It rises immediately from water, so that there is no space for cart & horses to form, but they must face the hill directly, & a worse bit before the top—an additional horse was added but jibbed in spite of lashing &c. At last got up safely. Kitty went over twice, with me & Sophy.

Over river, a neat verandah & shuttered hut kept by one Andrews who has store & public house &c.—had no flour on hand. Walked with Dr Hobson about ¼ of mile or more to hut of Mr Brodribb,[100] formerly of VDL whom he knows, to see if he had flour. There are 3 brothers in this country, engaged in same concerns—one living at Goulburn, another going to a new station at head of Murray, the youngest brother here. Dr Hobson went ahead to warn of my approach, thinking they would not like to be

Our arrival here has anticipated our expectations. Every thing seems to have prospered with us. If it rains heavily, it is not while we are upon the road; if the permanent water holes are so far distant that a forced march is necessary to reach them, the same heavy rains have filled some intervening ones, which could not have been calculated upon, and which abridge our exertions. The rivers are still so low, that the water in the deepest has scarcely come above the axle trees, and the difficult banks of the creeks, which if concealed under water would be really dangerous, are so completely exposed that the tactics of our drivers and our well trained horses are sure to enable us to surmount them. Then as to our commissariat, neither our horses nor ourselves have become emaciated on our daily diet, which though simple in the extreme seems to have been wholesome and sufficient; or if the luxurious propensities of our quadrupeds lead them sometimes in spite of their hobbles and tethers in search of richer pasturages than such as were assigned them they are always sooner or later recaptured and brought back to the bit and the harness.

The late showers have already given a doubtful hue of green to the brown surface of the earth, giving us promise for the future, and while the dust is laid for us, there is scarcely moisture or mud enough on the beautiful natural roads we are traversing to cool the horses feet, or clog the motion of our cart wheels.

We have had no bushmen to present their guns or pistols at our heads, and thrust their hands in our pockets, and you have seen that the best of the flock has been tendered for our acceptance, and that the flour which silver and gold could not purchase has been placed in our hands as a gift, and obligation expressed at our gracious acceptance of it.

Thus favoured as we are by nature, and circumstances, and not able any longer to doubt, in spite of our modesty that there is something in our very selves, which captivates all who come within our influence, we are journeying on to Yass, which we hope to reach on Thursday next.

Letter, Jane Franklin to John Franklin, 27 April 1839

taken by surprise—& after a little time the young man came out clean dressed & making a profound bow. Being asked whether he liked this best or VDL he said this—more room. They came from elder brother's farm on the Black Marsh on the Clyde where they did not do very well but were well conducted young men—they have 4 stations here—going for better grazing under mountains at head of Murray but blacks there bad. They have both sheep & cattle. One brother is taking 4000 sheep to Port Phillip. Dr left something for bad eyes of one of brothers—he says it is very common to have eyes affected in this country. We asked about native dogs. He said they had had 9 sheep only killed by them since here—shewed him pod of tree found by us—natives call it Corryjon [Kurrajong] & cut the seeds which are in bed of fibres—which if get into the eye, never see again.

We heard that the Brodribbs are going away because they are eaten out of house & home by being by the road side. They fenced, of course at considerable expense, a paddock for themselves & during 2 or 3 days of absence to bring up their sheep found it entirely eaten off by persons who had let in their flock there—not their flocks only, but themselves, to be entertained.

Thunder & clouds when we arrived—in the evening the wind rose— sheet lightning & thunder, but the clouds blew over & tho' a little rain fell, it was very slight—a team passed & crossed the river next day. Dr Hobson, foreseeing a storm, went to lodge at Brodribb's & asked many questions about natives.

Brodribb's Account of Natives[101]

They believe they shall live in another world, a great country where there will be plenty of kangaroos & opossum & where they shall meet with one another again—also think that the great eagle is the spirit of one of their deceased & worship it—latterly Mr Brodribb or another white man killed an eagle. They came to him, congratulated him on the rain which had fallen & said it was owing to their having dipped some of the feathers in the river. They kill the eagle themselves. These 2 accounts seem somewhat inconsistent. What is more outstanding & is unparalleled in the history of savage notions is the singular attachment they pay to their dead offspring. When an infant dies under 6 months they carry it with them & make a pillow of it when they sleep, till it will no longer hold together. This feeling seems to extend even to their adult offspring—or in a late meeting between 2 tribes in these or adjoining parts, an old woman, in one of these was told by one from the other tribe that her son who had been with them, was dead—she immediately snatched up a tomahawk & cut her head open & was proceeding to inflict further wounds when the instrument was wrenched from her—she then seized a burning brand from the fire—thrust it into her flesh, but was prevented I believe from destroying herself.

A sense of justice & honour seems to exist among them. Two hostile tribes from the Goulburn & Murrumbidgee met to fight—but the Goulburn being much weaker than the other, the Murrumbidgee picked out 18 of their men to be opposed to 18 of the other, the rest remaining as spectators. The Murrumbidgee tribe, I believe, had the advantage from their use of the Wamara [woomera], a stick which they use in throwing the spear & by which they send it to great distance.

They acknowledge to eating their enemies.

Their worst trait is their ill treatment of their gins.

Their best, their respect to old age.

They are very much afraid of deep water—will not go into any water holes that are deep. They think there is some terrible animal at the bottom which they describe as big as a horse, but resembling a pig.

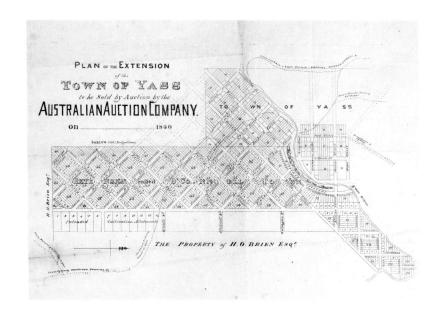

Edward David Barlow

PLAN OF THE EXTENSION OF THE TOWN OF YASS.

TO BE SOLD BY AUCTION BY THE AUSTRALIAN

AUCTION COMPANY ... 1840

one map; 28 x 49 cm

[Sydney: Barlow Litho. Bridge Street, 1840]

Ferguson Collection Map F453

V

Murrumbidgee River to Yass

28 April – 3 May 1839

As Lady Franklin proceeded on her way after crossing the Murrumbidgee River, she began to encounter the pressure of hospitality. She was expecting to be met at Jugiong by a carriage from Henry O'Brien, one of the principal squatters of the region, who held an estate, Douro, on the Yass Plains and a sheep station at Jugiong. But the theft of O'Brien's horses gave Richard Hardy, Police Magistrate of Yass, a chance he was swift to take, and it was he who appeared at Jugiong to escort them on their next stage. From this point in her journey, Lady Franklin was increasingly surrounded by those who wished to do honour to themselves and her by their attentions. Courtesy, as well as her particular feeling of responsibility as the governor's wife and in a sense his representative, compelled her to accept many offers of hospitality she could well have dispensed with. Gone was the freedom of sleeping in a tent; now her fastidious taste and sensitive skin shuddered at the best comfort that could be provided in local homes. For a few days yet she could relish the casual encounters of the road, but by the time she reached Yass the traveller was giving way to the distinguished tourist. Still, civilisation had its compensations, and most welcome was the opportunity to replenish supplies that had become mouldy, rancid and very sparse.

Very sultry.

10 miles to Coolook Station. Kitty got sore back—obliged to give her up. Tinker now always in the cart. Road hilly & often on sidelong slope—left river behind—passed several creeks & iron bark tracts. Mr Elliot remarked of the dark trunks of the latter, that it continually seemed to him as if they were in the shade while white gum trees in sunshine.

We met two horsemen, well mounted, with guns—they looked at us & passed on—a team of 8 bullocks drawing dray—the drove divided as neatly as a regiment of soldiers might have done right & left.

Encamped on bank of creek, near a field with one or 2 huts. Seeing 2 or 3 clean dressed persons here who seemed disposed to accost us, we lingered a moment, & one, the master of the house, Mr Batts, came forward, asked if we would enter, at least till our tents were put up. Accordingly Captain Moriarty, Sophy & I went in & found he was going to keep an inn &c.—a respectably spoken man—the 2 others were Dr Parsons & Mr Dudley.

Mr Batts was 23 years seafaring man—some of his family at Sydney urged his coming out to them—3 times he attempted it, 3 times cast away—but 3rd time contrived to arrive—afterwards 7 years in command of ship from Sydney—18 months ago was put in command of the *Louisa*, laden with oil for London—bad weather in Bass's Straits—driven off Maria Island, took refuge in Hobarton—ship had been in whale trade—was condemned by commission at Hobarton. Her owner desired her to be sold—she was bought by Mr Andrew Haig—tired of being skipper & sick of all this, he determined to set up in these parts—he has a licence for public house to commence in July—built house himself last December or January. His wife has not come yet. He has taken the last man's stores—he did not do well here during the year he was here—the store is attached to the hut, which is not allowed in a public house—so shelves &c are to be taken down, & place turned into bedrooms, & a new store built a little way off. He has flour, tea, sugar—nails, saws, knives, axes, pannikins, tin plates, pots, lanterns &c. The ironmongery was nearly useless—suppose his predecessor had not sold about dozen articles all the year—should send them to auction at Yass—tobacco, tea & sugar only thing they had sale for.

Mr Batts has a parlour with walls internally plastered & painted grey— the earthen floor is covered with tarpaulin & then with Kidderminster carpet, a chintz sofa, & shelves with jugs &c, tiny bedroom leads out, with iron bedstead & tableshelf with washing basin & jug & another bedroom, a trifle larger—such as it is, this is the best house except Mr Mundy's since we left Melbourne. The ground is beaten & smoothed in front of the cottage, which has small square glass windows of 4 panes, & fenced in—a table & a few benches here for drinkers & outside a pair of large scales. He had a storekeeper there—& there were 2 visitors or travellers—in usual white linen dresses & one with long black beard & some light coloured Mustachios. Moon beautiful, at full or nearly so—read with ease by it unaided by fires or candle.

Monday 29 April

To Murrumbidgee flat 17 miles—off at ½ 8. Had much difficulty in heavy carts—very indifferent feed at this place & country as we proceeded very dry & arid. Came to a hut station on eminence by the road 5 miles from the last—a white-washed hut of 3 rooms, built by & inhabited by a couple of name Keane who have been here a year—found young man cleanly dressed in straw hat & blue striped shirt, & his wife a very nicely dressed, pretty-looking woman. They had 2 children, girls—the eldest had lost an eye & the other seemed diseased—[Dr Hobson?] advised her to be guarded from sun. The Keanes have been 3 years in the Colony from County Clare—1 year here. We found her with hair dressed, without cap, & looking very neat & respectable—rooms swept out. This might be accounted for by Dr Parsons having gone forward in this road, & probably announced our passage—it certainly seemed as if we were expected. The hut is whitewashed—has 3 rooms.

Continue up long & steep hill. Bad ascent on for some miles, road tolerably good & level—ground remarkably bare of vegetation. Another ascent—fine view from top. Descent steep—saw 2 women sitting on trunk of tree—both without caps or bonnets—stopped to speak to them—one excessively burnt & freckled, but fine features & animated countenance—her speech betrayed her, but being asked, said she came from Western Highlands, Isle of Mall—had been in colony 8 or 9 weeks—after 10 days in barracks had been hired by Mr Munro, 40 miles from Port Phillip where going 'now'. Mr Munro was from 'a place called Adenborough (Edinburgh)'. Asked if she had a family, she replied she was married only just before she came out. Ah! said Captain Moriarty you married to come out—she did not deny this—(Captain Moriarty thought she might be confined on road). Her husband was a blacksmith—I asked his wages & she did not know, had not cared to ask him—feared there was much drink in the country for blacksmiths—was Port Phillip better country then this—we thought it was—'then why do you go away?' We did not belong to one more than the other—we came from another part, a fine country called VDL—had she ever heard of it—she had—had we heard of, or seen her husband today? he was ahead with cattle—we had not. Went on to foot of hill, when found the dray & team of 6 bullocks to which she belonged—

here saw young man of a higher class in plaid dress & disagreeable countenance & other men & women—took no notice of them.

Passing on, came to a bark hut & blacksmith's shed adjoining, where the Sergeant went to get shoe put on. In meantime, I entered the hut where I found a pretty delicate young woman with an infant scarce a month old in her arms—& another child apparently of 3 running about—also a coarse looking woman who on being asked, said she was an assigned servant & who had a larger baby at her breakfast. This woman was the younger's attendant in her confinement. They brought us milk & water, the common beverage to offer when they have milk. Name is Burton—on my questioning her she said she was a native of Colony—had brother named Smith, a prisoner in VDL. She said she was not yet 20. This is the first blacksmith since left Melbourne. They acknowledged that it answered very well here. 10 milking cows & 7 horses—blacksmith's price much the same as in Hobarton—6 shillings the set, probably 6d for single shoeing—place is called Jubion Creek.[102] Just beyond it, the Murrumbidgee came upon us unawares. On the way passed a large ploughed field circled by rails & boughs before which stood 2 drays belonging to Mr Shelley, of the Doomot,[103] one going up & other down. The man who used this expression & who was reading a book, as he said, on Mediterranean history, being asked what he meant by up & down, said it was customary to say up or down according to the course of the river he was following—otherwise he should say down to Sydney.

On a dusty bare flat beyond Martin Ready's hut by edge of river bank, the ugliest place in which yet encamped, we halted for the day. As we were sitting at dinner at stretcher under shade of the gents' tarpaulin, a wild cow, which had strayed from a herd we saw pass by belonging to Mr Brodribb, was driven in by a stockman or horsekeeper—it was approaching us & he called out 'Boys, be on your guard, or she'll make a rush at you'. The gents laughed & took no notice—& 2 times the man called out in vain, till seeing the animal nearing us, I went under the tarpaulin, followed by Sophy. In another instant, the young cow was close up, & rushing at the gents. Mr Elliot took up the cover of Dr Hobson's bird box. Captain Moriarty seized a heavy club or log, with which when the animal was about to butt him, he struck her between the horns & brought her on her knees—a 2d blow, or even the first would have dispatched her if more violent—she rose again & seemed prepared to renew the combat & might have made rush at the tent but was diverted & got off. I was glad to learn in the evening that the whole herd, including the cow, were folded in stockyard at Marr's.

After dinner we went into adjoining hut of Mrs Ready, or of Martin Ready's, where we found the Sergeant had been grinding some of our wheat & was now making a damper of it. Mrs Ready told me her husband had gone to clean himself, but we did not see him. She was decently dressed, but without shoes or stockings—had sprained her ancle. Dr Hobson examined it—advised her to soak it first for 15 minutes in very hot water then plunge it for same time cold. The old woman said nothing—she would, I believe, have liked something more out of the common way. She has 14 children all living & around her, & 11 grand children—one, half-naked, she was dangling in her arms. She told me she had been (I think) 2 years here but 24 in country 'having followed her husband out'. She added, they have never yet been before a magistrate, nor been in any trouble whatever. She is from County Kildare, her husband County Westmeath—she 72—he 67. They have about 200 head of cattle & make butter & cheese—for the former, she got 3sh 3d per lb at Sydney.

We walked on to Jack Marr's—has lived 12 years on different parts of this river—had kept a store, now had a licence & sold spirits & wine— offered us beds. A grog & water jug was brought in & candle placed on table—when we declined, he hoped at least I would let him treat my servants—I begged to be excused, & when he saw I was much in earnest, he looked serious too & immediately & with good grace gave it up.

Mrs Ready had offered us bacon & butter—I accepted a little of former [if she would allow us to pay for it]—she accepted. Our own bacon, brought from Mr Tinsdale, had been long uneatable, except by 1 or 2 strong stomachs—our Melbourne bread had lasted for 10 days, at least for me who, dreading the hard biscuit, picked out to the last the bits untouched by mould rather than come to biscuit or damper, then ate soaked biscuit & rice & potatoes. The latter failed 2 or 3 days ago—biscuit failed today & nothing but heavy damper left with rice or macaroni which it was a trouble to them to boil. At the same time Snachall broke my tumbler & obliged to drink tea out of pannikin. Captain Moriarty stiff necked today with rheumatism. Codfish taken in river.

Tuesday 30 April

Leave before 9—19 miles to Bogolong—horses were said to be feeble & tired—arrived however by ½ past 2. Follow course of Murrumbidgee 1½ miles, come to Jubion Creek, where leave the Murrumbidgee behind & ascend. Met a moustachio'd man on horseback who rode up to Sergeant Rose, with a letter which latter shewed to us—stating (from Mr Green of Bogolong to which station we were going) that a carriage was to meet us there tomorrow from Mr O'Brien—afterwards, a man overtook us going to Yass—Captain Moriarty spoke to him & desired him to say he was coming—'I will, Sir,' says he, without asking whose name.

On to Bogolong Creek, where is Green's station, an inn established there by a retired Sergeant of the 4th regiment, which went on to India when he got his discharge, still quite a young man. Green was 14 yrs in the army. Sir George Gipps has favoured him by allowing him to purchase here 5 acres of land at £2 the acre before the land is put up for sale. Green bought the good-will, huts, fences, not the run. He has a wife and one child.

They offered us the use of the house—I thanked them but said we had tents. They did not remonstrate—but sent servants with fuel for our fires—& when asked at our fresco dinner if they had bread, they sent us 2 beautiful loaves & a plum tart. Thought on second thoughts it would be [right] to sleep in her house, Sophy & I—when told her so, her countenance expressed much pleasure. She told me they wished to get a name & were anxious not to be mistaken for last occupier who was a prisoner, not of good character. Had tea in house.

About half past 9 at night while going to bed, we heard the noise of a fresh arrival, asking if Lady Franklin had come & Mr Elliot. The Landlady came in to say it was Mr Hardy, the Police Magistrate of Yass.[104] Sophy, who was in a little inner room of the general room, was asked if she would object to his sleeping next door—heard that he went to our tent where gents were lying on ground & sat some time in front.

Wednesday 1 May

Went in to breakfast next morning. Mr Hardy told me he had lost himself or should have been here 5 hours before—met with a stray horse which set him right—apologised for Mrs Hardy not coming too, she was not well, & could not ride above a mile. We heard nothing from him about O'Brien, but Mr Elliot said he found they had a carriage but only one horse. Mr Hardy is a youngish man, thin, sallow & lined—black lanky hair. He had smartened himself & was not in bush costume & looked the worse for that.

We were in general agreement that it was one of worst nights we had had—great many fleas for us—gents did not use our stretcher nor peg down the tent, so were very cold. Mr Hardy asked if we had not been examining sheep stations along the road for ourselves—I replied we seemed to be too late. He has a brother lately gone with Captain Sturt to South Australia with sheep or cattle, meaning to squat within 50 miles of Adelaide—nothing would check squatting there & a general expression of rejoicing that so it was—labourers in these colonies mad about South Australia—such high wages—about 200 had gone from these parts, accompanying the sheep & cattle droves.

He asked if we did not draw very odious comparisons between this country & VDL, as respects the roads particularly—I said I would not say that exactly—we were perhaps prejudiced in favour of VDL but tho' the made roads there were excellent, the unmade were impracticable—ruts &

gullies & scrub. 'You have seen nothing sublime here?'—no. Dr said that within 5 miles of Hobart you might see sublimer & finer scenery than in all the country we had passed thro'—here you might be put down on any part of road & could not tell it was not the same. Talking of houses, he had heard our houses in VDL were better 'It was said so,' I replied—talked of squatting. Townships are to be formed at Gundagai, on the Murray, Ovens, Goulburn &c—but intermediate land would not be sold—it would put settlers to great inconvenience.

Mr Hardy has a farm by the river which he calls Yarra Corella. We followed the stream or mud channel by an awkward narrow road, & came into nook of township, crossing the mudbank & drove up to courthouse—where shewn into parlour, & presently Mrs Hardy, pretty little girlish person, came in, blushing—but speaking well & fluently. After some time she said 'you'll see my brother Alfred before me'—I enquired—did I not know she was sister to Mr Alfred Stephen?[105] I now saw the strong resemblance, but had never heard of her before—she had been married 2 years—had been 13 yrs I think in these colonies—had lived in Hobarton with her mother, but left before we came to colony—they invited us, turning out of their bedroom to make room for us—& went themselves to an inn.[106] Mr Elliot & the 2 others were lodged at another inn—a letter was at P.O. for Mr Elliot from his cousin—I found a long one of many note sheets tied with green silk cord from Mr Forster[107] dated 4th April—very interesting & satisfactory—also an exceptionally kind note from Sir G. Gipps congratulating me on setting foot within boundaries of the colony.

Mrs Hardy is in bad health in consequence of an extremely fatiguing journey she took some 2 months ago on horseback to Sydney & back—accomplished, with fatiguing visit of a week there, within a month. In returning she lost her appetite & with it her strength—has no family—he also was very ill during the heat & lost entire sight of one eye by inflammation—was attended by Mr Cullen who consoled him by saying it would not disfigure him at all. Dr Hobson gave him hopes he would recover it. Mr Hardy spoke without a word of reproach or censure regarding his Dr of whom however he has but a poor opinion. Mr Cullen—I was told, for tho' I saw him twice I did not hear it—cannot finish a sentence without an oath. Captain Moriarty told him he would be fined for using one of them, if he was in VDL. There is another medical man here (Dr or Mr James Ellis) who with his wife left cards for me when we had gone to Yass—they are both very poor ones—wished Dr Hobson to come & settle there—he would not for less than £3000 a year.

Mr Hardy is first Police Magistrate of Yass—he came 18 months ago or in November 1837, having entered the Court House on the 5th of the month—at that time, the only buildings were the Court House, a hut for a store & one inn. His salary is £250 a year & residence, I believe no forage—

some of the Magistrates' are rather more—I did not know till I went to Dr Gibson's[108] that he [Hardy] had been the Editor of the *Australian* & in this capacity was a zealous supporter of Sir Rd. Bourke & for this was rewarded by the Magistrate position—he & his little wife also are said still to be contributors—on evening of our arrival, knowing the posts have come in, I asked to see the papers, & I was almost convinced that he shyed at it— at any rate, he did not bring forward any—he told me with characteristic familiarity he hoped I would ask Sir G. Gipps to double his salary & then he would keep a carriage to bring me next time.

We dined in Court House, rather a well arranged dinner, & retired early to Drawing room where had long time to wait for tea. She shewed me a large collection of silk purses knit by her mother—& they both played with & kissed the cats or kittens of which there were 4—one was from VDL given by Mr Frankland[109] & she persuaded herself it was a sacred duty to cherish it. Two cats go to bed with them every night (happy that they thus agree)—& Mr Hardy did not know anything that would grieve him so much as the loss of one of them. We were very uncomfortable in our bedroom, which was dirty, full of fleas, crowded & untidy—the door never opened for a moment but in came the cats, & when shut out they came in at the window. The Hardys went to their inn. She apologised for not seeing us next morning as she left her room late & gave me the reason.

Probably Mr Hardy was the 'correspondent' who sent the following report of Lady Franklin's arrival in Yass to the *Australian*:

YASS: May 2—I take the earliest opportunity of informing you of Lady Franklin's arrival here from Melbourne yesterday. Her Ladyship and suite left Launceston on the 1st April and Melbourne on the 6th, performing the journey to Yass in twenty-five days (upwards of 400 miles), and this too with a heavy horse-dray necessary for the carriage of provisions, bedding, tents, &c.

Lady Franklin used her tent the whole of the journey until her arrival at Bogolong (within one day's stage of this) without appearing to have suffered from the effects of night air. It will be gratifying to Sir John Franklin, and her Ladyship's friends, to hear, that not the slightest accident has happened to any of the party ...

Our worthy Police Magistrate met Lady Franklin at Bogolong.

Australian, 14 May 1839

Thursday 2 May

At 10 am Lady Franklin and Sophy set off, mounted side saddle on Belladonna and a borrowed pony, to visit the 'caverns of Cavan', as the Colonist *grandly put it. They were escorted by Richard Hardy and the local Anglican minister, Charles Ferdinand Brigstocke, and were to lodge for the night in a bark hut belonging to a local pastoralist, Mr Sharpe. The gentle plains and ridges near Yass demanded little description from Lady Franklin's pen, but she was interested by talk of Hamilton Hume, some of whose sheep they passed by.*

Mr Hume discovered these plains & had considerable grant of land given him—2000 acres. He is a remarkable man for his instincts in travelling, almost like the blacks, as the natives[110] are said to be. He always knows how to make his way straight to any place—more than the blacks, for they only know their own district—he [has the same ability] in countries he has never seen before. He is a plain & simple man in his manners, & like other natives, said Mr Hardy, Mr Hume is tall, thin, lanky & pale. The climate seems to have same effect on personal appearance as it has in America on Yankees.

They reached Mr Sharpe's hut for luncheon, then mounted their horses again for the caves, seven miles off. Crossing the Murrumbidgee, they noted the limestone cliffs as they passed, then ascended steep and grassy heights to an 'opening beyond a rock', through which they descended.

Then down into Judgment Hall—a white projecting rock is called the seat of judgment—water in spring under rock on side—pistol fired off for echo—lofty & grand room at further end, get over bad place & pass Pompey pillar & crawl past on hands & knees. Beyond introduce to Altar Cave—so named from convex-sided, flat-topped mass of stalactite [sic] exactly like an altar, perhaps about 4 feet high, quite smooth—hanging over it from top of roof against the wall suspended by space of about 1 foot, a convex canopy of drapery in plaits at top about 14 feet high each deepening into deep folds or pleats below—it is said lower of these is musical. The altar room is spacious & grand—at farther end a narrowed passage brings to a natural, rather shell-shaped basin as for holy water—obliged to use edge of lipped basin to get along—narrowed passage brings to Ball room, spacious and level—some chandelier stalactites hanging down on one side—then slippery ascent, like mud on which snow is melting, to farthest extent, to Robing room—not past. Our torches were of stringy bark with canvas dipped in pitch wound round—we were in about 1¼ miles— Dr found ammonites, corals, starfish &c in the rocks petrified, of an antedeluvial world. We did not get out till ½ 5—sunset, got over some bad plains, my horse being led—gents before on foot feeling their way & in the thickets of the river breaking away the boughs—arrived as the moon was rising.

Supper of pork again &c—gents retire—some to barn, others to Scotch woman's hut where they were devoured with fleas, so that Dr lost his patience & scolded the squalling children. We were in Mr Sharpe's hut in stretchers—gaping boards—Mr Sharpe has 70 acres in cultivation—wishes to get in 100. He has paid 50 shillings per acre for clearing—Margaret the Maid is paid £20—is Scotch from Perthshire—has 4 children—her husband is the ploughman—has large poultry stock—had 150 fowls—of which 80 stolen by prisoner servant who had charge of them. Mr Sharpe's sheep are 10 miles off on the other side of the Doomot—has 4 or 5000, 3 or 400 head of cattle—& 20 horses—mutton is scarcest thing to be had on the farm—beef, fresh or salt, pork & fowls are the usual food.

Friday 3 May

On our return to Yass we found Mrs Macdonald's carriage driving up—she & her daughter came out of it. She is mother-in-law to Mr Henry O'Brien who is now at Sydney—and is in mourning for her daughter his wife—brought an unmarried daughter with her.[111] The O'Briens are an Irish Catholic family. I learnt from Mrs Macdonald that she had expected us—everything ready & for servants also—I told her when I had an opportunity that Mr Hardy had led us to believe some change of arrangement had taken place—said she had but one horse &c. That was true, she said, for the day before her horses in paddock had broken their fences, as it was said, & run away—probably they had been planted in order to get a reward for finding them again—but she had borrowed another. The night of our arrival, she sent a formal invitation to dinner for next day which had only the more convinced me we had done right in not going there; this we were obliged to decline as we were going to the Caves. I begged Mr Elliot to apologise to her for not calling before we went as time was short & we wanted to get on a stage—afterwards I found that Mrs Hardy was writing to her to come to luncheon after the caves, as she was now doing.

Apologising for leaving her for a short time, I went out with Mr Hardy to look at the town & as we returned we found another carriage driving up to the door, at the hour appointed for luncheon—whether by invitation or not, I cannot say, for Mr Hardy pretended not to know who it was & then only 'guessed' it must be Mr & Mrs Hume. I suspected notwithstanding by their so nicely hitting the time, by their not explaining why they came & by the smartness of their dress that it was all arranged & perhaps in consequence of my having once or twice expressed a desire to see him. Why should he have affected to conceal his having asked them to please me? Mr Hume is a tall man, looking about 40—dark & rather lanky black hair, blue heavy eyes & rather a good countenance—simple, unpretending & almost countryman-like in his manner—ate nothing. I believe his travelling fatigues have laid the foundation of ill health. I said I thought he was the discoverer of these (Yass) plains—he believed so, he said—Mr Hardy said he had been well rewarded for it—got an enormous grant—Mr Hume denied this—said he had got only 2000 acres—'was not that enough?'[112]

Dixon's map of the Colony[113] was brought out—pretty, with settlers' estates coloured—all praised it. Mr Hume said there were a few inaccuracies in it, not very important, but these he was now correcting in a new edition. The map was mostly done from his own surveys & those of others. Dixon is gone out again to North, hopes to find dividing the continent East & West, the source of waters falling Northwards into Gulf of Carpentaria &c— & South—either a dividing range will be found, or else depressed land in centre with lakes. Mr Hume had seen but little of Mitchell's book,[114] but did not quite approve of it. It appeared to him he had not said quite the truth. We spoke of Dr Bland's pamphlet[115] of Hume & Hovell's journey—Mr Hume had not a copy of it—did not much approve of it—some inaccuracies in it. Mr Hardy gave me his copy—Dr Bland is a scientific naval surgeon, transported for killing in a duel. In speaking of the rivers we had crossed, I mentioned the 'Hume', in speaking to his wife—had hitherto called it the Murray—but Mr Hardy told me it should be called the Hume, & not the Murray till the Murrumbidgee had joined it. I was asked afterwards if I had called it the Murray in speaking to Mr Hume. 'No—the Hume'. They all laughed heartily—Captn Moriarty said 'did you ever know her at fault?'.

There were some questions asked by Mr Hume about VDL. He thought it was thoroughly explored & known—I thought not—room for him to make discoveries, but very inaccessible & difficult country—recommended him to come & see us in VDL—he listened with entire complacency & satisfaction. He wishes to see Port Phillip again & thought he should go in the spring—I said that would be the best way—then cross over to Launceston & cross the island to Hobarton. He thanked me. His wife at a little distance appeared to be listening with interest—she told me afterwards she had heard me endeavouring to persuade him to visit VDL & she was quite delighted—she had long been trying to persuade him to do so.

Notes on Yass[116]

Yass was begun about 2 years ago. When Mr Hardy came 18 months ago there was the Court House, which he entered 5th November 1837, 1 inn (Hanley's) & 1 store—now 4 public houses, 2 stores, & some huts. Mr Hardy has a farm below the township on the Yarra, where it makes a long strait reach, between high sloping banks—rather pretty. It is called Yarra Corella, or long reach or river. The river comes from about 10 miles above & goes about 10 miles below to join Murrumbidgee. The hot winds here blow 7 or 8 days together here in December, January & February. They were worse than at Sydney—helped to increase the illness of Mr & Mrs Hardy latterly.

The township of Yass is about 120 acres—extends a little way on both sides of stream & then in direction at right angles to stream where town is to be—6 streets said to be laid out—3 inns & a 4th building of brick with handsome stabling detached of brick also. A little beyond the township, towards the plains & on an elevation, is the foundation of the new Catholic chapel, a long oblong—bricks & stones about & a wooden cross erected on the foundation—Bishop Polding came here to consecrate it—the priests' house is rising rapidly by side of brick & seems of good size, 2 priests appeared—one will be almost always moving about the district—one of the priests is rather a gentlemanly man—they are both from Maynooth. The Catholic priests' house is to cost £250. The Protestant Church is to be on hillside immediately opposite but foundations not yet begun—Roman Catholics sure to be first. £1300 for church & parsonage—Bishop gives 200 from Christian Knowledge Society—600 are for house—700 for church. Mr Brigstocke[117] is paid £150 for himself, 80 for forage for a horse, & 60 for a house till he has one of his own. He is in hopes he may yet get 50 more from Christian Knowledge Society. I heard Mr Brigstocke had not been at Oxford or Cambridge & had been ordained expressly for the colonies.

The population of Yass is said to be about 100—perhaps more Catholics than Protestants—in whole district however, reverse is case—Mr Brigstocke's congregation on Sundays in Court House is about 30, including some from country—preaches there once every Sunday & Catholics the same. Mr Brigstocke preaches 30 miles off in one direction & about 12 miles off in 2 others. There is at present no school of any description at Yass. Mr Brigstocke told the story of a man here who is an inveterate drunkard—tells his priest, 'I'll not steal—I'll not fight but I must get drunk.' Mr Brigstocke has heard a convict say, 'I'll do any thing for a convict—I'd die for a convict—I'll not do more than I can help for a free'.

The Court House at Yass is a brick building stuccoed white. It has a heavy pediment in the centre of its façade rising over a sunk centre supported on 2 pillars, & within which is the central door into the court. The sloping roof of the wing on each side is hid by a square sham façade—one wing contains 2 rooms of Mr Hardy who lives here, viz. a sitting room & a bedroom, no more, the former opening into Court House which they use as dining room & where Snachall slept—there was not a closet or other place for her. There is a detached hut at the back in which is the kitchen & a closet or small room for the 2 Irish maids, viz, the Cook, & the waiter or housemaid—besides them the jailer, who was once a servant, helped to wait at table & cooked the best part of the entertainment. The Court is a lofty

& large room & semicircular at the upper end where the floor is raised a step & where 4 javelins in a stack in their box—fire place here—room is lighted by 3 oval windows on upper part of side walls in each side. The other wing of Court House contains a lock up room for men, ditto for women, & a room for jailer & his wife—the prisoners, eat, live & sleep in same room—Mr Hardy has on an average about 12 cases a month—there are 2 men now in the jail 'both from the Derwent'—There may be about 60 female convict servants in the district.

There are no mounted police here—none between Murray & Goulburn—because there are no tenders for forage &c. I asked the history of the most wretched of the huts in the street & was told it was their barrack when here. Mr Hardy has only 2 constables for his whole district—which he thinks contains about 4000 people. The constables & mounted police have the right to question every man they see for his certificate of freedom or else may take him up. Mounted Police once questioned Mr Hardy. We were shocked at idea of every free man being taken for a rogue till proved to be free—we have no such thing in VDL. The answer was that the smallness of country rendered it unnecessary & that it was chiefly owing to the Derwent runaways coming here. Why the Derwent? This is the usual & degrading name by which VDL known.

A bushranger once attacked Mr Hardy—presented his gun & asked for money—Mr Hardy refused, said he had none—told him who he was. The man was exceedingly civil—probably wanted to have friend at court if necessary—when he had gone away, Mr Hardy rode after him & called to him, thought the man would have thrown away his gun which he did not, but ran off with it—he was afterwards apprehended in another case guilty of murder—he was a great ruffian.

The drunkenness which prevails at Yass is dreadful—stockmen, sawyers &c are engaged by settlers & having their wages accumulate, ask for an order for it in town & go & drink it out at the public house in a few days. In most cases they are cheated by the publican, who tells them they have drunk out their money, long before they have, but they will also order the most expensive wines, as Champaign, which soon makes it fly. Mr Brigstocke overheard 2 carters or draymen outside a public house here ask each other what they would have for breakfast—replied did not care—let's have a bottle of champaign—ordered 2 bottles at 15 shillings the bottle. This mixed with spirits makes them mad. Their being restricted to tea in the bush only makes them the madder after it—since we left Jugiong, broken bottles by way have shewed the prevalence of drunkenness. Mr Hardy saw however no objection to multiplying public houses—he would not do so in isolated places, but in frequented roads the more the better. The reasons he alleged were that he did not like monopolies & that by competition, the imposition of charges would be less. Mr Brigstocke, speaking of drunkenness, said Mr Hardy was very lenient, not quite so much so lately.

Walter G. Mason
*RAZOR BACK, A PORTION OF THE ROAD
TO GOULBURN* 1857
wood engraving; 14.7 x 21.5 cm
In Walter G. Mason, *Australian Picture Pleasure Book*
(Sydney: J.R. Clark, 1857, p. 33)
Rex Nan Kivell Collection NK2106/82

VI

Yass to Goulburn

3–6 May 1839

Friday 3 May continued

After our return from Caves, Dinner &c we took leave of party, Mr Hardy himself proposing our horses to be got ready. Mrs Macdonald's carriage was to take us as far as Reed's Inn (about 10 miles this side of Dr Gibson's), where we were to arrive the next day. It was a swinging little phaeton with hooded centre, the box holding 2 & back seat barely doing same. She entered the carriage with me, as it took her towards her own home, about 2 miles off & put her down at corner of road leading to it, Mr Hardy following on foot with her daughters. The man drove off at a furious rate & I thought he would have turned us over—he was a great brute & slashed & beat his horses which were very unequal in capacity—heavy cart had gone off early in morning—Dr Hobson & Captain Moriarty did not stay to dinner but set off in the light cart ahead of us. Our stage was to Jerrawa, Grosvenor's Inn, 14 miles—which we ran over in very short time, thro' forest—a small plain opens where the inn, called the Golden Fleece, stands. Mr Grosvenor declared he had had no rain worth mentioning for 4 years— he could not get plough into ground, and now grain was scarce.

To Coopers' at Gunning 13 miles to Reed's 12. Setting off with Mrs Macdonald's carriage & horses, the latter refused to go—at last they were lashed on, made to tear down declivities & lashed up opposite acclivities—one of the horses had a sore back & the brute beat him over it. At 13 miles came to Coopers', called the Stragglers' Inn—the place is called Gunning, and there are wealthy settlers in the neighbourhood. We stopt an hour. In the meantime I spoke to Snachall[118] & said he must decidedly leave us at Goulburn. The next stage was very hilly—the horses could not be made to go on—I got out at the steepest rise & walked, tho' very ill with a sick headache—a few miles on, came to a creek—crossed, & a long hill out of it—I tho' very sick had to walk up. On getting to end, Mr Elliot went back to look to the horses. [He] could not get the bad one on & had to take it out and bring the carriage up with one. The 4 last miles were not so hilly & we got on better. Within a little distance of the end of stage, passed a sheep station—there is cleared land here & a deep pond which natives believe to be without bottom & will not dive into—it is an object of dread to them. Arrive at Reed's—stopped here the night. Dr Gibson's carriage to fetch us next morning. Reed's is called Breadalbane Plains—the native name is Mutmutbilly.

The party set forth the next morning with the gents riding in the cart, the ladies following in Dr Gibson's phaeton. Their destination was Dr Gibson's estate, Terranna, five miles from Goulburn. Dr Andrew Gibson had been a surgeon of the 39th Regiment, and was now one of the principal pioneers of the Goulburn district. His wife Alice was a sister of George and William Faithful.

They passed through forest land and fenced property, and freely criticised the post and rail fences—'ashy coloured & rotten looking, but better than some'—later discovering that Dr Gibson was very proud of them, and 'much surprised to hear them abused'. Dr Gibson's house, though it was 'only ground story' and the lawn was 'ill kept', had some pretensions to grandeur. With its roses and honeysuckles in front, and a series of courts behind, formed by the 'pretty servants' offices', the 'whitewashed stables with centre pediment' and a handsome pigeon house, it was a far cry from the station huts Jane had previously visited en route.

We were received by Dr Gibson, a man about 40—pale or sallow, head or neck a little awry—gentlemanly, quiet & gentle in manner. He is in indifferent health, produced he thinks by the climate which affected him when living at his station on the hill here. He has been better since he came down, but seldom free from rheumatic pains in head—sometimes up all night from them—has taken great quantities of laudanum, to injurious excess, so as sometimes to seem stupefied—found it necessary to leave this off a great deal—his wife appears some years younger, but must have been married 12 years, since her eldest child, a girl at school at Mrs Harvey's at Sydney is 11 years old—has 5 other children, of which only one is a girl—a boy of 2 years old cannot or rather does not yet speak.

Dr Gibson came out in 1825 or 6—with his regiment the Veteran Corps, which before long was disbanded—he has about 11,000 acres of land, numerous flocks & herds at different stations, but all supplied from hence—his other flocks are nearer Yass—Dr Gibson's surplus produce is sold by him to government as he has a contract to them—he supplies the commissariat store at Goulburn & stockade or road gang at [word missing]. He has, I think he said, about 400 acres in cultivation. He placed himself first on top of hill where were a few huts of squatters—after 2 or 3 years built this below & came down—Mrs Gibson liked the hill best. She is colonial born—Miss Faithful—& has never left the colony.

We were taken in to luncheon—afterwards walked in garden, a large square or oblong, mostly burnt up—border of strawberry beds & pinks burnt—lightly wooded ridge runs at back of garden—apples flourish here—gooseberries do well—not currants—figs & strawberries destroyed—Asparagus good—many espaliers. The winds are cold. Frosts at night are now destructive to the young grass—this is the third year of drought.

[We met] Mr Sowerby, the Chaplain of Goulburn—humble kind of clergy—had performed church in morning at Goulburn. It was his turn to come here once in month for service to servants. Dr Gibson lets his Catholic servants go to Goulburn for church, but not the Protestants. Mr Sowerby was of opinion that the Bishop is excessively cold & distant.

After breakfast the following day, the party made their arrangements for the next stage of their journey. Snachall petitioned to be allowed to stay with her, and Lady Franklin conditionally agreed. Hobson and Moriarty were to proceed to Campbelltown, from where Hobson would go direct to Sydney, while Moriarty would meet the rest of the party again at Camden. Four of the horses were now sold or returned, leaving only Hymagamas, Dandelion and Kitty. Beds, tarpaulin and the heavy cart that had transported them from Port Phillip were also to be sold in Goulburn. Lady Franklin spent the rest of the day visiting the town of Goulburn and the site of the old township, and returned to the Gibsons for dinner.

Set off at 11 for Goulburn, 5 miles. Dr Gibson first took us up hill where his first bark cottage was erected & where he lived till his health suffering drove him below. It looks over the smaller cultivated flat & ponds where house is & on considerable extent of plain & undulation other side. Sir Richard Bourke slept here. The scattered brick houses of Goulburn soon appeared before us. In nearer ground presenting its gable end towards road was red brick steam mill for grinding flour erected by Mr Bradley, whose home is seen on elevation behind amidst cultivation. Mr Bradley is son of an officer in the NSW Corps or 102d regiment & is married to Miss Hovell, daughter of the travelling companion of Mr Hume.[119] Beyond this we came to the new brick parsonage of Mr Sowerby, with play ground in front—he has 13 boys, boarders, at £40 a year. Rate of clergyman's payment here is £100 for 100 people, £150 for 200, £200 for 500—as we were to lunch there returning, passed on after speaking to him.

The Plan of Town of Goulburn is that of a parallelogram. The town has existed only about 4 years—the old township may be 10 years old.[120] *Goulburn is the capital of Argyll—about 2000 feet above sea— much the same as Bathurst—but colder—not so good a climate—town has about 100 houses—about 300 inhabitants (more?) 16 sections— 12 allotments in each section & H acre to each allotment. It has a race course—latterly in dispute. Dr Gibson thinks it does mischief. Near it was a gibbet where 2 men hung in chains for murder committed till Sir R. Bourke desired it to be removed. There was till lately a subscription pack of fox hounds for hunting native dogs, about 15 couple [?]—subscription £5.10.0. The hounds often destroyed the chase by coming on track of kangaroo & preferring the latter—no conviviality—met only on field. Goulburn, Yass & Limestone Plains are the last appointed Police Districts. Limestone Plains the last— formed a year ago.*

Jane Franklin, Diary, 6 May 1839

The most remarkable house in Goulburn was built also by Mr Bradley for an inn, but whether or not he could not let it, he is now going to live in it himself, finding his house on the hill cold. The town house is a red brick building of 2 stories & many windows—there are 3 inns now in Goulburn & many stores including butchers, bakers &c—2 of the stores bear in great letters Australian Stores & Argyll Stores. The first street—if so it may be called—we passed thro' & which is called Sloane St contains the Goulburn Inn with verandah—the mail coach office, & a good brick house with green window frames &c & brass plate to door of Mr Hovell, above mentioned. He has come to live here I believe since his daughter's marriage—pursuing line of Sloane St there is the Commercial Bank, the hospital, shabby wooden building & 2 or 3 other neat houses, all separate. This Sloane St is on line of road to the old Township of Goulburn, about a mile farther, abandoned for the new as being more out of line of Sydney & Yass roads. Another street will run parallel to Sloane St called Auburn St nearer the hill. The Episcopal Church is built on sloping ground, which had to be levelled for building. It had been fixed for another elevation near Mr Sowerby's, but Bishop objected & insisted on its being in middle of the town. It is rather a large & substantial brick building on foundation of stone, will cost nearly £2000—tho' all this not yet subscribed, yet it is expected. The foundation stones are got here. Where the stone is not common it is of varied colours—the hewn stone for finishing & ornamental parts comes from 20 miles off, near Marulan.

As we were walking from this, the Presbyterian clergyman whose name I was told was Hamilton crossed our path & something in his manner seemed to indicate to Dr Gibson that he wished to be presented. I begged he would & he called him back. As he approached me, the name of Hamilton & his general appearance—tho' as I thought altered, thinner & paler & stiffer with white hat—reminded me he was the same who came above a year, perhaps a year & a half ago, with Mr Lilly & others & to whom Captain Maconochie said that this was strange country, all things turned upside down, Chickens had no bones in them, an observation which at first arresting his serious attention, ended by making him flush. I told him I thought I had seen him before at Government House &c—asked if satisfied—yes, getting on pretty well.

Dr Gibson himself is a Presbyterian by birth, but an Episcopalian by habit in the army & by preference tho' a subscriber to both churches. He said Mr Hamilton had had to struggle with a great deal, meaning I suppose to get subscriptions. Dr Gibson said he was excessively zealous, & had something of the old Covenanter about him; I think Dr Gibson thought it too much—I thought this strongly expressed in his countenance. Mr Hamilton holds his church in the Court House, having come a few weeks before Mr Sowerby, both about a year ago. When Mr Sowerby came

Mr Stewart, the Police Magistrate on whom it depended to offer it at all, thought it might do for both—but this Mr Sowerby would not agree to, & indeed unless alternate & not regular services had been used it could not be done. At first therefore the English service was performed in a room in the mill, but since then a cottage in the town has been hired expressly for it. Mr Faithful told me the congregation sometimes amounted to 70 or 80, tho' yesterday only about 40. We passed the site intended for the Scotch Church in pleasant position right of road to old township—Court House is a cottage-looking building skirting the plain nearer the hills. New one not yet begun—this & other public buildings, engaged for by contractor 1, 2 or 3 years ago, are not commenced, but with respect to English church, a committee of gents have taken it into their own hands & got their own mechanics & by great exertions have got on so far—nothing they say gets on by contract.

The burial ground is still farther on same road, in very pretty position, on bushy & lightly treed knoll. Opposite the cemetery is a very pretty looking gentleman's cottage belonging to Mr Stewart the Police Magistrate who within a few days is married to a daughter of Captain Gower in this neighbourhood, & on this score excused himself from coming to pay his respects. He is Presbyterian—but represented as a good natured, timid, easy man, who as his wife was of Church of England would probably follow her to church—as by example of Dr & Mrs Richardson, latter doing same. Dr Richardson is the Colonial Surgeon, an elderly Scotchman of fair ruddy complexion, round head, grey hair & small features. He was lately called to Sydney to take Senior charge of hospital, but declined—he has the hospital here, chiefly convicts tho' particular cases of free are taken gratis also. The average number of patients is 30 to 40—average number who die in the year 25. Dr Richardson told me this on my remarking to him the number of apparently new-made graves in cemetery—reddish gravel, fresh looking mounds—the dryness of the season preventing vegetation growing over may partly account for it. There are some Catholic stones here, some handsome plain table stone tombs enclosed in fences but without inscription—no fence round—is long way from church. Dr Richardson said prevailing complaint was rheumatism, proceeding from extremes of temperature—great prevalence of cold Westerly winds here—West & South West—North West winds brought heat.

Visited the old Township. There is a small brewery here, & the wretched hut & stable sheds of the Mounted Police, of whom there are 21 here under Lt Waddy. Ordered 2 for tomorrow. Saw 2 Wollondilly natives, called Billy & Polly or Ounong & Wollondi—in order to obtain this information I was obliged by their instruction to ask for white fellow name & black fellow name—'You speak very well to me,' said Ounong to me. He was in trousers & opossum skin, fur inside, & cut & coloured, patterns made in skin outside—woman in blanket—was small—silky hair with tinge of auburn or chestnut—his hair ropey—broad ugly features. They handled my boa & made exclamations of surprise when I shewed them the lining of my cloak—they guessed I was the governor lubra they had already heard of.

Their language thus:

Opossum—Willi
Squirrel—Bango
Man—Myan
Woman—Ballan
Physician—Karadji.

Drew money at Mr Sullivan's Agent for Commercial Bank, & parted here from Captain Moriarty & Dr Hobson who went on from hence 13 miles to Towrang—to adjoining station. I felt uncertain whether I should see Dr Hobson any more in the colony, & begged him to make a purchase for me at Sydney for the Museum[121] & sent [i.e. send] messages to Hobarton. Returning we stopped at Mr Bradley's Steam Mill & found him there, a gigantic man, very respectful in manner—he afterwards invited us to go up his house, a wooden building with verandah, which opens into parlour, & his wife brought in—her father's Mr Hovell's picture was over the chimney.

At dinner we were joined by Mr Faithful, Mrs Gibson's brother, a bachelor, living 5 miles off,[122] the same who had his men speared about a year ago at the Broken River. He had 16 men with sheep & cattle moving on West in search of stations—encamped here; natives were numerous around—about 300. His men had been intimate with them & given them much food—they had but 4 muskets among them—amused themselves with firing at target against gum tree—3 never hit—the natives laughed & shewed what they could do with spears—when they attacked them the first they speared was the only good marksman—8 were killed—whether this number included or not one who was speared a few months after, in August, I don't know—the latter had great confidence in them & no fear in spite of what he had witnessed. Mr Faithful described his loss as very great in sheep—should have only cattle—seemed a person of no great intelligence—a giant in size & young—his sister seemed to gain confidence by his presence & talked more & loudly.

Conrad Martens (1801–1878)
BUSH SCENE, ILLAWARRA,
NETTLE TREE AND CABBAGE PALMS
[Sydney: C. Martens, 1850]
hand-coloured lithograph; 18.5 x 15 cm
Rex Nan Kivell Collection NK872/17

VII

Goulburn to the Illawarra

7-17 May 1839

On May 7, 8 and 9, Lady Franklin continued her journey from Goulburn to Campbelltown via Camden.[123] Her diary for these three days consists of rough notes and jottings in pencil which are virtually indecipherable. In a letter to Sir John, Lady Franklin wrote a very brief account of her visit to Camden. The proprietors, James and William Macarthur, were absent, but she was entertained by James Macarthur's new wife, Emily, née Stone, and his sister. After sleeping there for one night, and admiring the house, though without raptures, the party went on to Campbelltown. There, by prior arrangement, Captain Richard Westmacott, former aide-de-camp to Governor Richard Bourke, awaited them. Captain Westmacott—'the person perhaps we have liked the best in our tour, kind, sincere, active, energetic, religious'—escorted Lady Franklin on a detour to the Illawarra, where he owned a large estate.

In her letter to her husband, dated from Wollongong on 11 May, Jane Franklin described 'the beautiful and luxuriant district of Illawarra'. There was some effort by the locals, Captain Westmacott in particular, to persuade her to invest in a piece of land in the district, on the assurance that it would rapidly increase in value. She was briefly tempted, but later realised that she could not command the necessary purchase price. The brief fantasy may, however, have given the region an added interest in her eyes.[124]

After meeting Captain Francis Allman, Police Magistrate of Campbelltown, and his family (he an 'elderly man wearing a sort of shovel hat—she elderly & fat—daughter disagreeable looking') and commenting on the 'appearance of poverty & discomfort in house',[125] Lady Franklin and her party proceeded on their way, scrambling on horseback through the glens and ridges, the thick scrub and luxuriant trees and ferns, through Appin to Wollongong. Lady Franklin commented on the rush of emigration to the Illawarra and the high wages paid to mechanics, and the amount of drinking that took place in consequence. Men evaded the law forbidding the sale of spirits to habitual drunkards, she wrote, by getting friends to buy the alcohol for them, and taking it into the bush.[126]

[From Campbelltown], by previous arrangement, we diverged into the beautiful and luxuriant district of Illawarra; a tract 60 miles in extent, between the mountains and the sea, remarkable for its soil of extraordinary fertility, its rich vegetation and singular shrubs and plants some of which, as for instance two species of palm which abound there, are of a tropical character. The land is of extreme value, but is mostly occupied, though only lately come into notice. During our stay of several days in this district, we were chiefly under the care and guidance of Captain Westmacott, (a son of Sir Richard Westmacott, the great sculptor) who has a fine property in Illawarra. Captain Westmacott was for eleven years Aide-de-Camp to Sir Richard Bourke, a proof of his good qualities which to us were very apparent without this recommendation. He is the person perhaps we have liked the best in our tour, kind, sincere, active, energetic, religious. He and all the other residents of Illawarra were much pleased with us for admiring the extraordinary beauty of their district which they pride themselves the more upon, as during the late drought, it was constantly well watered, and the harvest was as productive as ever.

Letter, Jane Franklin to John Franklin, 11 May 1839

She passed a restless night at Wollongong, tormented by the incessant mosquitoes, and wrote the same day to her husband: 'I must tell you that I have not the slightest fancy of ever inhabiting or even visiting Illawarra again, for in spite of its beauty and richness, it is not a climate to suit me, and wherever there are mosquitoes as there are there, I must run away; I could not live in such a country.'[127] The next morning, Sunday, she felt too ill to go to church in the school house, but recovered sufficiently to take a walk in the afternoon down to the harbour, to admire the beach and the views of the town to be had from the point. The convict barracks, on a tongue of land by the harbour, shocked her a little with their poor conditions. The prisoners lay on bare floors or wooden platforms, 24 crowded together into each windowless 'box', into which came no light or air, except through the iron bars at the top of the door. 'We were told they were locked in only at night' she wrote, 'but found them locked in now—no mattresses—have they none? he asked the soldier—"only the sick".'

They visited next Mr Charles Throsby Smith, 'the proprietor of the township of Wollongong', in his home, Bustle Cottage, on a hill just outside the town. Smith had held the land on which the town was built by grant for fifteen years, and when Governor Bourke fixed on the site of the town of Wollongong in 1835, offered to sell him 300 acres for only £300. Bourke, however, insisted that Smith should retain the property 'for his own advantage' and accepted only the tongue of land that formed the harbour. Lady Franklin and her party visited the recently widowed Mr Smith, admired the view from his house, drank his champagne, and listened while he 'talked of his town'. Then, after admiring the construction, at government expense, of a basin for steam vessels, and being promised by the stone mason some of the fossils the workers frequently extracted from the solid sandstone rock, she returned to the cottage of the police magistrate, Captain Plunkett, for dinner. Conversation (as conversations so often did in Lady Franklin's presence) turned on the diamond, brown and black snakes which abounded in the district.[128]

On Monday 13 May, the party set off, on horseback again, on a three-day excursion via Dapto to Kiama and then back to Wollongong. Jane Franklin's diary contains brief descriptions of the striking scenery, and summaries of lively conversations about snakes and schools. There must have been some dispute, which she did not record, about the length of this diversion. At Illawarra, as she wrote later to Sir John, she was told that 'we should not see the whole of the district, nor the most extensive and interesting agricultural establishment in the whole colony unless we went to Shoalhaven'.[129] But she did not do so. A later diary entry suggests that this was 'in consequence of the discontent expressed, or implied rather, by my companions, who made me feel that they were being dragged along on my account & that in their eyes I was never satisfied with wandering'.[130] But at the time, her brief diary contained no hint of her disappointment.

Lady Franklin slept one night at Captain Westmacott's house at Bulli, before returning to Campbelltown on Friday 17 May. On her last day at Wollongong she was warned that she would be approached by the Presbyterian community of the town for a subscription to their church, a request which threw her (understandably perhaps) into a state of some concern, for she knew not how to refuse, but feared that if she once began subscribing to churches of all denominations, there would be no end to it. Captain Westmacott, indignant, declared that if she did subscribe to the Presbyterian Church he would ask her to put her name to the Anglican list as well, but pay the subscription himself. 'Is not he one of the right sort?' she asked Sir John.[131]

Meanwhile the Sydney papers were watching her progress closely, and beginning to anticipate her arrival.

This Lady-Errant is advancing gradually to our capital, and may very shortly be expected to make her appearance. After so long and arduous an overland journey to come and see us here in Sydney, the least thing we can do is to receive her ladyship with every mark of honour and respect which her rank and personal virtues deserve ... Lady Franklin is known to be a woman of considerable mental accomplishment; and it is expected, not without some foundation, that her ladyship will favour the literary world with an interesting narrative of her numerous travels, and peregrinations in various parts of the world, and among the rest her over-land journey from Hobart Town to Sydney, with her observations of men and manners, and also on the natural phenomena of the various countries and climates through which she has passed.

Colonist, 11 May 1839

By 15 May, in an edition which Lady Franklin read on her last morning at Bulli, the Colonist had heard of her intention to 'alter her route, and visit the far-famed district of Illawarra, before bringing her journey to a close. Her Ladyship and party', the paper continued, 'were in good health and excellent spirits, having enjoyed their over-land expedition with great pleasure, and without any accident along the way. What a romantic and interesting narrative may we not expect from her Ladyship after this! We have no doubt but her Ladyship will meet with a hearty welcome and honourable attention when she arrives at our metropolis.'[132]

This all seemed very complimentary, but some elements would have made Lady Franklin flinch. She knew too well what the Hobart papers thought of her *imagined ventures into the literary world, how distrustful colonists in general were of a 'bluestocking'. Nor would it take long for the Van Diemen's Land papers to give the apparently harmless playfulness of the 'Lady-Errant' a savage twist.*

Both Captains, Plunkett and Westmacott, saw her on her way to Campbelltown, beyond the unfenced boundary of Westmacott's property, and as far as a 'large tree, I believe a black butt gum'. There they said their farewells and the party proceeded on their ascent, through disappointing country, where the scrub was too thick to get a good view of the sea below, but the plants and shrubs seemed inferior to those they had seen on their road down. Jane 'regretted we had let the descent into Wollongong & brush of Kiama pass without picking things'. They came at last to Appin, where they found 'many people were assembled, hats off, glad to see me back &c, & a disposition to cheer'. After lunch at the inn they returned to Campbelltown, where they 'excused ourselves from dining with Captain Allman & thought he was not sorry', but were a little offended when 'his ladies' did not call.[133]

On Saturday morning, 18 May, however, they found the ladies at Captain Allman's gate to greet them as they went by. On this morning they were escorted by Lieutenant Waddy with '6 or 8 mounted police in full dress … how or where they were got together I cannot tell'.[134] *Thus accompanied, they set off for Liverpool, en route, at last, for Sydney, which they would reach before nightfall. Lady Franklin had been exactly six weeks on the road.*

Unknown artist
[*GOVERNMENT HOUSE STABLES,
DOMAIN, SYDNEY*] [183-?]
watercolour; 17.4 x 24 cm
Rex Nan Kivell Collection NK2455/35

VII

Sydney

18-27 May 1839

*F*eelings in Sydney, as Lady Franklin approached, had been mixed. A few days before her arrival, the Australian had protested 'against the people of New South Wales being saddled with one fraction of the charges of the overland journey'.[135] There was, however, a greater tendency to welcome her with honour and to applaud, as did the Sydney Gazette, 'the resolution exhibited by Lady Franklin and her determination, not to be stayed by difficulties'. A 'large number of gentlemen', said the Gazette, had intended to ride out to meet her on the day of her arrival, but there had been too many rumours, and perhaps too many changes of plan. The message that she would visit Shoalhaven had reached Sydney, and her arrival was therefore not looked for until Monday. When Lady Franklin arrived in Liverpool she found Sir George Gipps' carriage in readiness, and his aide-de-camp, Henry Elliot's cousin Gilbert, there to meet them. But, because her arrival was not quite expected, there was no guard of honour. Possibly she was relieved. For this last stage of her journey she was attended by 'six or eight orderlies with an officer' and escorted by a carriage and four sent from Liverpool to meet her by Henry C. Sempill, Esq., complete with roses and cards of greeting. When the party reached the police office in George Street she was met by the First Police Magistrate, Colonel Wilson, and his daughters, on horseback, plus 'a few gentlemen who had intimation that she was approaching', and these attended her to Government House.[136]

Now that she was in Sydney, the great speculation was how long she would stay. The Gazette *reported that she did 'not contemplate making any great stay in our capital. It is expected she will return to Hobart Town by the* Eudora, *Captain Addison, to sail on Sunday next.'*[137] *But the* Colonist—*in a tone which seems heavy with irony—declared that she must stay longer:*

[W]e can scarcely think, that after taking so long and so fatiguing a journey, her ladyship would leave us so suddenly. No, no; the public expect to see Lady Franklin some night at the Victoria Theatre before she goes; and her ladyship must go all the way to Bathurst, to Maitland, Windsor, and Parramatta, before she can form an adequate conception of this colony, and without that she won't be able to do us justice in her forthcoming book.[138]

On her progress from Liverpool to Sydney Jane Franklin's own diary is silent. She picked up the story at the moment of her arrival at Government House, where she made her first acquaintance with Sir George and Lady Gipps. Sir George Gipps (1791–1847), a veteran of the Peninsular War and a Whig, had arrived in New South Wales as governor of the colony on 24 February 1838. He had married Elizabeth Ramsay in 1830, and they had one child, Reginald, then eight years old. In later years Gipps was to find governing a colony at least as difficult as did Sir John Franklin. During his term of office New South Wales began the difficult transition towards representative government, experienced the gradual abolition of transportation, and was beset by disputes over land tenure. His relations with many colonists, particularly those in the Legislative Council, became increasingly bitter and hostile. But in 1839 those relations were still on the whole cordial, though signs of future trouble were certainly visible.[139]

Jane Franklin's descriptions of Sydney throughout her extended visit show both the rapid growth of a colonial society and its limits. She was soon occupied with calls and dinner parties, through which she met the principal military and civil officers and clergy of the town: the Anglican Bishop, William Broughton, the Colonial Secretary, Edward Deas Thomson, Commander of the Royal Engineers, Major Barney, and the commander of the forces in New South Wales, Sir Maurice O'Connell. The elite group whose acquaintance a visiting governor's wife could cultivate was small indeed, and, amongst the ladies at least, littered with the relatives of former governors. Among the first to call was the former governor's wife, Anna Josepha King, two of whose daughters had married and settled near Sydney. Mrs Deas Thomson was the daughter of the previous governor, Sir Richard Bourke; Lady O'Connell still bore grudges against colonists who had played any part in the arrest of her father, Governor Sir William Bligh, in 1808. This tight-knit group, with all its petty rivalries and discontents, formed Lady Franklin's principal society, but she was more interested by the rapid growth evident in the town itself, and the range of public institutions, churches and schools being established. Though she herself was struck by the size and diversity, if not the beauty, of the buildings, what is now most striking is the large spaces of wilderness or wasteland which still existed at the heart of the municipal centre.

Although the Colonist had so confidently predicted that she must patronise the newly opened Victoria Theatre, and some of the actors were also hopeful that she might do so, Lady Franklin steadfastly refused. She had enthusiastically attended plays in London in her youth, but colonial theatre did not meet her standards of quality or morality, and it was no part of her desire as governor's wife to encourage or even countenance it. She did not patronise the theatre in Hobart, she firmly informed the actors Conrad Knowles and John Lazar, and therefore could not do so in Sydney.

Saturday 18 May

We were shewn into a small drawing room, where presently Lady Gipps came quietly in, walking like a woman of much more advanced age— extremely quiet, gentle, easy & pleasing—she shewed us presently up stairs to rooms, 3 in old part of the house, which she left us to apportion— dressed for dinner, & on going down, Sir George Gipps was in the room & came forward cordially to receive me—short, self confident manner, grizzled hair—small, sparkling dark eyes—does not look you in face—Mr Parker[140] youngish, pale, meek-looking—rather obsequious—Captain Moriarty & Elliot there. Dinner—large room—Sir George & Lady Gipps opposite at table—Parker one end, Gilbert Elliot other. Servants handed wine— Sir George asked champaign &c[141]—questions relating to journey—little said by others—2 home gents somewhat under awe. A short time after dinner a note was received by Mr Elliot from Dr Hobson, stating he was to sail in the *Augustus Caesar* tomorrow morning at daybreak & asking at what hour he should call for my letters—told 9—that evening I went to write to Sir John. Dr Hobson called in evening. Sir George told me Dr Hobson had been 3 or 4 days here before he called & when Sir George heard this, he exclaimed '"Why, what the Devil have you been doing?" I begged him' [continued Sir George] 'to come every day to dine, & from that time to this, when you say he is going to sail, have seen nothing of him—curious fellow that Dr.' I replied, 'You frightened him—that's very clear.' 'Yes— I said,' repeated Sir George, evidently a little pleased, '"what the Devil have you been about?"'

Dr Hobson had not been well since he was at Sydney & told me privately he did not like the place & would not be here—he ought to go to a warm climate. Dr Officer[142] had written to him to say there was no appointment for him in VDL.[143] He had almost made up his mind to go to Port Phillip. He had seen Mr [Alfred] Stephen who had early entered on the duties of his office—he had not been well since he came—&

Mrs Stephen was covered with mosquito bites—(Lady Gipps had called on her—admired her beautiful children—did not admire Mrs Robinson who was there). Dr Hobson had had no occasion for my draft[144]—the Museum had but little. I begged him to call early in the morning for letters & wrote long one to Sir John & a note to Dr Hobson himself about chemical apparatus, & to Mr Gunn to introduce him & to Tobin to give him plants & seeds &c—was up very late writing.

Sunday 19 May

Slept late & did not wake till past 10—not feeling well, did not attempt to go to church, but felt should have been able afterwards. Opened packet of newspapers brought by Mr Stephen—received the party on return from church—Lady Gipps & Sophy in close carriage which afterwards took Newport, the ladies' maid for a drive. Sir George always walks to church— talked to Lady Gipps & sat down to lunch till time for afternoon church when went without the Gipps but with other gents—2 chairs in the pew— I would not occupy either—Bishop preached—new reader, no responses. Sir George agreed with me afterwards that it was impossible to preserve attention—he for his part thought of his despatches. Drove round & from domain by moonlight evening & on return found Sir George at door & walked [with him] to Mrs Macquarie's stables[145]—'she was 13 years Governor of the Colony' [he said].

Monday 20 May

Sophy went to breakfast at ½ past 7. There was much amusement about the Melbourne address,[146] which Sir George spoke of & said another was coming—for the gents of Sydney would not be outdone by Melbourne. It was reported I was going to the Red Sea. At 12, a message sent up to know if I could receive visitors—obliged to reply in affirmative—went down & found it was Mrs King[147]—not grown so old as expected—very red & spotted—coal black false hair—hoped she would go back with me to VDL. She made no difficulty. Agreed with Lady Gipps that we would be not at home to the rest [of callers], & ordered carriage at ½ 1. Went out in carriage with Sophy & Elliot about straw bonnets & into Tegg's shop—smart books—son of man in Cheapside—no work in New Zealand or Colony— taken into printing press at back & into place below at back—saw his Hopkinson's patent press, which prints the Theatre Bills, Bishop's pamphlets & Catholic pamphlets—no newspaper—bought his almanack.[148] Walked along arcaded street—George St to Clint's map shop[149]—saw only a woman there—gave orders for mounting maps of Mitchell & Dixon. Return to Government House, where Sir George waiting to drive us out in phaeton to South Head light house—Mr Elliot with us.

Pass before Catholic Church—gothic, without a tower, many windows—near it Catholic Seminary or Clerical Barrack where all are received on coming to Colony—pretty building, cottage style. Bishop's residence [Polding's] is in hollow near—on in road, pass Sydney College. Beyond, turn to left in road to South Head—overlook a pretty portion of harbour—beyond pass high stone walls of gaol, & new Court house—6 feet Doric columns support pediment.[150] Pass stone quarry—on right is seen part of Botany Bay, on left pass a large house belonging to a distiller, commonly called Juniper Hall—now the Distiller has cut me, said Sir George, ever since I have been a member of Temperance Society.[151] Scrub on each side growing in white sand—road covered with gravelly sand of a more brickdust colour—the garden soil here is made of rock pounded into sand & manured—such as this near Sydney will fetch £20 the acre—no land said Sir George is sold under £10 in County of Cumberland[152]—on left, a view of the bay & an island—on right, an ugly staring white house, the Catholic Orphan School built 2 years ago. It does not answer very well—healthy situation, but far from town for provisions—formerly Catholic orphans were in a general establishment, till Polding desired separation—now he wants another building that boys may be separated from girls—Dr Polding is an extremely polished & polite man, even finical—but never satisfied with what is done for him—always thinks more is done for other denominations than his—our Bishop feels similarly perhaps, but too much tact & too much man of world to shew it in same way.[153]

On, see Point Piper left, ascend from flat winding up in green scrub—much Banksia &c & stunted or cut gum trees—also grass trees—get ocean views front & right. Come to lighthouse—inscription goes round 2 or 3 sides of it—completed in 1817, Gill designed it—Greenway, Civil Architect[154]—is 76 feet high—round tower rather smaller at top than bottom—lantern gallery & dome at top—tower is bound in squares by iron hoops—rises from centre of low building which forms sort of wing on each side having dome on each—looks like Turkish dome. One side & front has verandah—the opposite, towards sea, has plain stone front—great simplicity—grass platform & small well of stones with battery places for guns & 2 end square embossed towers rising a little above—2 men here & a stone dwelling, & a few hundred yards farther is an octagonal building for signal station—signalling at the time for a ship coming in from Liverpool—the *Formosa*, with emigrants. Sir George asked why Union Jack was there—'In honor of you,' said man—'In honor of me,' repeated the Governor.

Went on farther, descending to see Watson's Bay, a pretty inlet, with points jutting out East & West. Pilot station here—Mr Hannibal Macarthur[155] has a villa here, just within the point of South Head—Easterly sea comes dashing against depression of cliff behind him & spray sometimes goes over his house—seems as if he had placed himself devotedly in the gap to prevent farther mischief.—See North head, fine cliff wall & passage between—went close to edge of precipice, fine cliffs about 200 feet—in some places worn by sea into ledges. Inlets beautiful, but tops of all level—seems as if some flattening weight had pressed all down to horizontal line.

Lady Franklin had met Bishop Broughton when he visited Van Diemen's Land the previous year and they were mutually impressed. She furnished her sister Mary with the following description:

I found him a most delightful person (the very personification it is true of High Church Orthodoxy in his ecclesiastical capacity but unassuming, amicable, attaching, and engaging in a most remarkable degree, as a man). The combined intellect, vivacity, and benignity of his interesting countenance forms the exact portrait of his mind. He has the great nose which Napoleon considered always to characterise superior minds—a very small mouth, with large & beautiful dark grey eyes shaded with black eyelashes. This fine head is placed however upon a very small figure, disfigured besides, by one leg being shorter than the other, so that he walks lame. Notwithstanding this defect, he has perfectly the look of a gentleman, & is thoroughly so in his demeanour and manners, being especially remarkable for self possession, ease & readiness with somewhat of a courtliness of manner, at least towards women. He is fond of humour, & has a fund of acute observations & penetrating perceptions.

Letter, Jane Franklin to Mary Simpkinson, 21 June 1838[156]

Returned rather late to dinner—a party to meet me—Mr & Mrs Thomson[157] & Major & Mrs Barney[158] & their daughter, Mrs Hutchinson Browne—Bishop & Mrs & 2 Miss Broughtons, Mr Clark from China (a young dark man, said to be very clever and interesting), Colonel Wodehouse of the 50th, assembled in Long Room or Great Drawing room—Bishop had called in morning & a heap of others—Major Barney lively & agreeable—Mrs Barney left England at 10—was 6 years educating in Germany, Hamburg, Altona, Hanover—married at 17—has been 9 years in Jamaica. Finds this country poor & dull compared to it.

Mrs Broughton lived 9 years a curate's wife, & would have been contented to remain—[I?] remarked on the important & interesting position she occupied. She has been very pretty—thin & dark.[159] Girls short—one very fat & clumsy—both have dark eyes & coal black hair. Spoke to Mrs Thomson—short, clumsy—expressive & clever face—masculine—fine singer. I asked after Sir Richard [Bourke]—she used to go about with him. I asked her to VDL—seemed as if she would like it. She begged me to fix a day to dine with them. I was told in her father's time, she did not forget she was Governor's daughter, & was a great quizzer. She sang—and the 2 Miss Broughtons sang a duet.

Major Barney told me at dinner, he thought Port Phillip pasturage like that of [all] these new countries. Generally looked fine at first, but soon eaten down. The supplies of wheat furnished by VDL seem to have raised us in opinion here.[160] I expressed to Mrs Barney & Mrs Broughton that I had a more exalted opinion of this colony than before, at which Mrs Barney almost shouted with pleasure.

Snachall, handing round cheese, could not make Mr Clarke see or hear—he poked it into his nose & stood thus with very earnest patience several minutes. Sir George noticed—reddened, laughed—saw I was noticing—we both burst out. He said he never saw any thing so ridiculous—I remarked he was determined he should smell it if he could not see it—Sir George, half ashamed, half provoked, at the thing, still could not restrain himself—I never before saw such an involuntary burst. Those opposite remarked it, but did not know what it was. Snachall thought the line of his duty was very plain—he must either make Mr Clarke take the cheese or refuse it & he could not succeed in either.[161]

Captain Moriarty told Sophy we had not only a better but a cleverer Governor. Mr Elliot said he would not be in any office under him [Gipps] for anything—he was frightened to death at him. Captain Moriarty had met [Judge Alfred] Stephen who said he could not afford to live here—had a hundred cases before him of the grossest description—extremely disgusted—meant to call on me.

Tuesday 21 May

Up in my room until called down to Major Smyth, *Fairlie.*

There are no further entries for Tuesday or Wednesday, perhaps because Lady Franklin wrote another long letter to Sir John over those two days. Her letter not only gives an account of these days but also shows her growing plans for a more extended visit. Her simple desire to stay was manifest. She did not want to miss the parties planned for her in Sydney, nor to 'give up' an excursion of a 'few days' with the bishop, who was going on a tour of inspection of churches and schools in the Hawkesbury and had invited her to accompany him (it proved to take two weeks). She was careful to emphasise the benefits which she believed would flow to Sir John himself from her activities, although she knew that her own uncharacteristic freedom from headaches and other illnesses—a sure sign that she was happy—would persuade him still more effectively. Sir John's own letters to her of about the same period show anxiety for her happiness and well being, but also for her safe and speedy return. On 14 May he had added a postscript to his letter: 'I hope you will not let slip any opportunity of returning—remember that but few vessels come from Sydney here'. And a few days later, in response to a letter of hers, he wrote: 'How much I should have enjoyed your excursion as well as that you contemplate taking to the Hunter and Port Stephens which I think you ought to accomplish if you can before your return but you must not make any unnecessary delay for I want you back ...'[162]
Jane Franklin had received neither of those letters when she wrote the following letter.

Tuesday 21 and Wednesday 22 May

My dearest Love,

I received yesterday your packet dated the 9th of May ... The *Eudora* and the *Medway* are ready to sail in 4 or 5 days but the *Eudora* would wait until Sunday the 2nd. This is not long enough for our objects and plans, yet at the same time I am unwilling to lose the opportunity, not knowing when the next will occur ...

If we go so soon as Sunday the 2nd, I must give up going to Port Stephens which I would like to see partly on the Parrys' account[163] but still more because without I shall miss seeing Captain King which I shall be very sorry for and principally on your account as I think he may require setting to rights as to the Maconochie question, he being in constant correspondence with Captain Maconochie.[164] I shall be also obliged to give up an excursion of a few days with the Bishop, who has offered to take us with him, but who cannot go until the 6th, also to forego the dinner parties which the Gipps were contemplating to have in order to introduce people to me, as well as invitations which other people intend giving me. I should much regret not dining with the Bishop, the McLeays and the Thomsons. The latter have pressed me to fix a day, but under present circumstances I could not do so—I gave them your message and told them how happy you would be to see them in Van Diemen's Land ...

On the day of our arrival we received cards and dinner invitations from Sir Maurice and Lady O'Connell[165]—(Sir George and Lady Gipps also). Lady Gipps said her answer depended on mine and the invitation was accepted. I believe it is the first time they have, or least that she has been there or anywhere for they do not go out to dinner, not even he, anywhere.

The same day also we received two cards of invitation to dinner from Colonel Wilson, First Police Magistrate in order that we might choose which day we liked best and if neither suited us, we were to fix our own, but we excused ourselves ... When I returned the visits of Mrs Broughton and Lady O'Connell I called on the Miss Wilsons and the same day being about to visit the handsome market place, we met Colonel Wilson at the identical spot. Upon which he offered to conduct me through it, as being within his jurisdiction. Closely adjoining it was the handsome building of the Police Office which he invited me to look at—the official business was over, except in one room where a man [was] being examined closely about horse-stealing.—he had a chair instantly placed for me and though I merely made a pretence of sitting down for one instant to acknowledge his civility and because having mortified him by refusing his dinner, I was anxious to satisfy him now, this lover of notoriety, who they say had rather be abused in the paper than not noticed at all, put an article in the 'Gazette' or 'Herald' which appeared this morning to say I had stopped in the Police Office to listen to the Case and describes me personally as a [']fine looking woman, with a very intellectual countenance and blue expressive eyes— vivacious and affable'.[166] What a fool has he made of himself and me!—and what fine food for the Hobarton papers. I am quite amazed at the figure I cut in the papers ...

A most untoward circumstance has occurred: Lady Gipps, though seldom or never she says, ailing anything, is to-day so unwell as to keep her bed and room. There is no chance of her going to the O'Connells' to-morrow [May 23?], and I fear very little of her being able to receive at the [Queen's] Birthday. Sir George says so many people have arrived in town for it, that it is out of the question to put it off now, unless it were a case of life and death ... The invitations this year are not so extensive as last year when they were sent over to Port Phillip—this year they do not extend beyond one day's journey ...

I have not been so well for a long time, as I have since I entered the colony of New South Wales and particularly since I have been at Sydney, and this in spite of some remaining mosquitoes, which we contrive to keep out of the bed however by gauze curtains. You will be the less surprised then if we are disposed to stay a little longer …

Yours in haste,

Most affectionately,

Jane Franklin[167]

Thursday 23 May

Had call from Mr John Saunders, Baptist Minister,[168] a person to whom Sir George had referred me as the best in the place for a Temperance Society as respects Snachall, & whom Sir George said he had the greatest regard for, as a high principled, conscientious, zealous, religious man full of enthusiasm—Sir George said Mr Saunders would stand on his head or do anything for him since he had signed the declaration of Temperance Society. Mr Saunders came with book in his hand—told him quickly what I wanted, for I found Bishop's carriage was driving up—he begged Snachall to call next morning—& begged me to use my influence with Lady Gipps, as female sanction much wanted. Bishop & Mrs were now in room & he abruptly left.

Bishop had sort of narrow landau or vis-à-vis —Sophy went in second, placed herself back[169]—Mrs Broughton third, placed herself by me, but when this ceremony was repeated, placed herself back, with a little hesitation & left place to him which he made no difficulty in keeping.

We went first to the School of Industry[170]—General Darling gave the house which was a Government one—subscription raised—Lady Darling's a very considerable one—some on foundation, some pay £12—all alike are kept till 15—then bound as servants till 18—3 years. Found Mrs Lethbridge there.[171] Two persons manage—schoolmistress & chief who receives £40 a year—& housekeeper who receives 20, & teaches to cook, wash &c. The girls do everything, the eldest only 14—all dressed in blue cottons with pinafores. The girls do not receive wages in service: clothing & food are enough. Sir George told me this school was not wanted. The gratuitous objects of charity in it are objects for the orphan School—stretchers & iron bedsteads—bugs exist—mattresses stuffed with seaweed cost 10sh 6d—reading, writing, arithmetic & household work.

Went hence to St James's—has a spire of brick. Drove from hence thro' George St to the site of new Episcopalian Cathedral—going on very slowly—area of church exclusive of tower 120 feet by 60. Tower is intended to be like Maudlin if found sufficient. The foundations of the Cathedral were relaid by Sir Richard Bourke—the first foundations, nearly adjoining, made the angle of the church instead of its Eastern face come on street. It is the Bishop's darling object. Sir Richard Bourke said you must have some painted glass—His Excellency must give it them—on this he found some hopes—he earnestly desires to have at Northern angle of Southern transept a chapter house & to give it a more perfect cathedral character—he acknowledged however there would be no chancel & nave but that it would be all chancel—on Northern side of cathedral is old burial ground—an ugly field with a small number of tombs in it.[172]

Bishop spoke of McLeays, and his wish to have shewn me Elizabeth Bay himself—when I expressed my intention of seeing it again on purpose, he proposed our calling there & telling him so—he lives in the second house in Macquarie Place—it is out of repair—found him at home. Mrs McLeay out but his daughter Mrs Campbell & her husband at home—McLeay made himself out to be 22—has been in the colony 14 years—large & fair & plain. He knew Sir John formerly, at Sir Joseph Banks'.[173]

Friday 24 May

Queens Birthday & very unwell. I was to have gone to the *feu de joie* in the domain, but gave it up—Levee at 12. Many carriages—were received in small drawing room. Lady Gipps was to have a consultation of physicians as to her coming down. In the evening, I wrote to her expressing my anxiety & desire to know the result—told her also my own state of suffering, yet that I would go down for an hour if I could overcome my sickness—no message was sent to beg me not to do so, if not well enough, but only an intimation of the hour Sir George would be ready to receive us below. No dinner was given today nor [arrangement?] made for it. I learnt thro' Snachall there was none, & a tray was brought up to Sophy & me. I was scarcely better when dressed, but sick again.

We went down to the small drawing room, word having been sent that people were coming—found Steel & Helys whom I already knew—Sir George not there but came instantly & after a few minutes & he had scolded people for not sweeping stairs & verandah, which were covered with dust, he made me & Sophy rise, gave me his arm & telling others to remain where they were took me into the large morning room, stript of carpet with benches round & 2 large chintz easy chairs which he said were

In a letter home Lady Franklin described her agonies of indecision about whether she should step in as hostess:

I had had the remark made to me before, that I should have to do the honors and in fact I felt in some dilemma whether I should express my desire to be of as much use as I could, (which was virtually proposing to take on myself the duties of reception) or whether I should be silent. I adopted the latter plan as being the least presuming and indeed till a late hour, I doubted my capability of being present at the party at all. After having been for an unexampled length of time freed from my usual ailments, I was that day seized with a sick head-ache. I wrote to Lady Gipps in her sick room to say I was extremely unwell and wholly incapable of any enjoyment, but at the same time if I could overcome my sickness I would go down for an hour or two with my niece who would not go without me. I was not requested to abstain from making any such exertion, and therefore I felt I was wanted.

Letter, Jane Franklin to John Franklin, 27 May 1839

for Sophy & me. They were evidently intended for Sir George & Lady Gipps. He was amused when we persisted in declining them, & then leaving Sophy behind & keeping me on his arm, stood a little way within door & in face of it nearby. The people came first to the aide-de-camp's room or Parker's room, thence to his, where ladies deposited cloaks &c— while gents cooled their heels in hall—they rejoined here, & passed above into long Drawing Room—whence it was intended they should pass on— if they did not move forward they were motioned or desired to do so. To most on entrance he presented me as Lady Franklin adding 'I am sorry to say Lady Gipps is very unwell & not able to come down stairs'—to some he did not repeat this eternal tale but let them find it out of themselves & to some he did not even mention my name. His manner was different— gracious with shake of hand to some, few words to another—only a bow to some. Mrs King did not come—she apologised to him one morning afterwards—hoped he was not offended with her—he seemed amused at her simple, half-shy way of saying this & said, 'I don't know, Mrs King, I am rather affronted' &c—Mrs Thomson absent & Lady O'Connell. Captain O'Connell came covered with orders, & a ridiculous & offensive sight in the eyes of other military men, who, however, all think him remarkably handsome.[174]

Ill as I was this standing by the hour almost killed me. He asked me at last if I would not sit down and I attempted to place myself near Sir James and Lady Dowling on a bench—all the rest of the people were standing. But this would not do, and I was forced to take the great arm chair. He did not choose dancing to begin till nearly two hours I think had elapsed, and everybody had come. I seized this moment to slip away to my room, where I remained an hour in quiet, and went back much better. The moment I appeared Sir George was at my side. He had previously expressed an earnest desire I should go in with him to the supper, 'else people would be disappointed' ... Only one toast was admitted this evening, that of the Queen. It was drunk very quietly, and the whole time we were in the supper room was only a few minutes of duration, and standing—there was not a seat in the room. The whole evening, Sir George never left my side: he was either walking with me from one room to the other, or seated by my side. I left him at last however about 2 o'clock, thinking that my departure might perhaps act as a signal to the others to go away.

Letter, Jane Franklin to John Franklin, May 27 1839

Saturday 25 May

Did not rise till ½ 11—at ½ 1, went with Sir George to School of Industry, where fancy fair ladies keep stalls in 2 rooms—great crowd.[175] Bought at Lady O'Connell's, Mrs Broughton's & Mrs Lethbridge's stalls & spoke to Mrs Campbell who kept pastry cooks—saw old McLeays there & was introduced to Mrs McLeay—Sir George said she was a ladylike old lady, but [said to be] very severe to her convict servants, the worst mistress in the country to them—did not know whether she is—it was the only thing he had ever heard against her. Mrs Somerset handed me some cakes & Mrs Lethbridge gave me a nosegay of camellias. Mr Elliot was required to pay half a crown for a note put in his hand addressed to me, in which I was compared to the Queen of Sheba (or Seba as they called her) visiting King Solomon.

Went next, on foot, to the Council chambers, held in a separate wing of the great hospital. The Legislative Council room is first on left in ground floor after entering passage—an oblong room with long table—& small gallery with 2 rows of benches in it for the public—Sir George said he would admit us on the 11th. Upstairs is the Executive Council—a very pleasant room. He made us sit down at the table, I in Sir M. O'Connell's place, on right, & Sophy in Bishop's on left. Saw there Mr McPherson, Clerk of the Councils, who looked like a common door keeper, & seemed to be scarce regarded as better. [Sir George said?] 'I can't tell Mr McPherson to read the report for it is not fit for you—I am sorry to say it is the heaviest we have had since we came to the colony—9 sentences'.[176]

We went to see the model of Hobarton in George St—it takes up a great space. It is raised, & looks well enough sideways, but when you go up into the gallery to look at it, it is very mean & all the houses made wretchedly so—the Custom House & Market are left out, Low having quarrelled with Peck & left it unfinished as appears by the advertisement. The Chief Justice [Sir James Dowling] was there & moved round a panoramic view of town. I was vexed at the exhibition & feared I expressed its badness before a man who afterwards appeared to be Peck—going out, he asked if his exhibition was satisfactory, but did not look up or address me.[177]

I took a little walk in the garden. Dinner & Evening talk of Egypt— Sir George there in 1821-2 up to Second Cataract.[178] Got ophthalmia, saw Caniglia, very enthusiastic.

Sunday 26 May

We expected Bishop to call for us at 9—his carriage did not come till 10—then took us to the St James's Sunday Schools, where Mr Wood, Chaplain of this church, a young serious man, met us in the court & conducted us up to School & Bishop. Classes were formed—girls on one side of great room, boys in others—all the catechism or collects—little creatures on sacraments & still lips, repeating commandments in a body, in short bits, after teacher, without book, not being able to read. The Bishop said, anticipating something from me, that it was mere repetition, mere words, but it was to be hoped that in time, the words being learnt, the understanding of them would come too—the very reason I thought why they never would. The boys' classes seemed better taught than the girls'— the female teachers did not appear to be really ladies. The Bishop said with complacency, however, that one was the daughter of a most respected merchant—in boys' classes, one was the schoolmaster, another Mr Wood, a third was by young man who seemed a good teacher. The Bishop thought so too, & wished to promote him—thought of making him catechist in Norfolk Island.

Visited next the schools under St Philip's Church where Bishop was going to preach. It was Trinity Sunday & Sacrament. Schools had nearly ended.[179]

Sir George on going home proposed a walk to see new Government House at ½ 3 & I agreed, tho' tired & limbs aching (it was thick fog in morning & we had all the windows open). Saw the new building, which led to long & interesting conversation (he would like to live 1 year in the new house)—this however must have been less so to him than to me as attention constantly taken off from it to a shrub, or a trifle of some sort or other subjects—Port Phillip, Maconochie, Transportation &c.

Had intimation given to me that Lady Gipps[180] would be glad to see me when I liked to go—I went after coffee—large room—door open, in bed— languid & exhausted, I think, before I went, tho' never above 10 minutes— prayers in Dining room by Sir George to 17 servants, 1 being out—some liturgy, some family prayers—well done.

Monday 27 May

Fresh drawings of Government House brought out by Sir George.[181] Sophy expressed her desire to copy them & he was pleased. A visit from Mrs Lethbridge about a manager of the School of Industry & from Mr James Wilson, artist, of the *Fairlie*, who seemed quite delighted to see me. He had gained at one time a rate of £1000 a year—for a few months was in Engineers Department till superseded from home—had been with 500 sheep to Menaroo [sic] plains & staid there till lost 410 of them by catarrh—now at his painting again—10 guineas for oil—spoke of [Conrad] Martens, landscape painter—15 guineas a landscape. He had asked him to do a dozen views of Sydney, & meant to send them to me as a present but had never got them—had painted Martens's portrait, had done a native & begged my acceptance of it—hoped I would see his wife.[182]

Sir George asked me if I would take a walk with him & I did. He begged me to understand we were no trouble in the house & no interference, & begged me I would not stay away on Lady Gipps's account—or his own account, more than on mine.

*I had a very long and interesting conversation with Sir George yesterday.
—I should say a confidential one, were he not so exceedingly frank and
open with everyone, that I can scarcely flatter myself with its being
confidential, though he did once use the term. The extreme magnificence
of the new Government House now erecting and the determination of
the colonists to have it grander and larger than any colonial
Government house existing elsewhere, formed the basis of our
conversation in the beginning.*

*We passed on to Port Phillip and I told him of Mr Latrobe which
he knew nothing about, and also (adding it was confidentially) of
Captain Maconochie's cause of failure. Sir George knew of his desires
and pretensions—knew that he was high in favour with Lord Howick
[a prominent member of the Whig ministry in Britain]—thought that
Lord Howick would come into the Colonies and that then, Maconochie
might succeed in his schemes. He said that Maconochie had been in
correspondence with him (Sir George) and that he was glad to tell me
of it in order that you might know it. His object was to recommend his
system, which Sir George thought well of in principle, and particularly
his 'social system', but believed that from its expense and the difficulty
of finding agents, it would be impracticable in this colony. Had it not
been for the expense, he would have had no objection to give Maconochie
a couple of thousand men to try his schemes upon in two or three
islands in the bay. Maconochie had not exactly asked for employment
under him, but he saw such was his design. He answered his letter,
and Maconochie wrote again rather pushing the matter beyond what
he thought quite right. The last letter he had not answered.*[183]

Letter, Jane Franklin to John Franklin, 27 May 1839

Dinner earlier than usual, as the boat [to Hunter River] went at 8—after hastily closing my letter to Sir John, I remained for a moment by permission to take leave of Lady Gipps—going into carriage Sir George said warm seal Coat [?]—you are not to return the latter &c—I intimated my gratitude. In our walk he talked chiefly of young Gilbert Elliot when we found ourselves alone—'would I swap?'—'No—& know His Excellency would be staunch'.

Robert Russell (1808–1900)
ENTRANCE TO WEST MAITLAND, 1837 1837
watercolour; 18.2 x 24.7 cm
Pictorial Collection R7209

IX

Excursion to the Gunter River and Port Stephens

27 May – 4 June 1839

*T*hat letter to Sir John, which Jane so hastily closed, on Monday 27 May,
when called to the steamer, had once again offered numerous excuses for
staying longer. To the prospect of the bishop's tour of the Hawkesbury region were
now added hopes that she might witness the meeting of the Legislative Council.
Sir George had given her an invitation to the gallery but her acceptance 'must
depend upon whether other ladies go also'. But 'though I may not have the
pleasure of being a spectator, the gentlemen [Mr Elliot and Captain Moriarty]
would be there'. Besides, the 'meeting of the Council is the signal for the dinner
parties, of which they have scarcely any, at any other time'. Once more she
insisted that this long absence was in Sir John's interests, and her heartfelt desire
to be 'of use' was apparent as she asserted: 'I feel I am deriving so much useful
knowledge to you by remaining a little longer, that I trust you will not regret this.
If I thought I could be of more use by being at home than by being here, I would
most willingly return, but I think the contrary.'[184] One plan, however, she suppressed.
The Colonist declared that after touring the Hawkesbury she meant to cross the
Blue Mountains to Bathurst, and added gleefully: 'This is something like a
traveller's tour, and will give her Ladyship somewhat to write about, and to tell
Sir John when she returns home'. But of this intention, Lady Franklin breathed
no word to her husband.

On the evening of Monday 27 May, Lady Franklin embarked on the steamer Tamar *for Maitland* en route *to visit Captain Phillip Parker King at Port Stephens. She was accompanied, as the* Colonist *reported, 'by Major Nunn, and a detachment of mounted police, who are to proceed under the command of Lieutenant Christie, to the disturbed districts in the Upper Hunter, and scour the country in order to put down the bands of bushrangers that infest the roads, and have been committing of late so many serious depredations'.*[185] *She was thus travelling under the escort of a man whose conduct was even then the subject of an Executive Council enquiry. Major James Nunn's barbaric 'reprisals' against Aborigines in the Gwydir River from December 1837 were thought to have been a model for the men (mostly convicts) who massacred over 30 Aboriginal men, women and children at Myall Creek in June 1838. Seven of the convicts brought to trial for the Myall Creek massacre had been found guilty and hanged, but the Executive Council duly reported in July 1839 that Nunn's actions were motivated by self-defence. The widest distinction, said the report, must be made 'between the case of the murderers of men, women and children, without personal provocation and in cold blood, and that of officers and men in repelling an attack made upon them, while under orders in the execution of their duty'.*[186] *Presumably Governor Gipps shared the faith in that distinction, since while he had insisted that the perpetrators of the Myall Creek massacre should be brought to justice, he seemed to see no inconsistency in entrusting Nunn with a military style campaign to 'put down' bushrangers in the Upper Hunter while the enquiry into his actions was still under way.*

On the subject of the Myall Creek massacre or other similar atrocities, Jane Franklin remains uncharacteristically silent. She travelled in company with Major Nunn, passed the estates of Robert Scott, who had argued strongly for the acquittal of the Myall Creek murderers, and dined with Edward Close, whose apparent indifference as a magistrate to the shooting of four Aborigines in custody by Lieutenant Lowe in 1825 had, to some, suggested either inefficiency or a desire to protect Lowe. But her remarks on these men were confined to their manners, appearance, property or good works. It seems impossible that the subject should never have arisen in any form—either now or earlier—when at Wollongong she had visited the estate of the Attorney-General, Plunkett, who had sentenced the convicts to death. But she was unwilling to judge, or even, it seems, to comment. Her silence is difficult to interpret, but certainly she displayed no disapproval of any of these men.

Monday 27 May continued

Carriage took us to Darling Harbour & were on board the Steamer which was along side at 8—went down into ladies' cabin to look at berths & found it crowded with ladies, servants & children—a broad table—a bed was reserved for us, but the sight & closeness, not a window being open, were sufficient, & we determined to sleep on deck, to the utter & incredulous astonishment of Major Nunn—who with Mr Christie of 80th[187] was in attendance on us. Passed the light on a hulk—moored on the rocks called the 'Sow & Pigs', leaving it close on our right, passed under North head, a fine perpendicular cliff, as well as South head. A little beyond, the coast becomes tame—it was a cloudy or thick moonlight night—I was introduced by Captain Moriarty to Mr Nowlan, of VDL who is said to have 8000 acres in the Hunter. He told me he thought of exchanging his property here for other at Port Phillip which would be much more convenient situation for him. He is an elderly, ruddy, stout man, and has a fixed, staring look—he told me Mr Threlkeld, the Missionary to Aborigines,[188] was on board, & had him brought up to me. As well as I could see by the light, he is a dingy elderly, plain man. He had been making a report to the Governor. His station is at Lake Macquarie—he was originally commissioned by the London Missionary Society when his establishment cost £500 a year— this they thought too much for the object & by some misunderstanding between them, his communion with them was dissolved & he has since received £150 a year from Colonial Government—his labours are having less & less fruits—at first, he had 160 blacks—now only 30 come to him, & those not domiciled—had only 1 living with him constantly. I asked after his *Grammar*—could not get it in book shops—he had none himself—the only 2 persons who had it were the Colonial Secretary & [illegible].

Mattresses brought on deck & tarpaulin covering—went under at 10— don't know how long had remained here, dozing rather than sleeping when the rain came on briskly—& could not keep from it & thus driven down to cabin where Snachall rose out of bed & Sophy & I lay down. A smell of bilge water here now added to former evils—lay considerable time in vain attempting to sleep—went again to look on deck—found rain had ceased, but deck wet—had horse-hair cushion or mattress brought up & lay down again without cover—got a little disturbed sleep & at last was woken by Mr Elliot a little before 6 as were approaching the light house of Newcastle—between the cliff on which this is placed, is Nobby Island which was changing its form as advanced, the murky morning twilight just enabled us to see breakers along rocks below. It is a question whether to blow up upper part of this island for completion of breakwater which has been begun from lighthouse point. The island is said to take wind out of sails as ships pass under it. Breakwater was begun 27 years ago.

Tuesday 28 May

After landing on jetty, we walked up the chief street. Its main 2 elevations are denuded of trees—on top of one on right was church—on left gaol—these, with the convict stockade where 160 men are employed on the breakwater form the chief public establishments—Captain Furlong of the 80th, commanding it, received us on landing & conducted us to his home.[189] He had been written to beforehand to give us a breakfast & as it had begun to rain in torrents, we could not reject that. We were obliged to sit down to it instead of seeing the place. The [steamer's] captain gave the boat 1 hour for stopping. I was alarmed at the sight of a lady at the tea tray [Mrs Furlong] so dark & plain, Hindoo or other blood—learnt from Captain Moriarty that she had, notwithstanding, been married before to a Major Hutchinson who was resident at Mocha, at or after the time Captain Moriarty was there. Rev. Mr Wilton,[190] the clergyman, a plain, queer-looking little man who possesses a collection of the natural curiosities of the place was there, with several ladies. They had all been hurried here by the premature arrival of the steamboat which was in sight before any of the servants of house were up.

One of the dishes at breakfast was curried Snapper, a fish caught in abundance here. I saw the creature which has a singular depth or width from dorsal line to fins & a lump or elevation on neck—it is very ugly. Great fun passed against Christie at breakfast for going out in search of bushrangers & the mighty efficiency of Mounted Police in their blue & gold. A view of principal objects is obtained from Captain Furlong's window (he is a very plain man also—one of their children was almost as dark, tho' not so yellow, as her mother, but with pretty features). We embarked again at about 8 in pouring rain—had to change shoes & stockings immediately. Cabin still full tho' some changed—after a time went on deck—awning was stretched over—rain had for the time ceased—came on again, but I did not move—the rain came on a good deal.

From deck, looked back on Newcastle Hill closing the reach of the river—wide river & flat wooded islands & banks around—passed close, almost grazing upon one called Mosquito Island. 'Mosquito Island' is said to be derived from a native name, signifying the failure of hitting the kangaroo which it is or was full of. Higher up on Ash Island, which we skirt close on left, is the home of Mr Walker Scott, brother of a Mr Robert or Bob Scott of this river, also called Count Robert from his large possessions or some other cause[191]—further on, same side, on main land, is house & estate of Mr Spark[192] & a little further up is public house & landing place called Sparkses. We meet the Maitland steamer coming down, 2 engines of 15 horse each—does not attempt against head wind. Come to Public House in elevation called Raymond Terrace about 20 miles from Newcastle, where mail is left for Port Stephens to which there is a road. Flat till come to Nelson plains, more clear, but not flat—some rising, wild pleasure-looking ground rises above on right. Pass entrance of Paterson's river, see Mr Close's white house on elevation above river on left (right bank) called Green Hills, where the boat stops. There is a good road from hence to East Maitland about 2 miles. From East Maitland to West by land is ¾ mile, by water, 25!

Mr Nowlan had been talking to me about Mr Close & his good works & how he had built a church & schools at his own expense. He was on board at our landing, a mean-looking elderly man, who asked us to take up our residence at his house instead of going to Maitland—I was disposed to do so, but saw gents did not like it. It was at last determined we should now drive on to Maitland in one of the stage-coaches in waiting, see Maitland, engage sleeping rooms there at the inn, & return to Mr Close's in time to see his church & school & dine. We went in a sort of omnibus to Maitland, overlooking cleared valley on right—passed very good-looking inn on left raised a little way from road which used to pass close to her [the proprietor] but is now cut through rock, leaving her on the bank. She complained to Sir George of the injury done & he gave her hope of making a bit of road for her. The inn is called the Family Rose by Elizabeth Mair, & the Rose Thistle sign is good. We drove on to Cox Inn & here fixed on our rooms.

Mr Grant who accompanied us here found some cases waiting for him in Court House, & was obliged to leave us under charge of Captain Adams of the 80th who took us first to the New Gaol, erecting of hewn stone on raised ground to form the termination of a street to be called, I believe, Newcastle Street. From hence we went to the Catholic chapel, of hewn stone. They intend having schools—have about 4 acres given to them—not far off is the English church, in course of building. Mr Rusden is the clergyman[193]—he lives in a pretty French-windowed house with verandah at the corner of one of the streets—sees few people—does duty in a small chapel near the stockade, used at other times for a school house. We entered this & found an active master teaching boys & girls—about 14 children present.

The stockade is as usual, a square area surmounted by huts, one of which is an open shed with tables & benches for dining, the other side 4 wooden boxes holding 24 men each, sleeping on ground & on upper boards—a passage across the box between the 2 opposite doors each of which has barred open space over it—I believe there are 90 chain gang men here. They have 1 blanket each—no bedding. From hence to Mr Grant's over high ground which gave us fine view of the green & cultivated valley & wood & chain of pretty tho' not very lofty hills—the end of one part, suddenly dropping, is called Broken Back. Beneath the pretty Government Cottage in which Mr Grant resides is the lockup house & the barrack of Mounted Police. Arriving at Mr Grant's he was sent for from the Court House & on his arriving lunch was served, one hot dish of finger fritures or rissoles—on which he appeared to pride himself. Sir George Gipps was here on his visit to Maitland—mention was made of young Gilbert Elliot's talent for caricature & Mr Grant spoke of one which was admired that he had—I said he should either not have told us, or should shew it & he instantly went to fetch it—it was His Excellency Sir George Gipps with all his titles hunting with a net after a butterfly, a scene Elliot had witnessed at Parramatta. Mr Grant who seemed to me *non compos* told me that as soon as Sir George Gipps heard of difficulties & dangers in a road which he did not care about before, he was determined to go. 'Surely, is he so boyish as that?' I said—I thought Grant looked half frightened. 'If the Home Government had sought all England to find the fit man for these colonies, they could not have found a better—quite a fit person for the settlers—a little abrupt perhaps—but the fittest man in the world.' I had been told this Mr Grant was brother-in-law to Lord Glenelg, having married Lord Glenelg's sister who was now living with Lord Glenelg.[194] He alluded to the humbleness of his position here, brother-in-law as he was to the Secretary for the Colonies, & that he should soon give up his poor pittance, & wanted nothing—again & again echoing praise of Sir George. He appeared to me, & it was afterwards confirmed that he was, more or less under the influence of liquor.[195]

We had the carriage brought up here & drove to Mr Close's by 4 pm. He came here 17 years ago—was a Lieutenant in Army, till lately was a Member of the Legislative Council—resigned—kept waiting in town merely to be told to adjourn. His place is called Morpeth. After Newcastle had ceased to be penal settlement, Mr Close was the first or one of first settlers—the grants made to emancipated convicts who had been working into knowledge & experience was of great use to first settlers. His wife, reddish-faced, grey-haired, but not old, has had 10 children and is evidently about to have the 11th. There are 4 living, 3 boys, 1 girl. He has also with him a family of orphan children of the name of Platt, 2 of whom came to the Queen's Birthday Ball with some chaperone. A little way from Mr Close's house is the stone church he is building, entirely at his own expense. He quarries his own stone—employs free workmen—has asked no aid whatever from Government & expects nothing but a clergyman—is not sure whether he shall apply to Government for clergyman's house but thinks by waiting a little he may be able to incur alone that expense also. He came here with nothing, and the least he could do was this work.[196]

Beyond the church, is a respectable house kept by Mrs Lakes as a boarding & day school for young ladies—her husband is habitually under the influence of intoxication, which abounds in this district. Mr Close told me that Backhouse & Walker[197] held a Temperance meeting here. It was a chilly evening, and many of his listeners spent the evening in intoxicating themselves—& he, Mr Close, on coming home asked for a glass of hot brandy & water. The inn here is the cleanest Mr Elliot said he had seen in the colony. We went to Mr Close's school, held in small house on water bank which the school master, who is as deaf as a post, has from him for nothing. He gets as salary but 1 shilling a week from the children—has about 14. There are a few Catholic children there—after going to mass they are allowed to come—to Sunday School.

Mr Grant came to dinner—he had never seen Mrs Close before. We waited 1 hour for him—he came in at the second course—and began almost directly of talking of interesting facial angle, indicative of intellect, of her little girl there (Anna Platt) of course believing it to be a Close—after incessant repetition of this he at last found out his mistake. He has a doleful look. During the evening we talked of slave—i.e. convict—owners, & the inevitable demoralising tendency on masters—Moriarty warm— Grant said he was going to bring out his views on subject. Mrs Close said her own children were taught by a female prisoner, a woman of accomplishments & good conduct, past 50. In order that nothing might be said about her wards, she sent little Platt to school at Mrs Lakes.

News of Lady Franklin's arrival at Maitland appeared in the *Colonist* a few days later:

The only news I can give you of any consequence is the arrival of Lady Franklin amongst us with a posse of military officers, dancing attendance on her ladyship. She has taken up her quarters at the Union Hotel, East Maitland, where the goodly matron of that establishment will do ample justice in the way of excellent accommodation. I believe her ladyship takes her route by way of Dungog, from thence to Port Stephens, and will visit Captain King, the newly appointed Commissioner for the Australian Agricultural Company at that place, before she returns to the metropolis.

Colonist, 1 June 1839

Wednesday 29 May

Mosquito-bitten—pouring rain all day. We could not go to Harpers' Hill & I, much affected by the recent change of weather, was scarce fit for it. We spent the morning in our rooms—dined at 5—visited Nunn, Christie, Nowlan & Grant. In the evening I had a letter from Captain King, who had received note intimating our arrival—he seemed pleased—he had more than once regretted his going away before we came. He sent Mr Ebsworth to conduct us [to Port Stephens], & proposed various routes—the most approved was by Colonel Snodgrass', a way I was determined not to go— (he has instituted law proceedings against Sir George Gipps about his salary).[198] But other circumstances formed their views—the steamer *Maitland* in which we might have gone to Raymond Terrace & hence to Port Stephens might not arrive owing to the weather (& did not in fact). Dire necessity, therefore, seemed to oblige us.

Thursday 30 May

Having had another bad night & not wishing for second gentlemen's dinner at the inn, I sent to Close's that we would dine & sleep there. First had carriage & drove to see West Maitland, about 1 mile—West Maitland is in perfect flat, liable to floods—one long continuous street, fewer gaps & more English-looking than any we had yet seen. The Rose Inn on the right, a brick house, is the chief inn—the small stone chapel erecting on the left is Wesleyan. At the other end of the street on the same side is an ugly tiny red brick chapel, & farther back a tolerably-sized stone English church is erecting. Small shops—not many good houses. A little beyond we enter the bush, which we were told continued to Harpers Hill, 9 or 10 miles—return, take leave of Lt Christie who is going after bushrangers. We went to Close's—arrived long before expected—dinner not ordered till 7—got an hour or two's doze. Mrs Close is a native—born at Woolloomooloo—her father came out in the first fleet—reflecting on this, she added he was the Commissary—after living here 10 years he sent for her mother—I think she said this to show she must be at least 10 or 11 years younger than the 'first fleet'. Another effort of the same kind, probably produced by consciousness of her grey hairs, was to beg me to remember her or give her love to Mrs King whom she had not seen for a long time—& who she said used to be called her young mama.[199]

We saw many native blacks about Maitland—they had just received the blankets furnished them by Government.

We waited for arrival of the *Maitland* which was seen coming up between 8 & 9. If she could have taken & landed horses & carriages at Raymond Terrace we would have gone that way, as avoiding Colonel Snodgrass which otherwise it seemed impossible to do—*Maitland* could not take them—she had been detained on the stormy Wednesday in Watson's Bay.

Set off with 4 miserable horses & 2 postilions. Proceeded along river banks in flat cultivation for about a mile when came to ferry immediately opposite the junction of Paterson's river—a carriage punt here, by dragging at rope, carried us across the Hunter to its left bank just below the junction. Proceeded up the Paterson on its left bank—met a messenger with letters to Captain Moriarty & me, from Mr Henry Carmichael who having been informed by Mr Nowlan of our approach had had lunch prepared for us yesterday & would have it again today, with a punt to carry us across Williams river. This opportune arrangement saved us from going to Colonel Snodgrass's. Left the cultivation & entered bush in which obliged to pick our way—proceeded thus till we came to the farm buildings & clearings of Mr Carmichael's and neared the house, a small red brick dwelling from which Mr Carmichael issued on road to meet us. In front he is making a circular metalled carriage road. The Williams river here perimulates a rich flat, which he has already partly under cultivation—on the opposite side is a steep wooded hill—a little below Mr Carmichael's house is the site of the Township of Seaham. He intends planting vineyards[200]—has been here near a year & a half—came out to meet us hat in hand—ushered us into small room where lunch was on table & a very ill-looking person eating whom he represented as the Dr—Dr Aaron—apologised. I hoped there was no sickness & was told Mrs Carmichael was confined—lunch was brought in & afterwards we were invited to go & see Mrs Carmichael who was sitting up in bed, the baby 4 days old by her side, she with a cap on which must have effectively prevented her laying her head on the pillow, though nicely dressed—has 6 children—the eldest holds stock. She told me Mr Carmichael had a book for me—supposed I knew who he was—I did not—he was the founder of the Normal Institution, nearly 5 years ago at Sydney—said it was a private institution & had been successful—he had sold it to Mr Gordon, his Assistant, who had been under him also when he was a Master in the Australian College.[201]

Mr Carmichael told us he came out with Dr Lang on the express condition that he should not enact his clerical profession. There were 6 clergyman on board—he had classes for the emigrants—one class of working men he took almost thro' Smith's *Wealth of Nations*.[202] In his Normal school, no religion is taught—that is left to their parents—I did not learn what he did with his boarders of whom he left 30 in the Institution on Sunday, but learnt that with his government men now, he has a Sunday service & reads to them Combe's *Constitution of Man!*[203] His principle was that the clergy should never interfere in education—nothing would ever be done in education, he said, with extreme vehemence & determination of manner, till all clerical influence was excluded. He had talked to Sir Richard Bourke on this subject, but he would not go far enough. Mr Carmichael had a bound copy of his little book, the 'Hints to Emigrants' ready with my name & other explanatory matter written on frontispiece.[204] Mr Carmichael is very diminutive & fair with blue eyes & a fine saxon wig—came out to us on the road, hat in hand, did not put it on till entered house—young cedars of the white species coming up near the house—called his place Porphyry Point. I did not know this at the time, nor ask why.

Crossed the river here in small boat & landed on Mr Mossman's estate—saw pretty water jar on his table—told it was of Mr James King's potting which we should pass going back. Re-enter bush beyond Mr Mossman's, passed some small plains & marshes & passed another farm. In bush casuarinas &c—saw waratonga, dwarf banksia, grass trees—crossed several small creeks much liable to overflow & passed thro' much sloppy marsh—sun sank down behind trees on left while we were yet only half the distance from Mr Carmichael's to Sawyers Point where we were to take boat—no moon—at last so dark that men quarrelled with each other & could not get on—logs in way, felt rather than seen—foot's pace—took off leaders to go better—for the last ¼ of a mile a red but not flaming torch was brought—some of the boatmen & a native soon came with blazing gun strips—arrived about ½ past 7 at Sawyers Point where we found a shed only. 4 men & boat here, the native being one. 3 miles to Carrington or Tahlee as they call the house—being native name—an island or two lie in corner of bay, near as we kept near left or Northern bank, covered with trees, behind which moon rose like broken artificial fireworks.[205]

Land at a small jutting & met in outskirt of garden by Captain King, who conducted us to the house—built on steep precipitous bank with 3 front windows, 2 under verandah, a chimney cross end & a pavilion with pointed front, built by Parry with 2 rooms. The one I slept in had one window at front, one to the side—Dumaresq added 3 rooms somewhere. The house commands a fine view of the capacious harbour, narrow pass to East coming from Northern shore folds over broken peaked chain of heights forming Southern side of harbour & hides the entrance. Opposite shores are tame & flat. Part of this shore also has a flat margin of mangroves growing in water—saw Mrs King—like Mrs Lethbridge but ruddy in cheeks & grey haired—he little, clever-looking, serious, yet expression as if sly humour lurked there—long & peculiar nose which was exactly imitated in one lad of 14 or 15 we saw there & softened & beautified in a pretty little girl of about 5 years old, 'Libby', abbreviation of Elizabeth, the youngest child & only daughter. They have 7 sons, the 2 eldest are keeping sheep— 3 others are at school in the country. Miss Annie Macarthur is tall & slender, soft skin but not clear complexion—dark hair, light eyes—fine features & very sweet expression—is about 20—engaged to Captain Wickham—who finishes his survey & goes to England—he is heartily sick of service—his surveying work is chiefly done by Stokes, his first lieutenant. He is said not to be liked by his officers.[206]

Captain King is somewhat older in appearance & much older in manner than I expected to see, having heard so much of his activity, energy and liveliness.[207] He was very quiet, not at all impressive in his attentions, but desirous to be kind—was communicative as to his own affairs—was obliged to remain 5 years but they might get rid of him earlier if they liked—his salary is I believe £1000 a year—no pension. Parry had difficult work to do. He found great extravagance & disorder—had to set things & people to rights & before the things began to pay his time elapsed, so that Dumaresq got the credit of the flourishing condition of the establishment, tho' as he himself said it was Parry's doing. The Australian Company, Captain King said, paid less than any other estate in colony but paid better than it had ever done before. 700 persons are employed up there, about 500 are prisoners—120 of them are employed in the coal mines. The Company has 1 million of acres divided into 3 separated districts— This at Carrington is the largest & consists of 400,000 acres. There are 300,000 at the Peel & the remainder in the district of Liverpool plains. They have not above 400 acres in cultivation, the rest in pasturage & for sheep, cattle, horses.

The 3 chief stations in this District are Carrington, consisting of a few houses & cottages on the beach East of Tahlee; the residence of Burrell where Mr Ebsworth resides at the head of the Carrington river navigation; & Stroud, the main station about 30 miles from Carrington, where are the storehouses, large buildings of bark, the residence of the Chief Superintendent of the Stud, Storekeeper &c &c, head carpenter, head blacksmith, head Manufacturer forming a square with neat brick church in the middle, built by Parry at his own expense. No public houses, or spirits sold, tho' Mr Ebsworth told me that at one of the stations, I believe the Peel, they had so many travelling visitors that it was extremely expensive, & they thought of having a house of entertainment including the sale of spirits. Captain King thinks the harbour of Port Stephens ought to become of gradually increasing importance owing to the opening of the new counties to the North, particularly New England, to which it seems the natural port. Besides their own vessels, whalers come in here to refit, lie in outer harbour in safety & are glad to come because no spirits allowed—get supplied here with beef, vegetables, & to a limited extent with small stores as tea, sugar &c. When the Company formed Carrington was expected to be chief station & was so called in honour of the Smith family who have great interest in the company—native name of the Carrington river is Carroa.[208] Tahlee is the native name of the point on which the residence is built.

I slept in Lady Parry's room—the house is not yet in order, nor furnished. A garden on the steep bank to the water was formed by her—on its slope is a raised hillock & black-painted head board on which is painted 'Poor Fido July 27, 1833'. It was one of the dogs which went with Parry to North Pole & died here just before they left. A dog of Colonel Dumaresq died just before she [his widow] left & she had him buried by his side.

Saturday 1 June

On Saturday morning, after breakfasting in room, I walked out with Captain King to an elevated part behind, where is a bench called Lady Parry's seat whence [one may obtain] a very pretty view of village, inclosing hills from outer harbour & whole capacious inner one & coasts—an island towards outer harbour is a very pretty object. We passed the foundations of the porphyry palace of Mr Dawson which he contemplated erecting here. It is a little below the ridge of the point & overlooks to South East some flats of mangroves into water—this point is singularly enough composed of porphyry tho' the surrounding hills are all sandstone[209]—Captain King broke a piece & ticketed [it] for me. I was then taken to the garden, a large space full of fruit trees & vegetables—sufficiently abundant to furnish the whaling ships when they come in—remarked many bananas in it. Day was close & threatening rain—time did not admit of going to Stroud & this consideration joined to my not feeling well which made me prefer inn quarters to company determined me on proposing leaving this morning & getting to Raymond Terrace, where, whatever the weather might be we should be safe for the steamer on Monday morning—no opposition was made to this as I explained my desire to be in Sydney on Monday & accordingly arrangements made for starting at 12.

I wished to have mentioned Captain Maconochie to him, but had no opportunity. I asked if he knew anybody in VDL besides Sir John & on looking at him, thought he colored a little. He replied he knew Mr Beaumont,—did I know his history? No—he was a sheriff's officer in London, & in that capacity touched Colonel Davey on shoulder in a manner the latter was familiar with, the day before he was setting off to take command in VDL. Colonel Davey said he was a great fool to be doing so to him when if he followed him to VDL he could make his fortune. Accordingly Beaumont embarked & was made in the first instance

Port Officer of Hobarton—Captain King said he knew also Mrs Scott—
Colonel Davey's daughter then a girl—the mother was a very gaudy dresser.
I asked Captain King if he retained his seat in the Legislative Council—
yes. When the seat was offered him, he expected the [appointment to the]
company & told Sir George so. The latter said that was no reason—at any
rate, it was better for him to accept if only to shew the estimation in which
he was held—& in fact it was his wish that he should do so. His wish was
sufficient—when he accepted the company, he tendered his resignation but
this was not accepted—he need not vote on any but financial questions.[210]
I spoke of Colonel Snodgrass being a neighbour of Captain King's & asked
if he would be much disappointed or cared much for appointment at
Port Phillip as I heard another, La Trobe, had been named. Captain King
knew from the papers of the latter appointment, and said he thought
Colonel Snodgrass did much wish for it. Mr Elliot, speaking of same
subject, went so far as to say Captain Maconochie would be disappointed
too. Captain King thought he never had much chance of it, but added no
more. I felt that in all probability no mention would be made of him by
Captain King & if publicly it would be of no use.

Captain King said the last time he saw Sir John was at small dinner party
at Sir Thomas Foley's at Portsea but he was quite sure he did not see me
there. A handsome luncheon was ready before 12 & as I could not eat any
meat, Captain King kindly set about cutting up a tongue into sandwiches
for us to take on road. Captain King has been only one week at Port
Stephens—came in steamer. He shewed us the last news from VDL—
I asked him how he came to take in the very worst paper in the island—he
did not know—it was the Company—he had never opened it.

Before we left Mr W. Cowper,[211] company's clergyman, called on me,
apologising for his wife's absence & bringing her card. He is a boyish
looking young man, son of Mr Cowper at St Philip's—has a little boy of
Colonel Dumaresq's whom he has so greatly improved that it is behind
Mrs Dumaresq's determination to remain 2 years longer in the Colony—
she is much concerned by her husband's desire that the child should
remain with him.

Took leave—Mr Ebsworth went with us to shew way to Raymond
Terrace—18 miles after landing at Sawyer's Point. Going to Sawyer's Point
in boat we keep near shore on right. Steep & wooded—as we approach
entrance of river, heights recede a little & become more broken & point
quite covered with wood—passed within some distance of 2 natives
paddling in tiny canoe—found carriage & horses & proceeded thro' same
bush road as yesterday for 10 miles. We saw now the obstacles which we
only felt the night before, bogs & marshes &c—bush swarming as it did
the preceding evening with mosquitos. The general opinion was expressed
that there used not to be mosquitos & they have come of late years—

Miss MacArthur expressed this, as derived from the elders of her family. Heard the bulbul thro' the bush.

Came to clearing & farm, vineyards & pottery of Mr James King, having first taken down a fence which he has recently put up across old road & which obliges people to go round—Australian Company & himself have dispute on this head.[212] We lifted the upright out of soft soil & disengaged the 3 rails, all of which we replaced—drove first to pottery, of which had seen water jar specimen at Mr Carmichael's who referred us to him—did not seem to be in very active operation, tho' sometimes 16 men are employed. Saw jars &c baking in kiln—2 sorts of earth used in composition.—King was out & his young wife after dressing herself hurried to the pottery—said Mr King was most anxious I should taste his wine, begged us to go in. After viewing the loft where things are kept & putting aside a few things, amongst which could not find Mr Carmichael's jar (saw covers & basins, butter & preserve jars, filtering machines & pedestals, water jars & wine coolers &c) we left via the adjoining vineyard & an avenue of orange trees in flower, & went to house to which Mr King had just returned—also her mother there—tasted white Rhenish sort of wine & a red wine in great haste having at first [declined?] entering & begged for a bottle instead as feared to get benighted it being between 4 & 5 o'clock & 4 miles to go. They invited us to stop the night & would have pressed us more had they not feared to be taking a liberty. A bottle was put in the carriage & we drove on at a great pace on pretty good road as it had been last 4 or 5 miles—road now more undulating—pretty— came before we expected & while still light to Raymond Terrace, situated just below entrance of Hunter's River with swamp land intervening. One parlor & a tiny bedroom beyond it which I had—Sophy slept on sofa in parlour—gents all together in another parlour where they were eaten up by fleas—Snachall came in in night to get out box of baby linen from under the bed, as the Dr's wife (Dr Aaron) was just confined in the house—note came late with a box containing wine & good glass from Mr King—wrote back, next day.

Sunday 2 June

Fine. The boat did not come from Mr Carmichael who had promised one so we took a heavy barge used for going off to steamer, no rudder nor pegs & failing in thwarts—4 men—not actually off till ½ past 4, & had 18 or 20 miles to go to Newcastle—sun only a little above trees on right as left. Getting on heavily, we stopped at sight of a similar & lighter boat drawn up against bank under cottage—asked to borrow it—'fine night for pleasuring' said the woman. Below Spark's came to 2 branches of river—

that to right for steamer—other for boats, shorter—they tried the latter, got on sand bank—again, ditto—not water enough—obliged to take steamer passage which at first they declared they did not know—got in sight of lighthouse many miles before we arrived & it never seemed nearer—other lights were from dwellings or native fires. Banks in many parts thickly grown with mangroves back to water's edge—tide turned again some time before we arrived & moon rose over on left.

Landed at stone stairs on side of quay, & walked to Commercial Hotel, up street on right with pointed chapel front—house shut up, & people knocked up—chambermaid came down in ragged shift & a single flannel petticoat, no shoes, stockings nor nightcap, house worse inside—2 parlors—chose the commonest as having fireplace where burnt a little wood & Newcastle coal of which the whole place smelled.

Monday 3 June

Next morning Captain Furlong was in attendance—he married the widow of Major Hutchinson who died resident at Mosha—all died but herself—she was brought to India in sloop of war—he married her afterwards in England—has 2 boys by her first husband who are at school in Sydney—and 6, I believe, by Captain Furlong, 4 boys & 2 girls. He is Commandant at this place. We set off sight seeing at 10, expecting the steamer *Sophia Jane* at 12—went first to see Breakwater—from lighthouse cliff extends about ½ a quarter of mile into bay about half way over to Nobby—which presents its steep wall angle to it. The breakwater is mainly composed of the friable sandstone of the hill. The outer stones however are of a harder texture & taken from round the cliff to South. Height of breakwater above sea may be about 30 feet, breadth of top, double, but at base much greater. At end of breakwater is great depth of water—6 fathoms deep—but greater part of distance beyond is shoal water which will make the labour of completing it less—3 railroads for carts impelled by brown & yellow gangs at work on it—has been begun Captain Furlong said 27 years—he is much vexed Sir George has given no order as he said he would do to knock down Nobby & commence breakwater that side.[213] Walked along sandy beach to this causeway, but river covering it is heaped of sand, hilly scoured by wind & tide—originally trees on it which some commandant thinking it was a harbour for runaway prisoners cut down & hence the drifts. Captain Furlong would like to have grant of it—& plant it with Guinea grass. Went up lighthouse hill—an octagonal wooden building of 2 stories held the lamp & burners which one day caught fire. Ever since, the light has been made by a huge coal fire on adjoining height close by—where iron post stands—& 2 poles—3 tons of coal are consumed per week in this—at 8 shillings per ton—G. Gipps said it cost more than the oil at South head. A flag staff here makes signals of ships—the flag is hoisted for first sight of steamer—coming down Hunter smoke may be seen 15 miles off so have plenty of time.

Next went to Church—not far off & one of the oldest in the colony—is stone & brick white washed—has a squat tower & small shingled spire, not projecting from end of church, but in centre & in line with its front—an inscription on a grey stone over the door states that it was erected A.D. 1817. Mr Wilton [the minister][214] has been 8 years here—has been in Colony 12. When Newcastle became vacant he asked General Darling to be placed here—has collection of stones, fossils, shells, zoophytes &c all from spot & neighbourhood in cabinet drawers—went to his house to see them—pretty—in garden full of aloes. New Barrack street will cause his house to be destroyed. I proposed his being Corresponding Member of our Society & sending specimens &c.[215] He thought he had 9 zoophytes—had 400 different katons [sic].

Steamer came in after 12 but went up to Coal Wharf—to take in coals, as we supposed, which promised considerable delay—had boat therefore to go to Nobby. Met a boat coming away from it which Captain Furlong more than suspected had been stealing his rabbits. Landed on small spit beach at angle of walk which rises perpendicularly along Southern side—other side is steep sloping grass—at top, a sort of porous pudding or sandstone formation overtops both the herbiage on one side & the different strata on other. We walked on the rocks & stones all round it—first in shade on Southern side, where it is perpendicular, so rough & angular in every part except lowest, as if violent disrupture of every portion had taken place. Cliff is 200 feet in highest part—then points to summit [?] & round towards harbour under the green steep slopes—here is ascent to top which I was told Sir George Gipps did as well as go round—Captain Furlong said it was difficult & seemed to wish me not—after picking up a few shells therefore & startling a black rabbit on the side (the rocky) where least expected to find it, we embarked. Captain Furlong put 9 rabbits on island about 7 months ago—someone told him the other day he had counted 90—there is no water on the island, but the rabbits continue without water.

Seeing steamer still quiet at Coal Wharf we crossed over to Mr Scott's salt works[216] the only thing Sir George had not had time to see. Mr Spears, a partner, was there—seemed heavy & stupid & not to know much about his own work. A scaffolding projecting into sea from sandy beach, supports a pump which pumps up sea water into horizontal whence it passes this building to the faggot structure which is the peculiarity of these works. Instead of evaporating the water in pans sunk in ground the salt water is brought thro' the aqueduct to summit of a wall or series of stages 40 or 50 feet high & about 100 long consisting of 5 stages of faggots laid upon just sufficient sticks or poles to support them but supported by side uprights as the whole structure is by pole buttresses—2 top stages closest together others 4 or 5 feet across. The aqueduct runs along top or length of this structure & has lateral branches on each side opening from it, the latter being pierced with holes thro' which the salt water falls upon the faggots crossways, the fresh water evaporating as it passes & leaving at last when the water has trickled thro' the lowest stage only the brine—from the lowest stage it is received on overlapping beams like a shingled roof sloping towards each other, so that the brine falls into a trough running lengthways between them like the aqueduct above—by this it is conveyed into 2 immense iron pans in the works heated by brick ovens. An adjoining plan is to store up the salt—faggots are very dry & stripped of leaves—hope to make salt at £2 per ton—imported salt is £5 or more—pump is to be worked by great wheel raised upon a mound of stone, to be moved round by 4 bullocks—adjoining sands are covered with Banksias. The loose sand here does not admit of salt pans as Mr Blaxland has.

Round to steamer & found they would be yet half an hour, as were taking on above 50 bales of wool belonging to Australian company, which had been for some time—drought had prevented their being cleansed from grease & were going with grease in which would diminish the price. Found Captain Moriarty. He had visited his friend Mr Forster & been to Booral & Stroud—at the place invited for me on Saturday—magnificent luncheon had been prepared for us.—Mr Wilton went to Sydney by this conveyance, also Mr W. Cowper with his little pupil Margaret. Sat down to dinner in steamboat (at 3) before she left the wharf—2 common looking elderly men at table & a younger respectable looking person who Mr Wilton at dinner presented us as Mr Stack, clergyman of West Maitland—dinner boiled leg mutton, fowls, ducks, ham—when wine asked for brought in pint bottles— Captain Moriarty in high spirits, quizzing Major Nunn.

Getting on deck, looked back at Newcastle & Nobby, latter very long visible with coast to North, sandy, white & low, with distant, insulated elevations & heads of Port Stephens rising like islands & apparently separated by considerable space from mainland. Bales of wool hid view— talked with Mr Wilton on scientific things. He once set up scientific journal alone, but [it] soon died a natural death.[217] Mr Wilton is widower with 2 children. The 2 other clergymen talked together on religion. Drank tea at 7—coffee & tea & meat which all ate—being cold went to cabin, where frightened from bed by being bitten by bugs beforehand—got black cushions of seat put on deck, & in spite of the cold lay there enveloped in my furs. Sophy there also & others, but all quitted it before morning except myself—anchored about 2 in Darling Harbour.

Conrad Martens (1801–1878)
VIEW IN THE DOMAIN, SYDNEY, SEP. 22, 1835 1835
pencil drawing; 12.2 x 20.2 cm
Pictorial Collection R4472

X

Interlude: Sydney
4-13 June 1839

Tuesday 4 June

Captain Moriarty went on shore at day break, & came back before 7, saying carriage was come. At Government House found Sir George on steps so went in—Lady Gipps had been worse, but better again—had been much more seriously ill than was imagined—had now left her room above & living in inner drawing room, while her own room was being painted & fumigated. Sir George as usual questioned us closely as to our travels. He spoke not very highly of Mr King & the Pottery[218]—he made great claims for having found out that there was green sand at Sydney. I begged enquiry to be made as to ships [for Hobart]—found *Eudora* sailed today with runaway convicts on board &c—wrote by her to Sir John.

We found we had hurried back in vain as respected the Bishop, since 6th was day appointed by him for Diocesan meeting & 7th Sir George wanted him for Executive Council—Sir George said he could not go till after 11th.[219] Lady Gipps admitted us into her room for short time. The morning was rainy, but in course of it walked to Bridge St to see [Conrad] Martens' pictures—he is a youngish man with mustachios—came here *en passant*, has got married & is a stock holder. He has painted chiefly landscapes in water colours and is now engaged on oils—native scenery. His sketches pretty in pencil on coloured paper—told him I would order a picture but must wait

145

till I had seen more scenery before I fixed on it—asked him if he would make me some sketches, pencil ones. [He said he] was not accustomed to do so, but would for me—it would hinder his painting pictures if he made sketches of them—talked of 2 guineas each—when I objected, said it would depend how they were done—perhaps one guinea—I said in the way I wished, 10 shillings each. He did not look quite pleased, but consented.

Mr Martens is in first storey at Mr Evan's stationery & book shop—saw well chosen & well-bound books here—respectable looking person in shop who seemed to be proprietor, was middle-aged or elderly, & pleasant looking—replied to my question that books were not for lending, but that I might have them.[220] Opened all the cases for me—at last told me his wife was sister to Mr Lempriere the Commissary & she had lately come from a visit to VDL while her sister-in-law Mrs Lempriere was here. Mr Evans then said that he had once been Surveyor-General in VDL. I recollected the name & that it was far from being in esteem. He was accused of being subject to gross bribery—I suppose my countenance & manner altered for his did & continued changed during the remainder of my stay.[221]

Wednesday 5 June

Unwell & in bed all day. Read *Vicar of Wrexhill* lent by Evans.[222]

Thursday 6 June

Went to Diocesan meeting—held in girls' School room—wrote to Bishop first to say we were going—he wrote polite note to Mr Elliot saying he had only just heard of my return, should be honoured by the visit &c. They had begun or Bishop was addressing them as we entered (we went into criminal court opposite by mistake first.) An aged gentleman seated at table advanced to meet me, & placed me in chair on right hand of Bishop facing all the company—there was one on his left vacant which Mrs King who sat next to it, pointed to me to take, but I could not well get to it [behind] Bishop's back—I had scarcely seated myself ... [uncompleted].

Friday 7 June

After Lady Gipps had taken her short drive, we set off to return some calls—Lady & Miss O'Connell called—& saw them, therefore left them out. Heard that Bishop had all the children of the schools at dinner, usually given I believe on lawn, but ground being wet they were in their school houses—Mrs Lethbridge said Bishop spent all his income in charity—she commented on want of patronage in exalted stations to their Society, in the son of a clergyman too![223]

Bought book at Maclehose's & walked in garden. Dinner party: Captain, Mrs & Mr O'Connell; Dowlings, Sir James, Lady & Miss Lady Dowling cleverish—sister to one gone to VDL. Count Strzelecki talked much to me—perceived VDL was a hit with me. Talking of English gambling, he said it explained beggary in England & wickedness here. Had broken his instructions coming here & to VDL & said we should give him a great deal of work.[224]

Saturday 8 June

Called at the Normal Institution, Hyde Park—saw Mr Grace. John Basanquet [illegible] the black boy was not at home. Mr Grace did not think him equal to European boys of same age—has been 4 years in institution—reads & writes pretty well & has notion of drawing & all the imitative arts—is deficient in calculating powers. He is a grandson of King Bungaree but comes from distant part of country, thinks it was beyond the Upper Hunter. There are 60 or 70 scholars in school—about 20 boarders.[225]

Went to James Wilson's—artist in Prince's Street—nearly dark when we entered ground floor room—saw one of his coloured chalk portraits—very pretty. He charges 5 guineas for a head. He gave me an oil painting of native young woman, seen by him in [illegible].[226] He thinks of looking for a farm in the upper Hunter district.

Party. Sir George took me out [to dinner]—he desired Mr Elliot to take Lady O'Connell, the first time that Elliot's rank[227] has been acknowledged, & Sir Maurice took Mrs McLeay & sat between her & me. The old lady is said to be rather crabbed & a very harsh prisoner mistress—Lady Gipps told me the McLeays had the School of Industry almost in their own hands & Miss McLeay was Treasurer but did not render accounts &c. Lady Gipps as Patroness ought to have most influence but did not like exerting it—children's diet had been altered—had had some days pudding called batter, a hard coarse mixture of flour & eggs, both now dear, no meat or vegetables—it is thought better to give them meat, but only half pound undressed allowed to each without pudding or vegetables—Lady Gipps wanted the girls' numbers increased, Mrs McLeay did not.

Mr Stephen sat on the other side of Sir George—talked to me a little across him. Mr McLeay sat opposite to him on other side of table—& Sir George remarked to me afterwards on the extraordinary way he [Mr Stephen] had been talking to Mr McLeay about the superiority of VDL. Sir George seemed excited & amused by this—I heard Mr McLeay say it was treading fast on heels of this colony, but did not hear the rest, &

Sir George thought he talked so that I & Sophy might report him in VDL. Mr Elliot who overheard him said it was quite ridiculous. Mr Stephen told Mr McLeay that in houses, size, wealth, population, this colony vastly superior, but in *la morale*, quite the contrary. Mr McLeay frowned—Mr Stephen went on to say that he saw a scene the other day of a description which could not be mentioned before a lady, a scene which never could be witnessed in VDL. Every day indeed, in landing at the Rocks & passing by Custom House, Gaol &c, he saw things which he supposed in time he should get hardened enough to pass by without notice. Mr McLeay looked shocked & vexed, & said nothing. I had quoted Captain Harding[228] who thought he had not seen above 4 drunken people in colony of VDL, tho' travelled 5 or 600 miles in it—'Perhaps', said Mr McLeay, 'he would not here have seen *one*.' I might have mentioned that 2 days running, the dead body of a black man was lying at door of a poor house, almost within sight of Government House & not removed. Mr Stephen asked me before

Lady Franklin delighted in comparisons between the two colonies, especially when they favoured Van Diemen's Land. She described this dinner-table conversation in detail to Sir John:

[Mr Alfred Stephen] thinks it better to be a public officer here than in Van Diemen's Land, because there are more enlarged views and feelings here; people here dispute, he says, on principles, there about persons. There is a party, he says, in Van Diemen's Land who would applaud to the skies any thing he said or did purely because it was he; another who would do just the contrary … When I saw Mr Stephen with Sir George at table, I thought he was a little under restraint. He spoke across Sir George to me of you and called you 'the Governor' (which I think was meant to honour you in mine and Sir George's eyes) and he talked across the table to Mr McLeay on the excellence of Van Diemen's Land in a way which made Sir George say to me afterwards, laughing, that he supposed he did it for me to repeat in Van Diemen's Land. I told him I had not heard it. Sir George has heard enough about the Colony lately from one quarter and another, and certainly cannot doubt one thing, that it has the power of exciting attachment and admiration in those who belong to it.

Letter, Jane Franklin to John Franklin, 15 June 1839

Mr McLeay what I thought of the model [of Hobart Town]—I said again I was ashamed of it—he told Mr McLeay how several positions were entirely left out. Sir Maurice said it looked to him like a large village of huts—extending however over much more ground than he expected. Mr Stephen said to me afterwards that as a public officer he preferred this [NSW], as a private individual than [VDL]—here there was strong feeling for principles, there for individuals—much more personality there. There was a party in VDL who would support anything he did or said because it was he, & another precisely the converse.

Lady Gipps was in drawing room when we left the dining room & remained till heard guests coming in—I asked Mr Stephen if he had seen her—no—told she was the nicest person in the colony. When everybody had gone, Sir George laughed at the way in which Mr Stephen & Captain Moriarty at dinner had been praising VDL—the people, the soil, the climate, every thing superior—& said he supposed he did it for me & Sophy to report when we went back. I & Sophy said we did not hear it—only heard Captain Moriarty declare he had drunk Tasmanian wine superior to Australian. I asked Sir George if he did not think there must be something very delightful in VDL to make every body so enthousiasme [sic]—I did not speak of myself, for he must observe I kept it all to myself. Mr Elliot had observed my discretion—'Oh,' he said, 'so you are the only actor among you!' The subject seemed to excite Sir George & good naturedly to touch him.

Remarking on the great size of the house[229] & the colony, [Sir George] said he did not think however this country (he spoke confidentially) would ever be the prosperous & important country the colonists expected—population must be dispersed for want of food—if much increased, they would starve. Port Phillip was hinted at as a ridiculous instance of wanting to be independent, tho' only 2 years in existence—Lonsdale had been disrespectfully treated there & in consequence he had written a letter to him which he desired him to read to the individuals concerned & to any others he thought proper.

Sunday 9 June

Sophy & one gent went to Catholic church to hear Dr Polding & singing—did not hear Burhill nor Dr Polding who was there however—prayers in English & sermon—latter on second commandment to prove what Catholics did was not idolatry. There were exceptions about not making graven images, even as touched Jews, & the commandment not addressed to us—making sign of cross, ancient custom as proved by St Paul saying should take up his cross etc!!! Sophy, who had never seen service before, was amused & shocked.

I walked with Sir George, Parker & Reggy to St James's—2 chairs—I went in pew first & took chair in angle which he pointed to, & which I concluded to be Lady Gipps', but which was his—so comfortable that I had a great inclination to sleep, as Lady Gipps has too, yet fully in sight of Bishop. Sat a little with Lady Gipps till interrupted by Dr Mollison who not finding her quite so well, said she had been near having a brain fever & would have it again if did not take care—talked to Mr Parker & afterwards to Sir George in a walk upon management of task work labour & probation gangs.[230]

Sir George spent part of evening out of room, & at prayers made one of considerable length on himself & household—praying for strength & a blessing to fulfil his duties so that he might not bring his station into contempt nor sanction others in sin—returned thanks for recovery of her with whom he was blessed to aid, support & encourage him, & for a moment, his voice faltered.

The illness of Lady Gipps has been on many accounts unfortunate. It has made Sir George probably give us more of his time than was convenient or pleasant to him, has I dare say been a constant little source of anxiety in her mind as to how we are getting on &c and to me has been productive of much embarrassment of feeling; for wishing to shew her every sympathy and attention, I had dreaded to be intrusive and troublesome to her, and the interest I have felt, and could have expressed to another, has been checked towards Sir George [the words 'by his sharp and repulsive manner' are crossed out in Lady Franklin's original manuscript]. I can dispute with, oppose, and even quiz him, but I cannot make speeches to him, and I may have appeared to both, indifferent to her, and engaged also in my own amusements while I have desired nothing so much as to shew my regard and sympathy for her.

Sir George's regard for his inestimable wife was affectingly shewn last Sunday evening, when he read prayers and repeated one of his own composition, praying that by his example and authority he might so govern himself and others, as not to bring contempt upon his station and then returning thanks for 'the recovery of her who was preserved to him to aid, support and encourage him'. This and other instances prove to me that he has a good heart and good principles.

Letter, Jane Franklin to John Franklin, 15 June 1839

About 12, went to Museum in Macquarie Place with 4 windows & door in front looking on a lawn—a room with 2 windows each side of a spacious passage contains glass cases, large & small, of birds & beasts, with sloping cases in centre—large cases cost £16 each—some foreign birds, presents—many of the things were presented by Major Mitchell & Mr Coxen—printed tickets—camphor & turpentine smell—Major Mitchell's 2 little mammals marsupial, largest immense ears—smallest like a little mouse—Catalogue does not refer to any thing, but contains classified list of things &c—some models & savage instruments, skulls, things in spirits, shells &c—many shells from round bay.[231]

At 2, went into Sir George's boat, 8 men well dressed and large boat 36 feet long across water to Mr Stephen's in Lavender Bay from name of boatman there with whom Mr Stephen contracts to bring him daily to & fro...[232]

On Tuesday 11 June Lady Franklin attended the opening of the session of the Legislative Council, in company with Lady Gipps and a number of other Sydney ladies. On the following day she accompanied Sir George on his barge up the Parramatta River to inspect Government House at Parramatta, his second official residence. The barge was for some time lost in heavy fog on the way.

Parramatta.

One of the lodges is in the cross street of town—drive up to house—a square fronted building of stone. Plastered. There is a porch to door of 4 coupled columns—2 windows each side—5 over good entrance passage or hall. Room on right is Dining room with 2 in front & 1 at side, opposite Lady Gipps's bedroom, similar, at back of hall, several sort of rooms—the chief is Sir George's study & dressing room within—a passage leading to good sized drawing room of 3 windows—1 at end & 2 side—wooden stairs—painted floors—I was shewed Sir Rd. Bourke's room. There are 2 beds now in house—and little furniture up stairs—things are taken from Sydney when they go up—Sir George comes to Sydney every Friday when at Parramatta—sometimes returns same day—a covered way crosses a garden court to a wing where are the rooms of Mr Parker, Mr G. Elliot & the chief men servants—view is open & scanty of trees, looking chiefly to town. Various buildings scattered about—an aviary—another thing nearer going to right observatory, low building with 2 small domes—near it an octagon bath. Second or upper story is cistern to which water pumped from garden—saw neither bath, nor observatory—asked about instruments—not so good as those of Cape—'Had Mr Dunlop done much?'[233]—no—thought it not unlikely he would be recalled.

At the back of house is edge of basin or depression, in which is garden, cypresses & olives in stiff beds, with patches of green barley for forage, fruit trees, amongst which many loquats & orange & vegetables. It is in a semicircular shape, surrounded by bank,—lower side is thick river stream with flat bushes on its banks dammed up—just above landing Wharf is a dam to keep in fresh water—not high enough for purpose in high tides so there is another above. In line of road beyond Bath is laundry house & beyond the thatched roof & sunk dairy with cottage of overseer, men's cottages opposite. The domain contains 3000 acres—cultivated land about 30 acres.

Took a ride in domain with Sir George accompanied by Overseer Carr, good part of it was in bush & forest—not pretty except the green hills of Toongabbie. The domain should support 300 cattle & 500 sheep—but is overstocked in a season like last—Sir George was induced to buy too many & is wanting to dispose of 50 of them. Does not expect to get above £2 a head—got £50 by his wool last year—sells sheep to butcher—saves about 2d a lb on them—20 persons employed. 'Includes ploughmen, shepherds, wood-cutters?' I asked—'Every body,' said Sir George. I suppose therefore it includes the 4 men for the garden. Sir George has not his cattle alone in domain at Parramatta, but perhaps as many as 50 belonging to other people—he should have stopped this when first he came if he meant to do it. Sir George is interested in all his little details.

Had breakfast when we went in. Walked in garden, rode in domain, left in carriage. I did not see Parramatta river all the way, tho' had been told it might be seen in one or 2 places—Sir George afterwards said he did not tell me to turn my head, because he found it was all mud—changed horses, Sir George having ordered a pair to meet us at the Star Public house about half way. Remarking on the number of public houses, Sir George said each paid £30 to Government yearly—I talked of superior dress of our factory women & remonstrated about the rice & maize—Sir George placidly & indulgently heard me. He shewed me Dr Wardell's house right (the same Gilbert Elliot had described as India horse purveyor) editor of newspaper—was scene of his murder—his monument at Clemelt's.[234] Sir George told me of his ignorance of scandal & even of the character of people & of what was said of him or his measures &c—did not know what Sir R. Bourke did, how he lived &c. He could not address himself very well on these things to Thomson[235]—was as if inviting contrast—Gilbert Elliot went out, but never got anything from him—if asked, he hardly knew where he had been dining—Parker went out & heard—but only smiled when questioned—was very prudent & cautious, and told him that Lady Gipps was beloved. I saw her when we went in—Reggy naughty—something amiss with him—dine alone—[Sir George] retired in evening.

Mr Thomson promised to give me papers, a survey map of Port Phillip & Threlkeld's Aboriginal grammar—also a portrait of Sir Richard Bourke better than one I had bought—liked him much. Before dinner, went to Barlow's Lithographic shop in Bridge St. & bought Aboriginal portraits—went to Evans'.

Thomson had brought Lady Franklin an invitation to a ball given by the 'Sons of St Andrew', which caused her some distress. In a letter to Sir John, she expanded on the causes of her embarrassment:

Since our tour with the Bishop was minutely arranged, a 'deputation' of which Mr Thomson was one came to me to request my attendance at the Ball given by the 'Sons of St Andrew' for the 21st. The day interfered with our tour, and we could only accomplish it by leaving the Bishop on the road and (as we desired to continue absent from Sydney till the time of embarking) rejoining him at the expense of much time and trouble. There were several reasons however why I wished to accept the ball. I thought Sir George some time back in anticipation of it had intimated an expectation if not a desire that we should be present. I thought also that as many people wished to invite us individually, but did not know how, in consequence of our peculiar position, we should by accepting this public invitation, enable them in some way to gratify their wishes and shew our sense of their kindness; and as the Sons of St Andrew in particular are not the least susceptible part of the community in some countries I felt a more than ordinary desire to shew consideration to them. Under the influence of these motives and having apologised to and requested the Bishop to pause for us on the road, I told the deputation we would accept. Almost immediately afterwards I found reason to repent. I determined on contradicting what I had said and excusing myself to Mr Thomson, who fortunately was to dine with us. Accordingly I got the private ear of Mr Thomson, and told him guardedly the real state of things. He seemed quite to understand and most kindly acquiesced, and thus we are free of the ball.

Letter, Jane Franklin to John Franklin, 15 June 1839

Conrad Martens (1801–1878)
FROM THE CURRAJONG
ABOVE DOUGLASS' FARM [c.1853]
watercolour; 23 x 32.6 cm
Pictorial Collection R3372

XI

Excursion to the Hawkesbury

14-29 June 1839

O n Friday 14 June Lady Franklin left Sydney with Bishop Broughton
for an excursion to the Nepean and Hawkesbury rivers west of Sydney,
where the bishop intended to inspect churches and schools. With passages now
secured on the Medway, which was expected to depart between 1 and 10 July,
her main desire was to remove herself from Government House until within a
few days of embarkation. Sir George Gipps had hosted all the dinner parties that
could be thought necessary to enable Sydney citizens to meet the distinguished
visitor, and with Lady Gipps still confined to her own room, Lady Franklin's
hope was 'that we may not again be a burden on the Gipps, and arrive in Sydney
a third time before we are expected, or before it was necessary, (as we have
already done twice)'.

Instructing Captain Wight of the Medway to write to them on the road if he
was able to leave earlier than expected, Lady Franklin and Sophy Cracroft set off
in the bishop's carriage, followed by Captain Moriarty and Mr Elliot in a hired
'pill box'. Lady Franklin looked forward to opportunities for 'interesting
conversation' with the bishop, who she was delighted to discover did not really
approve of Franklin's predecessor in Van Diemen's Land, Colonel Arthur. She
wrote happily to Sir John that the bishop had said 'Colonel Arthur was a man

who never forgave, that he never knew anybody who could less bear opposition, that he was a shrewd and acute, but a narrow-minded man'. The bishop, she went on, thought that 'Colonel Arthur knew every thing that was passing; every thing that was said and done. Whether this arose from actual espionage or only his extraordinary tact at getting everything out of every body, he could not tell, but so it was. The Bishop added that the more he knew of Colonel Arthur the less he liked him.'

With such an agreeable companion, and such apparent licence to extend her tour over several weeks, after her disappointment at the hurried visit to the Hunter, Lady Franklin's pleasure in the Hawkesbury excursion seemed assured. Within a day or two she was ensconced at Winbourne, the house of George Cox, one of four brothers, she said, who held 'good estates' in the Mulgoa Valley. Cox had visited Van Diemen's Land the previous year and delighted her with his praise of the country, with which he was so much pleased 'that his wife says he shall not go again, lest he take a fancy to live there'. On Sunday 16 June, she resumed her diary with all her usual minuteness and precision.[236]

Sunday 16 June

To Mulgoa church at 11—Mr Makinson went to do duty at South Creek & Bishop performed whole of duty. After church went to Mr Edward Cox's, about half a mile beyond, till evening service—had luncheon there in long dining room an additional room, & afterwards began writing letter in Mrs Cox's bedroom. Afternoon service at 3—Mr Makinson performed whole & Bishop sat on chair within Communion rail—Mr Makinson good voice & good sermon, wanted a little more emphasis. He has 6 Coxes at his school, 3 Kings, 1 Lethbridge, &c &c—school highly spoken of.[237] He takes much interest in the boys—he has 1 child—dined without company. After tea, I went into room meaning to return, but finding voices in next room disappeared, learnt all had retired to Drawing room for evening service which was prolonged by singing of Evening hymn &c. Sat up late writing to Sir John.

Monday 17 June

Showery. We made a short excursion before leaving to Norton's Basin, a little lake-like expanse of the Cowpasture river about 2 miles from Mr Cox's in the mountains—had not time to return by Mr Blaxland's bridge, in order to get back by 12 to the Bishop.[238]

Got promise of wine from Mr Cox who wished I would be president of a club to name them—took leave of these kind people to proceed to South Creek & Penrith. [The church at South Creek] is in bush or wood near road—Bishop is much afraid they should cut away too many trees—is a brick church—even brick foundations, which the architect said being very good of their kind were better than the soft sandstone of the country for the purpose—is to be finished in 2 months—hope to have clergyman of their own—at present Mr Makinson does duty here & at Mulgoa once each Sunday—church is to cost £1800 (that of Mulgoa £2000). Mr Copland Lethbridge, a cousin of he of Sydney & neighbourhood settler was here to meet Bishop. He is married to a daughter of Mrs King & it was arranged we were to lunch there.

Recrossing the creek towards Penrith, we turned off on right in bush, up to house—an ugly square stone house with one wide Venetian window on each side of door—3 windows over—no enclosure. Mrs Lethbridge is dark, and has the King nose—like her brother. They have been 5 years here—she has 6 children & has lost 3. 2 eldest are boys—2 next girls—2 youngest boys—eldest boy is 10—youngest 9 months—all brought up by hand— little girl of 6 makes all her brothers' & sisters' clothes—cut out & fitted for her—Mrs Lethbridge regretted much had not room to accommodate us. Had hot lunch—then drove on to Penrith 3 or 4 miles. The first cottages & indeed all the houses are by the high road side—2 or 3 only good ones— & these chiefly public houses. The church is of brick, larger than South creek, with stone ornament—3 arched windows of ugly shape & double courses of brick round. Row of brick cottages beyond—all either brick or wood—no stone here but alluvial clay. Court House on right—brick pediment centre—receding wings with white post verandah before them. Fine flat hence to river, blue mountain range over it—broad view near the eye—flat is divided by fence into paddocks, orchards &c, & many rude cottages at wood by road side—about a mile from town to Emu ford inn, a good brick house where dinner ordered at 6 by previous arrangement of Bishop—good upstairs rooms—closed our letters for post.

Tuesday 18 June

A doubtful & cloudy morning. Found Mr Dunlop, Police Magistrate of Penrith, in breakfast room when we went down. The 2 gents were there & had been speaking to him. Bishop looked displeased & freezing—no one but myself spoke to him—nor asked him to sit down nor take breakfast. He is a common farmer-looking man—had invited us in his house or to do anything & we had declined. Bishop went away in carriage to Penrith to settle about church. Mr Dunlop was left, & staid [sic] a little longer—a few more words said, then he rose as if offended & went off.[239]

While Bishop was absent we went in our pill box across the ferry which is close by and on road to Bathurst as far as the Pilgrim inn, about 5 miles.

Ferry is crossed by punt for carriage—5 shillings for passage to & fro—getting up bank over on Emu plains, a green flat extending a couple of miles, perhaps, to the foot of the wooded ridge of the blue mountains where advantage is taken of a natural gully to form road on left side. Another rift or gully to left is that thro' which Warragamba comes into Nepean—near this on opposite side is Regentville rising on hill opposite to river. Sir John [Jamison][240] has factory &c—house is seen on hill opposite an inn the Governor Bourke—kept by people of name of Wilson—Sir John Jamison wants to get road to come by his house, have suspension bridge across river & passage of mountains there—people here are alarmed. We passed a wood house in our way on the plains which I believe is Mr Dunlop's. He has been Police Magistrate here only 1 year—& has been but 15 months in the colony. Began to ascend above gully—fine wall of sandstone rock left, perfectly done by gunpowder—overhanging rocks at top edge—in one part it is guarded by post & rail fence—fine deep woody precipice right full of trees—little pools in it—up to sweep in on left of gully crossed by 1 arch bridge AD 1832–4, wound round, continued to ascend a little gradually, pass surveyors' scattered huts & little cleared nook in hills right. Get on level—pass this point to Pilgrim inn, wooden house left, a little beyond another on right. Between the 2, a road goes off left at right angles, the Lapstone or old road which, had we known it at the time, we might have taken returning.

Found Bishop was returned when we came back—Mrs Lethbridge had called with Mrs Sims, wife of Postmaster, a lady highly spoken of. About 1, or later, proceeded to Richmond 16 miles—there is a road by the river, the prettiest, which we were told could not take as being too bad—returned therefore to Penrith, where called at Postmaster's gate to acknowledge visit & on to 4 cross roads, where turned to left & thro' bush on flat ground—uninteresting, but little interruption of cultivation in view, tho' Blue Mountains were occasionally on left, of firmer shapes than at Penrith. The Grose comes thro' an opening in these to join the Nepean, & afterward called Hawkesbury—arrive at town of Richmond situated in open plain, green street, broad & strait, laid out at right angles & extending over considerable space—did not see one large or good house—[they range from] scattered mean ones to cottage & fenced paddocks. Very little new building—good deal of orchard ground.

Passed to left thro' town & back in road parallel to that we came, to Hobartville, Mr William Cox's house.[241] Enter white gate & short road to back of house & offices—fine white cedar here—lawn—loquats line one path—aloes also—garden front face West. On Northern side of house are some good sized oaks, above 20 yrs old, somewhat injured by late drought. Young oaks, smaller size, in road to house from gate—above the older oaks is hill bank on which new brick church is erecting—Mr William Cox has been here 21 years. Mrs Cox short, stout, has been pretty—8 children.[242] The 2 youngest girls are at school at Miss Deans, Macquarie Place, Sydney. (The Miss Deans are new arrivals in colony—were known to Kings— Mr King's youngest daughter was with them in England. Their mother is with them & they take charge also of a little boy, son of their brother, a widower who is settled as a lawyer at Port Phillip.) The youngest son is at the King's School Parramatta. Hall—steep stone staircase—confined passage on landing—had room with 1 bed given to me.

Company to dinner. 18 sat down. Drawing room, grand sized—3 windows in line—door on one side leads into dining room—1 end window, 2 side. Few servants—hired man to wait second course, all tasks, etc. Mr Cox does not make wine. Visitors were Mr North, Police Magistrate of Windsor & Mr & Mrs Stiles, from whom Bishop shewed me letter of invitation at Richmond. Rev. Mr Keane of Pitt Town, who succeeded Mr Mears now of Illawarra (Mrs Cox's 2 eldest sons received most of their education from Mr Mears). Mr Whittaker, a young man who lived 4 or 5 years in VDL which did not agree with him—thinks there are as many mosquitos there as here—thinks scenery there much finer—is a private surveyor. Mr & Mrs Betts—the youngest daughter of Mr Marsden in mourning.[243] Mrs Blatchford, an old lady, whose daughter Mrs Berwick was second wife of Mrs Cox's father & has been married again—she almost lives with these Coxes.[244] Mr North has 6 daughters & 3 sons—Mr & Mrs Archibald Bell of Patrick's Plains on the Hunter—(these came in evening).[245] Mrs Wyatt also came in evening & Miss North. Mr Edgar Cox, half brother whom we saw at Clarendon [in VDL]. Miss Smith, who was wrecked in the *Enchantress* in d'Entrecasteaux channel—Colonel Moriarty, who was then Port Officer, recognised her immediately. She was landed at Pembridge island, and after 6 weeks came up on *Medway* to Sydney.

Spent the evening seated upright on sofa, heated, sleepy, warm, bore it long & could not longer—begged permission to withdraw. They had piano & eating after I went. Sophy followed at Mr Cox's suggestion.

Wednesday 19 June

Next morning, I breakfasted in room & continued to write there (to Mr Forster) till 1 o'clock. Bishop was gone to Windsor & Pitt Town to visit schools & churches—he did not return, as we were to return to Windsor for dinner & sleep. Went down in Drawing room—all at books, quite silent—looked at revised Prayer book &c—luncheon—carriage ordered at 3 pm for Windsor.

Took leave of Cox & drove 4 miles to Mr Stiles'—Clergyman at Windsor. A review of the 80th Regiment took place somewhere near Windsor today, a misty damp, drizzling day—I saw nothing of them—I had been invited to Mess, & Bishop also, but we declined.[246] It is 4 miles from Mr Cox's to Windsor, open ugly, hard & fenced country. Outskirts of Windsor, or open space where church is, very ugly. The church is a large, ugly, red brick building, 6 windows & door in side tower at West & with white cupola lantern, a frightful thing, above it—they talk of wanting globe & cross, but nothing can mend it. Church was built in 1819 which makes it one of the oldest in colony.[247]

The Stiles's[248] landed 5 or 6 years ago at Hobarton— staid 3 weeks there—thought the scenery was finer than this colony—have been at Windsor ever since. They have 4 children. The house they live in was built for clergyman with design of having school—is in same line as church but at little distance. It is an ugly red brick house, said to be best parsonage in colony—it is probably the ugliest also. Though the house is large, the rooms are scarcely furnished & miserable looking. Stiles could not accommodate our servants, who went to public house. They are nice people—he quite clerical & clever looking, fine grey eyes—he preached the visitation sermon—his [wife][249] has pleasant & good & earnest countenance— Bishop spoke highly of her—said she had some talent, but thought her now rather out of spirits—maid said she'd given her mattresses away to the poor or to servants going away—for first time I slept in same bed as Sophy, there being no second mattress, no sacking to bedstead, nor sofa.

Mr North at dinner & Mr & Miss Betts—evening heavy & fatiguing.

Thursday 20 June

Next morning I rose with a sick headach which grew worse & worse. Today to Wiseman's ferry 25 miles—50 by water. Drove thro' town [of Windsor]—a remarkable ugly place—about the size of Maitland—is either

3rd or 4th town in Colony—houses nearly contiguous in chief street which not near so nice as Maitland—built of ugly brick. Continue in open country for about 2 miles when leave Parramatta road entering the bush strait on, & turn left to Pitt Town, in open country on skirts of bush. This is only a small collection of poor houses.

Mr Keane's the parsonage is low built building—Mrs Keane is represented as a very active zealous woman—great activity in feeble body. He is a little mercurial man, an Irishman, not very sound judgment but best hearted, & most devotedly kind & benevolent person in world. Church is not built; service performed in some usable substitute. Mr Stiles had rode with us here, now joined by Mr Keane. On in bush & bad roads—orderly with us—he left road & went side—we followed, got lost, met waggon & then sheep & shepherd who sent us back to road. In doing this, we had to go thro' bush where trees pretty thick—pill box in which were Sophy & 2 gents ran against wheel, drew it off. This caused considerable delay while it was mended with ropes. On in bush to Cattai Creek—rather pretty bit of scenery, cross it by wooden bridge called Roberts bridge from name of man who built it. Ascend sandy hill beyond to Roberts' cottage where got out for few minutes and took leave of Keane & Stiles. The good woman had tea things on table for us, but we had not time to stop—16 miles hence to Wiseman's Ferry.

We ascend sandy hill beyond & farther on come to cleared extent of ground right & left in wood—hence onwards, I noticed nothing—excused myself to Bishop & sank in corner, suffering & dozing from sick head ache. Found later part of road very stony, broken & hilly—an extremely bad road—Snachall was suddenly thrown off by pitch of carriage over end of log, which cast her on ground near hind wheel—fell on her knees & not hurt but bad bruises on them. The jolt roused me from my insensibility to see her on ground—I made her come in after this—Bishop expressed himself very thankful it was nothing worse—on—getting dark, & road very bad & horses tired—Bishop was continually in & out to relieve horses which began to stand still, so that I at last, ill as I was, & Snachall with the bruised knees were obliged to get out also.[250]

At last we descended by bad road to Wiseman's Ferry where a good house stands, built by its late proprietor, a rich emancipated convict of good character who kept an inn here or received people without charge. Before his death, he gave up the inn & resided here—as his widow, who is now in weeds, does still with 2 nieces. I retired to my room to be sick, but when a little better was taken by her in garden to see front of house, with its double story of verandah hung with coloured lamps, an arch over iron side gate, the same on upper part of summer house or pavilion in centre of garden. This was first done for General Darling—and has not been done since. The gents had a handsome dinner & good wines in upper dining room opening on verandah—[251]

Friday 21 June

Next morning, I found, tho' faint with weakness having eaten nothing yesterday, that they did not choose me to have any breakfast till it went into parlour—I then had to wait till their breakfast was over, for I was too weak to dress to go down.

Saturday 22 June [?]

About noon, finding Bishop in spite of bad weather was going in boat on his work, I determined to accompany him. Went down the Hawkesbury about 2 miles to a tiny wooden chapel in wretched condition on right bank of stream—scenery very fine. On flat or point on left is white cottage where lives an old blind woman of name of Dogherty who, tho' blind, can do everything for herself—cooks & threads her needle. Lower, another point on left with respectable cottage on it. Mr Edmonstone, the late clergyman, for some time resided here. Mr Edmonstone has quitted the district, not liking, the Bishop says, his accommodation—which being a single man, the Bishop thinks he should not object to & declares he is angry with him. Before Edmonstone, Mr Sharp, now at Norfolk island, was here—removed from bad health to Pitt Town, & again from same cause to Norfolk island, where he is better & his wife worse. Nearly opposite is perched a cottage on a terrace & the humble unpainted chapel adjoining—between these & promontory of rock is gully & nook of cultivated ground, maize & wheat cultivated by poor old man, called the Sexton, tho' without pay or even office, of name of Harding, going by name of Harvey—he & his wife looked very dismal, particularly when Bishop at first thought of fixing the clergyman's new

I went with him [the bishop] in the wet, and shocked those I left at home by so doing, while the Bishop, a man after my own heart in this, expressed no disapprobation and made no effort to deter me. Mr Forster tells me in his letter that I seem to make light of all difficulties. 'To be able to do so,' he writes, 'is a blessing only known to those who enjoy it, and I thank God that I am likewise one of those individuals.'

Letter, Jane Franklin to John Franklin, 20–21 June 1839

house on upper part of his cultivated land—this was changed, & place was measured out between chapel & cottage. This was the Bishop's object in coming, & accordingly he brought with him in boat, having commanded him to come from Sydney, Mr Williams, the builder who is to build it under orders.

Sunday 23 June

Divine service was to be performed at a little chapel above Milkmaid reach on the Hawkesbury 3 miles from Wiseman's ferry. Took boat at a large piece of rock on river, carved into steps. Came to small wooden unpainted chapel—3 or 4 windows without glass one side—partition divides vestry—inside white plastered, 6 narrow benches each side—pulpit & desk—earth floor—Bishop in robes—clerk Mr Penton, black silk handkerchief round his head—has been a prisoner—even then was Schoolmaster—has been so I think 12 or 14 yrs—has 12 scholars, 3 times a week. On alternate days he goes to Nelson's reach—42 people in church including this clerk & Bishop—people all come in boats—singing sermon. We walked to Mr Ayrcough's—looking down river, with cleared slope & flat below under cultivation—yielded scarce any return. He would lease it off—only did not like to be idle. Found neat parlour & table with covers as if waiting for dinner, but the young man was too shy at first to say it was prepared for us. His sister lives with him—he is cousin to Dr Nicholson of Sydney, and holds the property for him. Mr Ayrcough & one of Miss Wisemans seemed courting.

Found that the little black girl near me at Church was Mitchell's Baldinilla, whom he wished to take with him to England, but Captain wanting £50 with her, he left her behind in charge of Dr Nicholson. She could make writing & sign her name—did not say her age—looked about 7—curly damp hair—ugly nose & mouth—middling good—capacity superior to what could be expected—some of her questions surprising. She is learning to read.

Back [to Wiseman's]—discussion of plans. At past 2, set off to cross ferry & go up part of grand road towards Hunter. Bell bird—fine shrubs & plants, pass wooded deserted hut of stockade & above several chimneys of others. Continue ascending—came to view of new valley to North West, perfectly flat, cultivated & varied, narrow, white building in it—steep sides of wood with little intermixture of rock & at upper end beautiful faint mountain of striking appearance rises in distance. Tho' no water seen, I think this valley, seen to end & thus finally terminated, the best of all— all most lovely & exquisite—went on beyond, seeing ridges & gullies of wood till road began to descend.

There are no entries for Monday 24 and Tuesday 25 June. But it seems that Mr Elliot returned briefly to Sydney, while Lady Franklin, Sophy and the bishop decided to return to Windsor by water. On Tuesday 25 June they travelled up the Hawkesbury River as far as Cyrus Doyle's property, Ulinbawn, at Sackville Reach, where they spent the night.

Wednesday 26 June

Breakfasted in room at Mrs Doyle's—she is second wife—Spoke of Mr Doyle having 6 sons & 2 daughters—place is let for 5 or 7 years to Mr Lambert—she hopes it will not be sold, but kept for one of Mr Doyle's sons.[252] Left at 10 for Mr Tuckerman's, a little above here. Found Mr Tuckerman, an unpleasant looking man, at landing—enquiring for church land, he said it was a mile above by land. We went by water, he & his 2 daughters followed—Mr Keane from Pitt Town met by appointment. A little discussion as to whether this was the church land given by Mr Palmer or not—settled it was—a burial ground here, on sloping ground, 6 or 8 stones or tombs enclosed in square rails, besides a few others not so guarded. On one of stones were these lines:

Farewell dear husband & relation
Since God 'as caused a separation.

One acre was desired by Bishop to be measured out. He had much difficulty in bringing to the point the fencing of this—where were fencers to be got? they could not be got—they were so scarce. Bishop would get 2 at Sydney if any body would ration them—Mr Tuckerman knew of no one who would—they had barely grain for own families—would be obliged to buy if they did—Bishop agreed to provide sufficient store if Mr Tuckerman would superintend giving it out—if left to procure it themselves, would eat it up at once. Where was wood to be got? none here—must come over water—where did his come from? this side of water? why was the church timber to come from different place—how was it to be carted? Mr Tuckerman agreed to do this himself—as to the building, stone was abundant—it had better be built of coarse stone—stone for doors & windows to be done at Sydney, almost as cheap as wood. At present, the service is performed in barn of Mr Tuckerman by Mr Keane. I expressed to latter my hope to see him in VDL going to or returning from England which he was planning for his health. He would return [he said], dereliction of duty not to do so—I was glad to hear it as knew Bishop could not do without zealous clergymen & knew he thought him of the number—I said this because Bishop had not time, [with Tuckerman?] interrupting him & rowing away from point—Keane seemed pleased & also Bishop when I told him.

[Continuing up river towards Windsor] come to Stubbs's ferry & punt on left beyond, a fine perpendicular wall of rock—Cattai Creek enters on left—banks are like pleasure ground—green & swamp oaks. On, stop at boat building under cottage, Grono's—7 miles from Windsor[253]—on landing found dinner going on of mutton chops & tea. A fine-looking man is Grono, native of Colony & she also native. 4 children & a brother or sister's child—are of Welsh origin & Presbyterians. Man & apprentice, plain and dark, are building boat of 14 feet keel for Mr Marsden of Windsor—to cost 12 guineas with a pair of sculls—built of Blue Gum from banks of Colo—talked of worm which perforates the trees here—was told that if boat lay at anchor 3 weeks, she would be eaten up with worms—are like small beetle. They roll themselves & eat their way thro', making perfectly circular hole under the ledge of the planking. These worms are chiefly found in parts of river where it is sweetish or brackish, not quite fresh—much better to use boat than lay it up on account of worm. Boat should be kept dry & turned keel upward in sun, when worms come out—then pitch the hole. Snachall told the woman in our absence who we were, the Governor's lady of VDL & the Bishop of Sydney—indeed! On being asked by Bishop, she said she was fond of reading & her husband too, & they always read of an evening. He promised to send her some books—rooms neat & children dirty.

Proceed, romantic character of river quite gone—grassy bare banks & wooden unpainted cottages scattered pretty thickly along edge. The Curajong[254] or blue mountain range across head of river. Pass as we approach Windsor the narrow entrance of South Creek—see the ugly church rising above bank. We land below the yellow verandah cottage, called Government Cottage—residence of Mr North, Police Magistrate, who was down to meet us, as well as Bishop's carriage from the inn. Notes put into my hand—one from Mrs Stiles, expressing pleasure when had to receive us, but heard we preferred going to Cross's—another from Mr Cox urging us to return to stay at Hobartville [at Richmond] & saying the innkeeper Cross had wife ill & inconvenient to him to have us there. Our rooms at Cross's were ready, but not having made any other particular preparations, he seemed quite willing to excuse us—& we prepared to go to Hobartville.

Mr North also put into my hand a letter from Sir George Gipps dated 25th saying he was glad to see Mr Elliot night before, as previously had not the smallest idea where we were to be found—(why did not he ask Mr Parker?) Lady Gipps had been back several days from Parramatta was quite well & was to reappear at Dinner table at party on Thursday, asked if we should be there? at any rate confidently reckoned on our being at a ball they were to give on Thursday 4th of July—all this shewed him utterly ignorant of our arrangements with Bishop & of my note to

Lady Gipps & sent by Mr Elliot who was in the house, but with whom as it would seem Sir George had no communication from evening of Mr Elliot's arrival on 24th to morning of 25th. Determined on not answering this till saw Mr Elliot.

While we were at Mrs Stiles', where called till carriage ready, Mr Cox came in having rode over to fetch us—proposed what Bishop had already done, that we should visit the Kurrajong next day—& sleep again at his house—arrived between 5 & 6 at Hobartville—the 2 girls Jane 14 & Rebecca now 13 with Miss Smith, the youngest son Sloper [?] home for holidays from the King's School & his companion Lumsden from the same—latter & his brothers came out with the Bishop & are under his superintendence—in evening Lumsden called me to hear the boys' address to Mr Forrest on latter's retiring from School & on presenting with tea service of plate bought at Irving & Lamb's, Sydney—with Mr Forrest's answer which was very good—the boys say they fixed on tea set on account of his 'amiable partner'—their wording is very boyish. Lumsden said he did not think they would ever have a master they liked better—Mr Forrest is going to Campbell Town to be succeeded by Mr Clark.[255]

Thursday 27 June[256]

Sophy went with 2 girls to Richmond School to attend examination by Mr Stiles—Mr Stiles not there, it being a mistake & she saw only schoolmaster & schoolmistress—asked him if he ever asked the children questions—he hesitated—sometimes when had time—did not often &c—asked if she was Lady Franklin—hoped we were pleased with the colony—was sure every body would be pleased to shew us respect.

Mr North & Mr Archibald Bell came to accompany us on way to Kurrajong Country in tandem—Mrs Cox & I in pill box—others on horseback. After first space of bush, found the country intermixed with cultivation & queerly broken & hollowed—a wooden cottage or hut perched here & there shewing subdivision of land into small farms—some farms of 10 acres are leased & support a family—this country on account of mountainous character & fine soil was reserved for small settlers, who had small grants made to them, lowest 50 or 30 acres—largest farms here are 2—of 500 & one of 550—latter is Mr North's, Police Magistrate.

After about 6 miles came to Schoolhouse of stone not mortared & cracking from each other—large glass window in it broken by hail storm. Bishop's School is attended by children, from distance of 3 miles—number averages 30, tho' 45 on books—today only 22—Why? because Mr Stiles had been there the day before—thought this should have acted the other way—he performs divine service & preaches there every alternate Wednesday. No mistress—children seemed cold tho' weather beautiful, & looked dirty—many were barefooted. They were divided in classes, boys & girls teaching—torn cards & paper on walls—schoolmaster's dwelling, the former schoolhouse (a wooden cottage), adjoins—fine view hence of the undulating mountain country & of the extensive horizon all around—Windsor & Richmond & Mr Cox's part of view. There is no view of such extent in VDL.

Proceed above a mile higher, ascending on ridges & steeps. Left carriage, tho' it might have proceeded—came to inn by road on left, Mrs Douglas's, an impudent, ugly woman who was not supported by gentry—but has neat clean house where we might very well sleep, & good eating also—tho' had brought our own provisions. She put out roast pig, fine potatoes, the growth of her own country here—being particularly good for potatoes, beautiful butter & light excellent damper different from & better than any had seen in colony before. The woman was very familiar & communicative as to behaviour of certain young officers who had lately been there. Her husband was originally a prisoner—she with family came out to him & Darling gave them 50 acres here. The husband is a scourger—a girl of hers goes to the School—why not there to day—because she was wanted to clean the house. She wanted us much to stay the night.

Only 1 mile farther come to what is called the Cut Hill where road winds round & round own precipice—river seen other side—14 miles from Douglas's is Tomah Mountain, the highest I believe in range. Snow sometimes rests several days on it—splendid views from it—carriage can go so far as 15 miles from Cox's river which is 45 from Bathurst. Mr Bell who was with us discovered this passage in this range in 1821. In 1825 this road was begun by Government. Since then, a better sweeping line tho' a little longer has been found by Mr Bell & if road is finished, latter will be taken—would be much easier line of road for Bathurst produce than that from Penrith & would bring it to water carriage to Windsor where it might be shipped to Broken Bay. Penrith opposed to it of course & Sir John Jamison & Mr Blaxland in company—Mr Bell got grant of 1000 acres for discovering it—& afterwards another grant on accomplishing this road at Government expense from Governor Darling—his first grant is at Hunter.[257] Did not see the Kurrajong trees—it is very tough, fit for chains & leather. Returned part of way by full moon to dinner—disappointed in evening not seeing or hearing from Elliot to whom Captain Moriarty had written in morning by orderly to Penrith where he & we expected to meet this evening, desiring him to come on or send if had anything to say.

Lady Franklin was now juggling her desire to place no further burden on the Gippses with her fear of missing her passage on the Medway. *The lack of any letter from Mr Elliot, and the continued absence of Mr Elliot himself, led her to turn her steps back to Penrith, where she hoped to meet him. But in departing so hastily from the Coxes, she in turn missed receiving a letter the bishop had written from Parramatta on his way home—a misfortune which would later cause her considerable social embarrassment.*

Friday 28 June

Mr Elliot not arriving & it being necessary to see him before decided on our plans, we took leave of Hobartville for Penrith again expecting to find him there—we were to go the river road, which as going thro' private fields & farms for most part is difficult to find, & Mr Cox was kind enough to go with us. Our road led first towards the part we had crossed yesterday, when turned to left up course of river where navigation is interrupted by fall or rather a rapid—on opposite side is Belmont the residence of Mrs Bell, mother of Mr Archibald & of Mrs George Cox[258] standing on projecting steep hill & said to command very lovely view. On—pass the rudiments or site of the village of Castlereagh, founded by Governor Macquarie & consisting but abandoned—there is house, a church & a parsonage which was seen thro' trees—parsonage is red house. The clergyman is Revd Mr Fulton, originally transported as Irish chapel—being respectable & man of education, he was sent as Catechist or Chaplain to Norfolk Island. He figured in no way discreditably as witness on Governor Bligh's side in the trial—his daughter is married also to an original convict, of name of Fraser, who was an assistant in his school when he kept one, & who is now a settler living near him, but not very respectable. This must be a sore passage in Bishop's history of his clergy.

Got into a very miry strait road, fenced in. Had many pools & puddles before us, & as soon as he had plunged in, Mr Cox's horse invariably stood still, disliking the water, & was obliged to be dragged thro' it by the collar. As we proceeded along this flat road we found some obstruction beforehand. A carriage had passed us on road & preceded us & now stood still before us—got out to see & found a cart with several bullocks sloughed in deep miry place where one bullock lay dead, its nose, mouth & eyes caked in mud so as to stop every inlet of breath & to make its head a uniform mass of mud—another attached to the cart was more than half buried & was evidently preparing for the same fate—one or two were detached—the 2 or 3 men belonging to it looked brutal, hardened & apathetic—As we could neither encounter the same, nor pass, some fences were taken down & we passed thro' field & got into road again leaving the other carriage behind.

Road tho' in plain took sharp turns at right angles, sometimes up to hills left then straitforward—over the river on right appeared the Bathurst road going white up the hill & up the river in front appeared Regentville—come into Penrith & drive to Governor Bourke inn where heard Mr Elliot had arrived late evening before & was now out. While speaking of this, our pill box drove up with Mr Elliot, picked up in road, making a third with Sophy & Captain Moriarty—he had hired a horse & gig yesterday at Parramatta—could not make it get on & so was late. Deliberated what to do—finding Captain Wight was to be ready to sail Sunday week, I determined to go at once back to Sydney. I had no inclination at all to go to Weatherboardedhut on road to Bathurst without going farther, as it was expense for little purpose, tho' I could not help thinking Bishop wished it on his own account, not wanting us to come to him immediately. Against this, was my repugnance to urge on my companions on road, when I saw they disliked it—& thus we resolved to sleep at Parramatta tonight & get to Bishop's tomorrow—letting him know by post that we should arrive so much earlier than expected. Mr Elliot brought me a note from Lady Gipps, expressing she would have great pleasure whenever we returned to her & not otherwise alluding, if this was alluding at all, to the Bishop.

Had I received the letter which the Bishop wrote to me yesterday from Parramatta in his way home I should have acted quite otherwise, (tho' should not have gone to Bathurst) & been spared much pain & embarrassment.[259] The Bishop gives some hints for our guidance in case we did not go to Weatherboardedhut, as I hinted to him at the last moment was possible. He supposes we may pass thro' Windsor to Parramatta on Saturday & remain at Parramatta on Sunday. As Lady Gipps has left Government House he presumes we can have no objection to go to an inn & recommends Walker's as by far the best—its only fault being that the rooms are small & too near together, but we might write beforehand & engage the larger Sitting room & 2 adjoining ones for myself & Sophy—says at Parramatta we would see the King's School, Factory, the Church in which is Mrs Bourke's monument & all else that is worthy of notice in a very short time & shall find the clergyman, Mr Bobart, & the master of the King's School, Mr Forrest, prepared to show us any attention & lend every aid in their power in furnishing means of conveyance. In the neighbourhood is the church at Hunter's Hill & the Clergyman's house just commenced, which are worth going to see for the beauty of the prospect. A little farther on is the New Lunatic Asylum which as a building may be worth looking at—Bishop has requested the Revd G.E. Turner who is the resident clergyman to give us safe conduct thro' his territory—begs us to look into church at Windsor & at the tombstone of Andrew Thompson erected by Governor Macquarie—'This is an historical document [he says] which no one who desires to know New S.W. as it has been, should omit to examine.'[260] At Baulkham Hills are the orange groves of Macdougall on one side of the road, & of Sutton on the other. These are worth stopping to see & near Parramatta are Mobb's which are very worthy of a walk thro' them. 'Whatever may be your intermediate proceedings, we shall hope to see you on Tuesday with Miss Cracroft: for which I shall prepare Mrs Broughton on seeing her, as I hope, tomorrow: & I assure you your visit will give her & myself the greatest pleasure—Pray let me hear from you at what hour you will be with us.'

Before we resumed our journey, we ordered some dinner at which Mr Cox joined us. Took leave of him & late in afternoon set off for Parramatta, I going first half of way in gig with Mr Elliot. In way, seeing church of Penrith open, we went in—it is very spacious. On road are the smart lodge & white house on left of Major Druitt.[261] Arrived late at Parramatta & drove to Walker's inn, which without knowing contents of Bishop's letter (intended by him to have been received by me at Mr Cox's) was recommended to Mr Elliot. We found it full of gentlemen of the hunt come up that day to Parramatta. It seemed a low long pretty-looking snug building—went next to where found admittance, a large & more shewy-looking house than other on outside—parlour well furnished but ceiling had lately come down—bedroom indifferent. The people almost had gone to bed, tho' very early for that—tea & cold beef. Feeling myself unwell, got Mr Elliot to write to Bishop to say we should be with him next day to dinner after calling at Government House on way.

Saturday 29 June

Next morning, begged gents to call early on Mr Bobart whose carriage Bishop had told me personally would be ready to take us about Parramatta. Accordingly after breakfast he arrived in his gig or double gig holding 4— is a serious tall clerical looking man whom I liked very much. We drove first to the church with its 2 towers containing 4 stories of small windows in foreign style—on Northern side of building over entrance is inscription stating that it was founded in 1800, in time of Governor Hunter (finished I suppose by Macquarie according to the story of the twin towers)—In interior 2 rows of columns—windows on each side & chancel—In latter on South side is monument against wall to memory of Mrs Bourke, wife of Sir Richard Bourke, who died about a year after her arrival here. The monument is an area in relief with following inscription below.

Sacred to the memory of Elizabeth Jane Bourke, wife of Major General Rd. Bourke, C.B. Captain General & Governor in chief of NSW & VDL. She died at Government House, Parramatta, on 7th May 1832, in the 54th year of her age. Her remains are deposited in the cemetery of this town.

Reader, she was the most gentle & affectionate of God's creatures—Correct in all her duties, she led a life of unassuming benevolence & practical piety—she was the comfort & solace of her husband, the friend, teacher & nurse of her children, & a blessing to the poor. He who places this marble to her memory would indeed be the most wretched of mankind did he not feel the Christian's hope of meeting in a better world her whom he has lost in this.

I also noticed a new stone on same site to Captain Foreman who died 1836 having made 5 voyages round this world.

We then went to the King's School, a large stone house, shallow, opposite the river & near the new bridge—taken into private apartments of Mr & Mrs Forrest.[262] She appeared older than he—he respectable, tall & elegant—told them I had heard the boys' speech to him read—he said had they chosen for the composer several other boys, there were those who would have done it well—he is much beloved, but is said not to be a great disciplinarian.[263] Mr Clark was present, his successor—is said to be very clever. Seeing or asking for a prospectus, one was shewn, which I said I supposed I might keep—this was yielded at first, then urged it [sic] being their only one—I begged to give it back but not allowed. Bishop no doubt had more—I said I was going to him today. 'Going to his house!'—I observed they seemed surprised.

Next to Female Factory—Mr & Mrs Bell not agreeable—women at dinner—went in—all standing at cross tables—tin dishes with pieces of meat given to one woman at each table to distribute—with her fingers she laid out 9 or so many different portions on bare table & they took it up with their fingers—some did not eat then but put it in their pockets or aprons—exactly like brutes. I asked Mr Bell about knives & forks & plates—he did not instantly answer, then threw back head & body & burst into a loud hoarse laugh or fine hysterics, perfectly affected in order, no doubt, to prove to me how supremely ridiculous was the idea of making them do so. He said they would not do it—I was much disgusted.

We went also to Government Garden & House—tried to enter latter but found door closed & nobody at home—windows however were not fastened & Mr Elliot & Captain Moriarty climbed in thro' the Dining room ones, unlocked the door & let us in—I took Sophy hastily over the house. We went also to Observatory which Sir George, I thought, seemed to have an objection to my seeing when I went with him, & did not speak well of the labours of Mr Dunlop—nothing to be seen could be less recommendation than the appearance of the place—2 small rooms with domes scarce weather-tight & with ceiling tumbled down—dirty, dusty & untidy & confused beyond description—books on shelves lined the room, tumbling apparently with rottenness. Were first shewn into a small parlour where Mrs Dunlop came in, middle-aged woman, & then her husband, a tall, gawky, philosophic looking man, dark & clever-looking, simple in his manners. His instruments are small & some useless—one so awkward for manual management that were he not so tall as he is could not use it—he made no observations or explanations about anything & none of us made any, being all perhaps as well as myself too ignorant, except perhaps Mr Bobart. Of course we stayed but a short time—house surrounded by blooming china roses—he shewed the spot on ground where his spider issued & searched for it—but did not come—it seems a great pet.

Mr Dunlop gave us the melancholy news of Mr Allan Cunningham's death—heard that morning. He was to be buried on Monday from the Botanical gardens where he died. When we had left I told Mr Bobart I wished to engage Mr Dunlop to correspond with our projected scientific society, but did not know to ask him—& engaged him to speak to Mr Dunlop for me—hurried back to inn & regretting leaving Mr Bobart who had hoped he said we should have stopped over Sunday & that he might have taken us to the orange groves &c. He told me he had been in New Zealand & had there found the curious vegetable & animal production, a reed growing out of back of a caterpillar—which had been called Bobartia after him tho' he was not the first to discover it—he was descended from those however who had had a distinguished botanical reputation—he would see if he had a specimen good enough to send me. On mentioning this afterwards to the Bishop he said I or he was quite mistaken—for he was not the discoverer of it (that he had avowed)—nor was it called Bobartia but Bebertia (I think the Bishop said for a different person)—that the production in question was common enough in New Zealand &c.

We left Parramatta in time to get to Government House (in Sydney) between 4 & 5 o'clock, intending to pay our respects to Lady Gipps & get clothes &c for the Bishop's. Arrived at Government House—entered Drawing room & saw no one, but presently Lady Gipps arrived, not looking very glad to see us, but we were expected as Mr Elliot had written beforehand—presently she asked me if I had a letter from Bishop & on answering in negative she said he had called on her that morning & was extremely sorry to say he had sickness in the house—that a child of Mr & Mrs Clark who were staying with them was seriously ill so as not to be able to be moved & he was therefore under necessity of deferring our visit for a day or two—she therefore hoped we would stay with her. How deeply was I mortified!—for I was now confirmed in what I thought before, that for some reason or other the Bishop did not wish us to arrive at his house till next week. I did not know that Mr & Mrs Clark (the former of whom I had seen at Parramatta & on whose account no doubt surprise was expressed at our going to Bishop's) had been staying with them. Thus we found ourselves cast back again upon the Gippses; when not only in all probability they did not want us but when they knew besides that we wished & arranged to go elsewhere. No doubt I looked hurt & mortified, & I had not courage to express my obligation to Lady Gipps for letting us thus remain, feeling too well the awkwardness & unmeaningness of these compliments. When at last I did laugh out something of her kindness to take us in again & took her hand in saying so, she received it very coldly. I then said the chief thing which vexed me in the matter was that I had acted against my better judgment in coming in to town today for I had received an impression from the Bishop himself that for some reason or other, he did not wish us to come till next week, & now the thing explained itself. I did see this observation had a good effect on her mind. I found 2 notes waiting for me (alluded to by Lady Gipps) from the Bishop & Mrs Broughton, with expressions of their regret & hope to be able to receive us on Monday, & immediately sent off an answer to them. Dined alone—Sir George made no observation upon what brought us back but asked about our journey as usual. They were displeased at the house at Parramatta being empty—& rather shocked at my account of what was witnessed at the Factory.

Thus a third time have we arrived at Sydney sooner than we expected & when we had better have staid away, & both this time & the first time, it was in consequence of the discontent expressed, or implied rather, by my companions, who made me feel that they were being dragged along on my account & that in their eyes I was never satisfied with wandering. I felt with them as if an apology was necessary for all I did & as if I did not dare avow that curiosity had any thing to do with it—as indeed it had but a moderate share, for my strongest feeling was a repugnance to burdening the Gippses with our constant presence. I found it necessary to tell them that this might be a matter of indifference to *them*—because no responsibility was attached to them, *I* was supposed to control the movements of the party—but to *me*, the responsibility was thus painful.

Conrad Martens (1801–1878)
[*VIEW OF TEMPE ON COOK'S RIVER,*
NEAR SYDNEY, N.S.W.] 1845
watercolour; 22 x 34 cm
Rex Nan Kivell Collection NK1191

XII

Sydney Again

30 June – 16 July 1839

*L*ady Franklin's one desire now was to return to Hobart. But there were still vexing delays. Her passage was secured on the Medway, but the ship waited more than a fortnight for a hearing at the Supreme Court in which her commander, Captain Wight, was involved.[264] Ultimately the hearing was postponed, and the Medway sailed on 16 July. While she waited, Lady Franklin made her preparations for departure. In a round of farewell calls, she once more pressed invitations on the favoured to visit Government House in Hobart. Those invitations pointedly included wives, though they excluded children. Perhaps she hoped that now that she had demonstrated the practicability of intercolonial social calls, they would become more frequent. Perhaps she hoped that other ladies, by following her example, would remove the appearance of eccentricity in her own behaviour. But she was to be disappointed. In return for her scattered invitations, she received expressions of regard and esteem, gifts and mementoes, and a series of apologies and excuses.

Jane Franklin's frame of mind in this final fortnight of her visit is difficult to gauge. In many ways, she seemed happy enough. She was now on terms of familiarity with many new acquaintances, some of whom she valued and admired. She was venturing further afield without the escort of Sir George: climbing the lighthouse at South Head, visiting Mr Spark's grand home at Tempe, crossing the harbour to call on the Berrys at their north shore home, Crow's Nest. She was busy, active and cheerful in her preparations for her departure, settling accounts, disputing bills, purchasing souvenirs and ginger drops for the voyage. But there were signs, too, of stress and anxiety. This third descent on the Gippses included more than its fair share of awkwardness. There was, for example, the question of Snachall. Lady Franklin's maid had been taken ill with a fever and could not be asked to face the long sea voyage. Lady Franklin did not want to leave her behind as a continued burden on the governor and his wife, and made arrangements for her to be moved to a hospital. Sir George was equally anxious not to have it said that he threw Lady Franklin's maid out of his house as soon as Lady Franklin herself had left. Tensions rose over this, and also over Lady Franklin's use of the governor's carriage. Perhaps both disputes were symptomatic of the fact that, as Jane knew full well, she had long outstayed her welcome. Courtesy and affection increased rapidly towards the end of her stay, but their farewells were exchanged with mutual relief.

Sunday 30 June

Lady Gipps went to church—I not.

Monday 1 July

Sick headach & kept to room all day, looked at Hobarton newspapers. Dreadful weather, wind & rain—funerals of Cunningham & Leahy, fixed for today, did not take place.

Tuesday 2 July

Mr Cunningham's funeral at 9—numerously attended—also Colonel Leahy's later. Bishop read services—Sir George sent his carriage to first, & had given orders for second, but when I went in to luncheon, I found Lady Gipps warmly contesting with Sir George the propriety—said it made no distinction between respectable man & others. Sir George said on my entering, 'Now, Lady Franklin, let's hear what you have to say!' I was entirely for Lady Gipps—Sir George said women always work together & must have their way. Colonel Leahy died in a manner consistent with his life—half-intoxicated, fell up stairs, fractured his ribs and died in consequence of being afterwards moved in or out, when part of fractured ribs is supposed to have touched his heart. A post mortem examination is said to have indicated a life of 20 years more from healthy appearances— his impatience & swearing on his [death?] bed are said to have been dreadful. He had remarked just before his accident, on hearing of there being sick people at the club, that they ought not to be there—it would be pretty thing if funerals were to go from the Club—he was the first! He had been highly elated at the excellent bargain he had made about his property—having engaged to sell part at high price & kept the best himself. The only time we saw him at Wollongong, he was talking of the value of his life & how long he thought he might live.

Went in boat to Darling harbour to see *Medway*—Mr Grant, mate, elder brother of Surgeon in VDL shewed us—fixed on cabins—heard there was some uncertainty as to her departure. Took boat round part of Sydney Cove. Made calls & purchases—restored books to Evans—called at Clewetts & saw model of Sir Richard Bourke, cloak on shoulder—entered Dunsdons Confectioner in George St, no native preserves—Tyson's mercers in George St like private home—on right linen, mercery & furs—on left Howell & James—trinkets, jewellery, perfumery—upstairs, furniture, music—bought a rug—here & at Beady's in Pitt St asked for Tulip wood from Moreton Bay—to Irving & Lamb's about vase of £50.

Captain King to dine—spoke much of Cunningham—whose funeral he had followed today—said it was singular that he, Captain King, had been the last to speak with him. Previously to his death he was aware of his danger, yet believed in the possibility of his recovery—at last sank rapidly—died 27th June—Captain King persuaded him to make will & sent for Mr Norton. Left £100 to Anderson the Gardener—plants in spirits & Manuscripts to Robert Brown—herbarium & books to Mr Hebert of Kensington? & £1000 left to a gardener at Kew. In the whole, he left about £3000, of which 600 not accounted for in will—Captain King says he meant to leave it to Presbyterian schools—but thinks as this was only a verbal expression, it will revert to the Crown. Anderson was with him when he died, holding his hand—funeral procession moved from the Botanical gardens—a branch of his favourite tree—the Azuria Cunninghamia or Moreton Bay Pine—from the Botanical gardens was placed by Captain King amongst the plumes of the hearse. He was resigned & died most quietly.

He was 5 years with Captain King in his expedition,[265] and exhausted himself with his own energy—rose at day break, would take no food with him because of the weight, & returned at night fall, exhausted & unable to eat—pressed his flowers & shifted the others & went to bed. Being told he would kill himself, replied what was the use of living if he could not work?

Captain King spoke of Major Mitchell, only person in the Colony whom I have heard speak well of him—did not deny his bad temper, but knew how to treat him. Spoke of the extreme accuracy of his map—said it might be enlarged to 4 times its size & would be equally accurate.

Sir George, when dinner announced, told me to my dismay that Lady Gipps was not able to come to dinner. When I asked, Sir George said I might see her after dinner—heard how things arose—advised her to begin & see Dr—saw her a second time.

Captain Moriarty having had a letter from Captain Brodie, saying Wilson the Artist was going to have sale of his pictures & effects & desiring him to tell me, I went after 10, as the sale was to begin at 11, & saw the bad landscapes &c in oils he had in his parlour & which he estimated would bring him in about £40—result was not one half. I begged Captain Moriarty to stay & bid—he got Peggy for me & Mrs Wilson, & several for himself.

Next set off for Woolloomooloo, to see Bishop &c who had called yesterday, but their carriage being seen coming into town, we turned back & went to Bishop's Registry office where he was & went in & sat down— he still hoped if our ship did not go Sunday, we should come. Passing near Catholic Church, saw group of prisoners on ground & a priest standing amongst them on bank under Eastern end of church & found them one reading to others a tract, other questioning another verbally on catechism, others learning it. Saluted the priest who looked shy & said something about strange face—& their being in deplorable condition. I thought he meant spiritually, but found he meant as prisoners. Bishop walked over with me to cellar under church & here left us—Mr Elliot & Sophy looked over & selected books—spent a good hour there—then drove home to luncheon—saw Lady Gipps lying in bed & expecting crisis.

Went out again & left cards—or rather left slips of paper, having left card case at house. Ordered frame for native girl picture at Lewis's, mean little shed or shop on Brickfield Hill, the upper end of George St. Bought a work box inlaid with Tulip wood from Moreton Bay, made by prisoners at Norfolk Island. I bought this at a large furniture warehouse in King St, all their furniture of cedar—all the wood of picture frames of New Zealand Pine—he had a little of Huon pine.

Just before dinner, heard of Lady Gipps' crisis. Gentlemen's party— I spoke to Captain King of our intended Scientific Society—Mr Thomson tried to revive theirs 2 years ago, but it would not do. They quarrelled the first time—hurt themselves by asking for correspondence of great folks in London. When Peter Cunningham, assistant-Surgeon, sent his account of some fossils from hence, Mr Murchison who read the account turned it into ridicule. Captain King told him he had learnt a lesson—would never send home or write anything—Mr Murchison apologised, and said it should be last time.

Captain King agreed with me as to Mr Gould being an entirely uneducated man. He said when he came here he brought verbal introductions from Sir John to different individuals & went up to them & said 'Sir John Franklin desired me to give his compliments—he is in very good health & hopes you are the same'.[266]

In boat with Captain Moriarty to Point Piper & Watson's Bay & lighthouse—intending to ascend the lighthouse. Landed opposite Vaucluse, a house of Mr Wentworth, in a nook of Watson's Bay—house is irregular building, not large, in domestic gothic style—did not go close up to it but bent to left towards lighthouse & crossed a fence into sand—had about a mile to walk, chiefly up hill. Ascended stone stair to lighthouse—81 steps of stone, then wooden, making 95 in all—in part of the stone ascent it is almost quite dark—dome small—contains 9 burners revolving—3 different degrees of velocity can be given to the revolution—usual is one revolution in a minute—at this season 1 ½ gallons of oil is used nightly—6 men are kept here—very cloudy towards sea. Beneath the tower is placed 2 square towers, one at each end of a strait line with 5 embrasures between—a stable is at another angle & lodge for man at another—light is said to be visible 12 leagues—walked on to what is called Outer South Head, where the Semaphore or Flag Staff stands near edge of cliffs with a residence—the man here shewed me by his speech that he recognised me—told me there was a ship outside, the *Augustus Caesar,* arriving soon from Hobarton.

Scrambled hence on rocks & towards Mr [Hannibal] Macarthur's, which we went up to at back, & ascended thence to edge of cliff & looked over— sea here comes over from ocean into bay when wind sets in outside—this is narrowest part of the promontory of South head. Returning & none of family being there, accepted invitation of a man to pass thro' house— Mrs Macarthur, who has indifferent health & thinks Parramatta does not agree with her, is often here with one or two of her daughters. It is quite a small house of 4 rooms with central passage—towards bay has a pretty verandah & flight of stone steps—a neglected garden & paddock hence extend to beach. The dwelling of 4 pilots is also here—took to our boat here, & rowed back to town—have sketch of view from lighthouse by Mr Martens.

Dinner party to day—the Gibbes, Mr & Mrs Berry[267]—Mr & Mrs Manning[268] —he, a large & rather heavy-looking man—she small & *eveille* & gracious—Mr & Mrs Therry who did not arrive till dinner had begun— Mr Miller, Commissary who lives, as well as the Berrys, on the North Shore, Mr Spark of Tempe,[269] a highly respectable merchant who had been mentioned to me by Miss Williamson & whom I got introduced to me in order to speak of her & to arrange for going to see his place at Tempe—he is very quiet, rather slow in manner, but both shrewd & amiable in countenance & bears a high character—he comes from Elgin which is Miss Williamson's place. He did not seem as well acquainted with her as she seemed to be with him—said if it was the same family he supposed they were highly respectable.[270]

Mr Manning sat by me at dinner—he had led out Mrs Berry who was on his other side, who is a great radical & flirted with him about their ages—she acknowledged afterwards to be 59—saw but little of Mr Berry who was however brought up in evening to me—I was amused with him, something made him say 'I'm thought to be a radical, but instead of that I'm a pestiferous Tory—' I told this afterwards to Sir George who laughed & who did not seem to think very highly of his talents, but said he was good honest man—I believe others rate his abilities higher, & so should I. Sir George flirts with Mrs Berry who is not frightened at him nor at any body. She tells him she should be the happiest woman in the world if she knew what to do with her money or had relations to leave it to. Sir George told me Lady Gipps was very fond of her loquats, which were remarkably fine, & cultivated Mrs Berry's acquaintance in consequence—when this was said before Lady Gipps she looked at me, half uneasy lest I should suspect there was some truth in it—Sir George did not indeed know whether she did not look beyond the loquats to the relief of poor Mrs Berry as to her money.

Mr Manning spoke to me about Mr Stephen. He evidently disliked all the family very much & was disposed to think ill of Mr Alfred—had met him in company & did not like his flippant manner. Might he ask me the grounds on which he had ceased to be a member of the Government before he left VDL?—there was a story that in a case which he mentioned, he had not acted the part of an honest man—I told him I had never heard a word of it before—that he was subtle & vain & perhaps vindictive, but was a man of warm & impetuous feeling. I had never heard his integrity impeached—believed it to be intact—I could not enter into his motives for resigning, but it was scarcely possible to doubt but that private pique & enmity had something to do with it—he could not succeed in supplanting his enemies in Sir John's government, & certainly resigned at a time when he must have meant to embarrass it. 'That's exactly what I should think of him,' said Mr Manning—sedulously picking out the evil from the good & dwelling alone on it. I mentioned this afterwards to Sir George who eagerly said, 'There is no foundation at all, is there, for such a report?'—I believed there was none.

There was card playing as usual in the evening which kept the people late.—

Saturday 6 July

To Cook's River & Tempe. Major Smith & Mr Steele with us—turned beyond Parramatta St into road left—come to Mr Simeon Lord's handsome house right. On—distance of bush & peeps of river left. Come to Cook's River [church] right.[271] Sir George laid stone not a year ago—its cost about

£3300—is in bush on right of road—Mr Steele is its clergyman.[272] It is of brick plastered, pinnacles of which are at each corner of stone—tower to right square embrasured with lofty arch in front opening into it but closed in lower part by square partition of door—it enters a vestibule formed in tower—over the entrance is seen the Western window of the church—over the square tower rises octagonal base of spire with 5 small windows & over this is a smooth spire of wood with gilt iron cross on top, so this in one direction is scarcely to be seen—side 6 long windows—not gothic, & ugly, divided by buttresses—battlement along top—1 larger Eastern window in flat Eastern end with Gothic tracing at top—flower points of gable—Inside 6 octagonal columns each side reach to ceiling which is joined in centre & flat at sides—the tops of the windows are of stained glass. Clergyman's house is close by, near Western end—2 windows & a door in front with gothic ornaments corresponding to church.

On 23 May Lady Franklin had met Mr Steele and found:

he was the person mentioned in a letter I believe I have in my possession, when he was mentioned if not recommended to us as tutor—he then wanted to get ordained, & thought office in Governor's family might secure this—but this could not be promised—afterwards thro' the Archbishop of Canterbury he got ordained by the Bishop of London, with only a half hour's examination, especially for these colonies, & came out with Sir George Gipps which had been of great advantage to him. Had got the new church at Cook's River, of which stone had been laid by Sir George—had no family except his wife.

Jane Franklin, Diary, 23 May 1839

On—see house of Tempe, Mr Spark's, where we were expected, at end of road, river intervening—arrived & descended to ferry on banks of river— met by Mr Gill, a nephew of Mr Spark's. On the other side of the river is swamp or white flat overflowed, half land, half water, with hard dry pleasure path curving to it to foot of the bank on which is Mr Spark's villa. Mr Spark has been here about 8 years—built the villa himself. At front is door & Venetian window each side, from which projects a circular colonnade & supporting pleated roof or verandah—wall over this is ornamented with medallion containing Prince of Wales's feathers in plaster. To left & behind, rock rises steep, but is of modest height, tho' styled Mt. Olympus—forms a sort of small promontory at foot of which is small wharf or jetty & bathing house—the intended dam begins a little higher on opposite bank, takes a curve or bow upwards, & is to abut on this promontory—Sir George begins to think it will never be done for want of convict labour, no ships having come in for some time—he wanted two gangs or ship loads of 200, one on each side, for the stockades erecting or to be erected each side. Major Barney calculates 1200 millions of gallons of fresh water will be in the Basin. River goes up 6 or 7 miles above this & 4 below, where is Mr Lord's mill & the well first discovered in colony called Cook's well—2 of the gents went this way, by heavy sand not fit for carriage, & then pulled up river in Mr Spark's boat. View from Olympus of winding of river—in flat bush & swamps, & see heads of Botany Bay—all ugly enough—up river there is said to be some pretty scenery. Mr Spark has a large garden on flat—white soil—walks crossing at right angles & Norfolk Island pines at intersections—one very bushy with upper spindle lath also a Moreton Bay pine. Orange & lemon trees. Some fine Wattle trees—one long trellis-covered wall of vines, all differently marked—6 or 7 Norfolk Island pines. At side of house are aviaries, of wooden cage work. Casuarina trees stripped of leaves with convenient branches are planted in aviaries for perches of birds—parraquets [sic] do not do so well as pigeons, ducks & pheasants.

Mr Spark with Mrs Duguid, the banker's wife come to do the honours, arrived after us. 2 rooms—Dining & Drawing room prettily furnished—pictures in each—one of Martens', a view of Tempe in water colors. I told Mr Spark I had a sketch of it—he seemed surprised & pleased. We had a handsome luncheon. Very pretty china—oysters from bay brought here to fatten—an immense pineapple of his own growing, juicy but scarce any flavour. He has a small library, containing some tolerable pictures & small plaster antiques with busts of Canning, Brougham, William 4th & Napoleon—means to build a room with lights from above. Mr Spark is a bachelor—gentlemanly & quiet—from Elgin. He is one of largest subscribers to Cook's River Church, tho' not a parishioner. [I] asked for the consecration service of Mr Steele.

Sunday 7 July

To St James—Sir George did not go—staid for Sacrament—went in afternoon to Mr Cowper's at St Philip[273]—over Bishop's pew is a monument to Mr Cowper's wife, who died in 1831 aged 49—Mr Cowper is there called Senior Assistant Chaplain. In his sermon he said he or we could not, like deluded Romish priests, absolve them from sins, drag them from purgatory &c. Sir George said at dinner he was always surprised that 2 institutions were not formed in a country like England where Charities of all sorts abounded—viz. one to compensate those whose reputations were unjustly injured, & funds also, by imprisonments on things on which acquitted—the other to find places for prisoners sent back into the world. In America they went into back countries. Sir George had abolished cutting off women's hair—when women lost their hair, there was an end of them— he seemed to intimate it unsexed them. I thought this for women & flogging for men should be reverted to in desperate cases.[274]

Went to Lady Gipps before dinner, talked of servants.

Monday 8 July

[Sent Wilson's] drawing to Mr Stephen to look at—he highly approved of it. Mr Orton ushered in—came last week from VDL—he saw Sir John the day before he left—he went on board the *Eudora* thinking I was there— wanted me home very much.

Had carriage after luncheon & called first on Mrs Broughton—told her must propose coming to dine with her instead of [illegible] on account of Snachall. She seemed pleased—will you come tomorrow then—her manner kinder & somewhat nervous. Next to Mrs Thomson, at home—she also a little nervous. Court journal on table—her father sent it to her, she said—she was the last whom it concerned. Two little girls, Elizabeth Louise Deas & Susan—I reminded her of her intended visit to us in VDL—again said I could not take her children—but begged that would not be a hindrance. She looked pleased & obliged. Left card with Lady Dowling, out—called on Mrs Lethbridge, thanked her for native dog skin rug—cards at Wilsons & Shadforth—called on O'Connells—saw Lady, Mr & Miss— found she & ladies not likely to come to VDL—she pressed us to go again on Wednesday—declined.

Went, in returning from Woolloomooloo, to Sydney College. Centre & 1 wing finished—wing has 3 stories of 3 windows & parapet pierced with narrow open arches—centre, a handsome square door with high flight of steps to it, lancet on long narrow window each side—over, a tablet of some stone with carved inscription in Latin stating that this school of Literature & Art was instituted under the auspices of Sir Thomas Brisbane, founded by Sir Richard Bourke in 1831, Sir Francis Forbes president, Hallen architect. Enter door into great school—very large room in length of house—benches and desks—2 chimneys each end—a door between in the end on the left, & over it a portrait of Sir Francis Forbes, seated in crimson chair, resting edge of book in his right hand on his knee—flat, clever & rather cunning face.

Sir Maurice O'Connell waits to pay his visit to us till the next regiment arrives here. The O'Connells have been very anxious to pay us attention, but with the exception of Sir Maurice they are not much to my taste. Lady O'Connell is very gracious and prevenante *in her manners, but very artificial; a person whose sentiments I should doubt even from her own mouth. Captain O'Connell the eldest son and Aide-de-Camp is a handsome young man, ridiculously covered with Spanish stars and orders acquired in Christina's service as a Brigadier General under Evans. It is bad taste his decorating himself with these in the presence of the Representative of Majesty when he could not do so (in the absence of royal permission) in the presence of the Queen herself. Lady Gipps remarked to me also that it was rather foolish in Sir Maurice to assume the title of 'Excellency'. It appears that he asked Sir George his opinion about it, and Sir George expressed his desire that he would do as he liked; upon which he assumed it, waiting approval from home. I think I would have waited for that first. He seems however an unassuming, good sort of man, always calling Sir George 'Governor'. Sir George told me that the newspapers had tried all they could to get up a feud between him and Sir Maurice without succeeding.*

Letter, Jane Franklin to Sir John Franklin, 15 June 1839

Went in to Lady Gipps—spoke of her visit to VDL. It seemed as if she could not come without Sir George & he she supposed not possible—did not know—said it was a pity there was the nominal dependence there was existing between the 2 colonies, as otherwise the Governors might communicate & visit with more advantage—she said, no authority at all over that—if Governor here went, no authority—no—but a ceremony. She said that in coming [to NSW] Sir George would have liked much to have touched [at VDL], but was restrained by this idea—I said, Sir Richard Bourke felt the same—but I was sure Sir John would not feel it. In the evening Sir George said, speaking of visiting, he must come when Lady Gipps did— meaning not at all.

Mr Wilson came to retouch his chalk drawing, injured by being carried to Mr Stephen. He told me his 600 acres on Hunter were to be rented of Mr Blaxland junior at £90 a year, to begin next March for 14 years—600 acres, 400 fit for cultivation—he means to take in hand only 100—bad people on lease of it. I told him of the Huon[275]—he wished to take advantage of it—had fixed nothing yet with Mr Blaxland—would see if he would take it very ill if he got off his bargain. If he went to the Hunter he must go in a month, yet he had many portraits to paint. His sale of effects went off well, except pictures—sold off smaller things, as cut glass, candlesticks &c for more than he gave for them—this is usually the case with anything neat, pretty or well-made.

I saw Mrs Coney, wife of a prisoner in VDL going by the *Medway*, sent by Mr Mitchell the Emigration agent, to know if her services could be of any use to me in the passage. Drew £100 to pay bills & set off for Benevolent Asylum thro' Pitt St emerging near by Toll Gate House. Good houses in Pitt St—& some sheds—Victoria Coffee house & restaurant is one—went into the confectioner's shop & bought ginger drops &c. Called at Tegg's, remonstrated about prices & took about £10 worth—paid £7 to Evans. Neither he nor Tegg had Franklin's *Voyages*—all sold—neither could get Cunningham's portrait, nor Plunkett's *Australian Magistrate*.[276]

Benevolent Society—old shallow house of Macquarie. Two wings, of which one is new and of brick—saw 3 wards, old, infirm & sick men—old women are in another—several young ones affected with blindness, which came on in the emigrant ships; one had dropsy in eyes. Kitchen forms separate building opposite back of house—behind kitchen an open space, bordering on the Catholic burial ground, where old men loll about or sit on benches—many dismal-looking objects. It is a hospital for the distressed free—many come in to be cured & go away—received 900 last year—above 70 died of catarrh—have 1 lb meat daily amounting when bone & waste subtracted to about or little more than half a pound—1 lb bread given at breakfast & tea, not wanted at dinner, 1 pint of soup, & 1 pint tea at breakfast & another at tea. Dr Cottenham expected rice would be substituted for some portion of meat & said it would be for the better—1 oz of tobacco allowed to the old men above 40. House out of repair.

On return to house, after dressing for the Bishop's I went in to speak to Lady Gipps who had sent for Sophy in morning—her door was shut—tapped at it—Sir George's growl asked what—I just opened the door & spoke—he said I might come in if I did not mind seeing him on bed, where he was lying at full length, dressed. I went in—Lady Gipps on sofa, seemed displeased. I had not been 2 minutes in room before summoned to go away—I said good night or evening to Sir George as I passed foot of bed. He never rose, or moved—on reflection I thought Lady Gipps' manner probably proceeded from vexation at this.

At Bishop's, found the Steels, Colonel Wodehouse & Captain Harding. In dining room, on the floor stood a large portrait of Mr McLeay, a copy of one by Sir Thomas Lawrence in the Linnean Society. This copy was done at request of his friends on his removal from Colonial Secretary—they did not know where to put it—Sir George was asked to let it be in Government House, but declined. I [said I] supposed he thought it would look like favouring a party. Bishop said he did, but need not have, for he was a man of sufficient distinction & science & who had done much to illustrate country. I asked if Mr McLeay knew it—Bishop believed not—at least he had not told him. He had never told anyone, but found Sir George had himself, which made his own discretion useless. All gone to bed when we returned before 10.

Wednesday 10 July

At 12, Mr Miller came to conduct me over water to Mr Berry's— crossed diagonally to Berry's bay or wharf beyond Billy Blue's cottage— the headland of Berry's bay on left is called Ball's. At the head of the little bay is a stone shed where Mr Berry deposits his produce from Shoalhaven. Several cottages & plots of garden for his workmen. As we approached Mr Berry was seen descending the road & Mr Miller's carriage or spring gig cart—built for ladies, he says, tho' he is a bachelor. We ascended road in bush, in which went on for a mile to the green gate of Crow's Nest—lofty situation & exquisite view—harbour in portions, Botany Bay like river seen in all extent, Sydney in portion, church of St James in particular thro' opening in trees of foreground, & going more inland, ranges of hills. Cottage is white plastered brick—they have lived in it 7 or 8 years—it was her brother Mr Wollstonecraft's, who left it on his death to her with 700 acres. They ought, she says, to live at Shoalhaven. Her father was brother to the celebrated Mary Wollstonecraft married to Godwin & her [cousin is] married to Bysshe Shelley—house has broad stone pavement front & 2 old fashioned large windows each side of door which opens into parlour with 2 windows—snug & pretty—a tiny study with 2 front windows & tiny bedroom behind occupy the corresponding half of house—at back is broad stone pavement with verandah, on one side of which is a snug little dining room, on the other I believe a bedroom. Descended hill to garden, soil not so bad tho' rains cause gravel— best soil gets to bottom where fine oranges & loquats & lemon—also a little grove of bananas with fruit on branches. Had one cluster picked to keep—oranges fine—ground overgrown with a sorrel bearing long tubed yellow flowers, stalks very juicy. We had a very pretty luncheon—much fun on Mr Miller for being of Temperance Society. Mrs Berry said she always told her husband he was cleverest but she had most common sense—had nothing to wish for but some relations to leave their money to—she had her own way in every thing—I asked them to come to VDL—seemed pleased & made no difficulty. I brought away a basket of fresh butter for Lady Gipps & some oranges. Sir George had told me Lady Gipps was very fond of her loquats & on this account had cultivated much Mrs Berry's acquaintance. When he heard of the butter, the joke enhanced in value.

Returning by another road thro' bush we passed Mr Miller's villa, called Upton, commanding most extensive & superb view of harbour. Mr Miller's house is small & rather elegant—outside of stone, 1 window each side of door, belonging to 2 parlors—was built with convict labour—all has been the work of 5 years. Leaving view of Mr Stephen's on left we landed by Billy Blue's cottage, where embarked. Landed at Fort Macquarie which presents to harbour on 3 sides, 8 guns—on 4th, 2. In upper room of the Tower, the Sailmaker of *Herald* was at work—saw his thimble strap. Walked home by path between Government domain on left & paling of new wharf forming on right. Here convicts at work, cutting away the bank of rock to make it horizontal. Excavated rock in slabs with hollow between, in side of which insert wedges to make it come off in slabs.

Went to the door—I was called up by [the maid] Newport to see Lady Gipps, having desired her to tell me the right time—she received me rising from sofa—talked of various things. She liked much the books I lent her. When Sir George entered, I had foot on chair & removed instantly & rose—he looked as if he remembered yesterday & [illegible] curious, anxious. I ran away to dress. At dinner he questioned me as usual closely about our morning doings.

On Captain Moriarty remarking how much wheat had come out of VDL, Sir George answered yes—his opinion of VDL had been greatly exalted by it—more exalted by it than by all Mr Stephen's high flown panegyrics—it had been done in a very handsome manner too—they have my best bows & acknowledgements if they are worth anything—to this I muttered, it cannot be doubted.

Thursday 11 July

Overslept myself, for want of the usual causes of being woke on firelighting &c, & Bishop & Mrs Broughton arrived before I was dressed or had breakfasted. When I went down I found them & the Count Strzelecki,

Elliot & Moriarty & presently, Mr Wilson came in—found the Broughtons were in the same mind as to coming to VDL. Bishop brought for me Admiral Bligh's Trial, carefully sealed in cover that it might not be generally seen— also some other papers—as he was going away I gave him my 'mite to his Cathedral' which he seemed pleased at, but said nothing. Had conference with Mr Wilson who said he had been refused assigned servants as Mr Blaxland had already his complement on that estate. This decided Wilson against it & he was anxious to accept the advantages of the Huon— did not encourage him—told him, as he wanted 300 acres, that I could not let this be, as it would shut out others, unless he could purchase 100 first— he thought this quite reasonable.

Lady Gipps went out today in carriage & Sophy with her—Lady Gipps asked after my family & name. I left cards at Barneys & Plunketts, paid bill at Clint's &c. Walked to garden & begged Mr Anderson[277] to pack me up a box of Sydney soil or sand. He quite seized my idea and said he would go for it to the Surry hills as being the purest—begged him to be fair about [it]. As walking in the garden, picked a daphne. The constable, seeing Mr Elliot do it at end of walk, hastened up with staff in his hand, saying 'Ay ay, that won't do—Mr Anderson won't allow that'—Mr Elliot coolly advanced towards him & said we came from Government House—he begged pardon.

I told Sir George this, as well as about box of sand—he seemed to like both stories—but said I should shew at some time what this soil would produce, the flowers & the colly flowers [cauliflowers] the latter striking him, because we had them to day for first time & he was pressing it on Sir Gordon Bremer[278] who came in when dinner was half over, as he has not seen vegetables for a long time—Sir George introduced him to me— he sat other side of Sir George which made it inconvenient for me to speak, & as he did not ask after Sir John I felt a little backward in addressing him. I asked soon however if he had left Mr Stanley at the settlement & was thanked for asking after him—he asked if I knew Mr Stanley—'A little' [I said]—'he was for a short time midshipman with Sir John in Mediterranean.' 'Yes, he knew well'—adding something in expression of Stanley's regard for Sir John, & said when he (Sir Gordon) was in the *Britomart*, he had Sir John close by him—I did not at first understand, but found it was Sir John's portrait.

Speaking of Melville Island & of his settlement there,[279] I asked whether any account of it had been published, or where I could see it—only in dispatches to Admiralty—he would give me a copy—& of his last expedition he had made a condensed account for Sir George which he dared say I could get access to. He seemed flattered—I said I should like to see *Alligator* & begged permission to go on board—wished not to keep him at home &c—he insisted on being there—fixed for Saturday.

Sir George alluded to my adventurous journey overland.

Sir George spoke at dinner of his desire to hear from England—his last dispatches are as far back as 25th December. He had nothing to say for Downing St policy in restrictions imposed on Governors, obliging them to refer home for every thing—he could not now make a Court of Requests at Port Phillip nor military juries, nor circuit courts, without reference home—when got home excuse would be sent that Ministers so much engaged, they must refer it to next session.

After dinner, sat with Lady Gipps & spoke of her coming to Hobarton—For some reasons, thought her coming now, would be the best. Dr Mollison called in evening—thought Snachall's state doubtful, if she could go—I proposed hospital.

Sir George left Sir Gordon & me in close talk & went to bed.

Friday 12 July

Began packing. Saw Dr Mollison—who told me Snachall could be admitted to hospital—told Snachall man & afterwards her—made no opposition. Bad morning, but seemed disposed to clear up, so ordered carriage at ½ past 1 for going to Mr McLeay's. It began to rain & looked worse—I sent to his house, but he was gone. I went to Lady Gipps' room to fetch a bill left there, & was detained by a conversation about Snachall &c—she wished us to stop a few days longer to judge of her state—I said nothing would detain me but her [Lady Gipps] going with us. She looked serious & said she feared it could not be—she had been once absent from George, & tho' with a dear sister, was unhappy—hoped we should meet again in some part of world—probably should in England—this brought tears to me who was previously disposed for it.[280] Presently Sir George came in & in a subdued voice & calling me by name said the carriage was waiting. I did not look at him in face, being ashamed, & ran out of room. I heard he had grumbled about carriage & expected the lining would be hurt. Before we had got halfway, it poured & the roads were very bad.

Found Mrs & Miss McLeay. Old gentleman was in garden, had been caught by rain & stopped in grotto—was very wet & had lumbago, she also—waited for him & then he proposed going over house which we did. Bronze balustrades about to be erected—bold stone brackets support stairs—observed door joints &c of cedar pilasters, wider at base than top, like Egyptian. I remarked this—he said the Grecian Doric was like Egyptian in this—Roman Doric otherwise—Breakfast room is oval at each end. He is evidently proud of house & particularly of staircase—agreed with me it was without a rival in the colony 'at present'.

The eldest son, Mr William McLeay, was introduced—a very plain, vulgar-looking man—is a noted man of science. Mrs McLeay told me she had heard from Mr Wilson he was going to VDL. He regarded me as his patroness but was frightened at £30 the acre—I explained nature of thing—she seemed surprised & could not wonder at his wanting to go—wished she had more time to talk of it—would we dine there tomorrow—could not—would we come & spend half an hour—had not time—I repeated my invitation to them to visit VDL—he pointed out to me large stone in pavement opposite door—God blessed me going away. Poured all the time.

When Sir George came into Drawing room before dinner, I did not attempt to notice him nor he me—I felt ashamed of my last interview, & I thought he looked displeased—this seemed to me hardhearted even tho' I had kept the carriage [waiting]—he said he should drink water. Mr Sargent [?] was first to ask me to take wine—butler being told to help me & not hearing the invitation was going to help Sir George as usual to drink with me—I made slight movement of hand to stop him which I think Sir George noticed. He did not ask me, (the first time he has ever omitted it) but in course of dinner, said he would take a glass & when had done so looked at me & I at him—he asked me no questions as to our visit tho' always asks & by this proved to me more than anything that he was displeased. In fact we had no conversation tho' he invited me to eat—& I was out of spirits & found myself unable to converse with Sir Gordon across table. Mr Parker asked me questions about Mr McLeay's house.

After dinner, I went up to Lady Gipps determined to make to her the apology about the carriage which I had not had courage to do to him for fear of repulsive or offensive manner—she seemed sorry to be interrupted, & when I expressed myself sorry at having taken out the carriage in such weather, said it was very bad indeed. I felt hurt & silenced—& when I alluded to it afterwards with slight additional explanation tears were in my eyes, which she noticed & her manner became kinder. She said Sir George would not suffer Snachall to go to hospital & had just said so before dinner. I represented my distress—hoped he would be persuaded—he was very open to conviction (yes, indeed he was). She hoped I would not distress myself—this again made me cry—Dr Mollison came in—I told him my desire she should if possible go on board, & left him. Met him again on staircase & had private talk with him—then went into Drawing room with red eyes tho' had strived to mend them—this prevented my looking to Sir George who on his side, did not look at or speak to me—asked Sir Gordon in his presence if they had newspapers at Port Essington. Sir Gordon said he had been asking things of Sir George who would give him nothing, absolutely nothing. I said you ask far too much at a time—you should go more cunningly to work—he is obliged to go to Treasury too—Sir George heard but said nothing—not a word passed between us—he heard me make fresh appointment with Sir Gordon & left the room for the night.

When all gone Mr Parker told me Lady Gipps wished to speak to me before I went to bed—went in, her manner exceedingly kind—begged I would not be distressed about hospital—was sure it was the best but hoped I would not mind leaving her [Snachall] here on account of the trouble. I said I was already so overwhelmed with obligation that a little more I had no scruple about—was glad of this opportunity of speaking—she remarked my nervousness—I said was out of spirits—this business, & also I was vexed at my conduct in morning in using the carriage & in keeping it waiting which I understood Sir George disliked very much—she said he was quite foolish in this respect—no cause of delay however important, was an excuse—what harm could it do?—I did not know but it certainly was not for me to act contrary to his wishes—however, resuming an air of cheerfulness & self-respect I said he had not scolded me, I was exempted from scolding.

Saturday 13 July

Sir George sent for me to small Drawing room—said an unnecessary degree of importance had been given to what he said to Lady Gipps yesterday about Snachall—he had said it was no use talking about it, it should not be done—it should not be said that Lady Franklin had no sooner gone than he sent her servant to the hospital—I remarked that this was only a home [?] & that its advantages were greater than any other— I therefore hoped he would be kind enough to reconsider what he had said, for I felt it my duty to remove her—Dr Mollison had told me if she remained, he should wish Reggy to leave—I therefore should feel extremely unhappy in leaving her there, tho' I felt bound to act so as not to displease him. 'I must do as I pleased—she was not his servant,' [he said]. I said it would distress me however if he were angry at my resolution—he left me I think more reconciled to it, but said I must do as I pleased—he would send the 2 Doctors to me—this was Mollison & Dr Dobie [who] called in to judge if she was fit for the voyage—he thought not & that she would be much better removed—they said Sir George had consented that I should have my own way, & so we walked to hospital to see the room—first went into Dr Mollison's house opposite end of Council building—then into hospital—2 rooms, fixed for inner one, but both hers—introduced to Mr Harnett, surgeon of hospital, pleasant, tall, mild man—engaged a convalescent free woman of hospital, named Day to wait on Snachall at 7 shillings a week, got Captain Moriarty to go & buy mattress, carpet, table & chairs—returned & told Lady Gipps & asked if I might have the carriage or should hire one—perhaps Sir George might object to his carriage appearing there or fear infection—then went in to luncheon where told Sir George I had seen rooms & that Dobie said she ought to be removed. He coloured, looked angry & said 'You do as you please.' I thought I had better not have renewed the subject—Lady Gipps sent for him at luncheon—he asked why she did not come to him—I knew it was to ask him about carriage. It was a long while before I was sent for—I was then told by her he had no objection to my having the carriage—she went out first for a drive & I accompanied her—on return at ½ past 3, changed carriage & Snachall, supported, got into it & drove to hospital, where met Drs Mollison & Harnett & established her.

Heard today that Mr Christie of Mounted Police had gone raving mad— Major Christie whom we saw at Liverpool, his brother, has insured his life, having a complaint of heart which may carry him off suddenly.

Sunday 14 July

Went to St James' with Lady Gipps in the carriage—Sir George & Mr Parker walking—as we got to church first, I took on entering the pew, the head of back seat, leaving Sir George's chair vacant. Lady Gipps, who took hers, earnestly begged me to take the other, saying she was sure Sir George would never let me sit there. I would not however & when Sir George entered, he very slightly asked me, & then seated himself. Lady Gipps looked displeased with him. Mr Walsh preached for first time here—short, energetic—talked of political expediency of the day, love of *lucre* thru' length & breadth of this land—he produced a great sensation.[281]

After church the Barneys came in, Lady Gipps having begged to see Major Barney to beg for a person turned off from being constable from letting prisoner escape & whose wife had been in great distress to Lady Gipps. While they were talking Mrs Barney addressed herself to me about the Wilsons, who are protegées of theirs also—he painted some portraits for them & has been employed by Major Barney as much as he can in the engineer's office in drawing—he was indeed appointed to an office in that department, but was superseded from home. The Bishop had been told by him I had given him a farm & advised him strongly to accept it—so also did the McLeays. Mrs Barney spoke with rapture of the Walshs—knew Mrs Walsh intimately—greatest friend I have, except you, [she said to Lady Gipps]—did a great deal of good.

I remained at home alone the rest of the afternoon, hoping Sir George would come in & ask me to walk. I waited in vain but at last found him & her come in together from the garden—sat & talked with her, till others returned from church when getting dark, & went to see Snachall— Sir George said at dinner he had put his last finish that morning to his financial minute—at another time told us he was always employed on Sunday on bringing up his papers of the week—& in church too often of thinking of his dispatches—has had none from England of later date than 25th of December—has not quite a dispatch a day written home—Colonial Secretary in last year had received 14 000 letters—'All of which,' Sir George said, 'I have read.'

In evening had prayers as usual—Sir George made the same beautiful prayer as once before on his own duties. May I this & that. Bless the companion of my fortunes that she may aid, comfort & encourage me— then prayed against his irritability of temper, a softer air turneth away wrath. It appeared evident to me that he was making the '*amende honorable*' for his ill humour & my suffering from it of the last few days. From today, his humour was entirely altered & improved.

Monday 15 July

Our last day—Sir George full of jokes about it & that we should not go—only thing in its favour was that the 300 000 oranges (this was the number Captain Moriarty at first mentioned, tho' afterwards reduced to 300 dozen) were on board. Visit from Wilson, his face radiant—his wife said he *must* accept my offer & he came to say he did—he had a female free servant whom he valued, but could not afford to bring over—I said I would pay her passage as a good servant was always wanted in VDL— settled with Snachall that he would go with us & his wife follow—he should think it ungrateful not to remain [with us]. Visit from Lady Dowling— I observed to Lady Gipps that I thought her rather clever & pleasant— Lady Gipps agreed but not so Sir James whom she believed to be of low origin & who shewed it. She said the Chief Justice came next to Governor by reference to home. She had remarked that Lady Dowling & Lady O'Connell never came together—Lady O'Connell staid away when Lady Dowling was expected.[282]

Going down to dinner, found the mother of a little boy of 13 who had been Reggy's play fellow yesterday & today—Mrs Bloxsome is a young woman, not very wise I should think—they have been out about a year & embarked on their property in New England, a cold district to North where have been very unfortunate, losing their sheep—all disappeared in country. When they came out thought they might have visited VDL & Dr Hodgson (friend) consequently gave her a letter for me, which she told me of in course of evening. Said accidentally at dinner to Sir George he was thought to look on gloomy side—who says so? he immediately asked—[I] really did not recollect [I said, though I] had no doubt it was Thomson—knew he thought so. When went into drawing room after dinner, sat on stool & read to the 2 boys Reggy & Oswald from a book I had that day given him, called 'Conversations of a father with his children'. It was delightful to see Reggy sunk in arm chair his beautiful eyes fixed with intent expression on me—interrupted by entrance of Dr Mollison whom I had seen in morning & to whom I gave a £5 note—his countenance & manner in evening convinced me he was satisfied with me. He was to write when Snachall better—going away tonight Captain Moriarty said to me good night. Mentioned 'to-morrow'—I said it sounded quite awful. On bidding Lady Gipps good night, asked her if might come into her room tomorrow morning—she said she should be down to breakfast at ½ past 7. It was said we were to go on board at 8 & sail at 9. Wrote to Bishop at night.

Tuesday 16 July

   Tomorrow came—found them at breakfast when went down—one side of table clear—took the middle of it, hesitating between Mr Parker & Sir George at opposite side—it was remarked kindly the rarity of my appearance at breakfast—said I had been there twice before—Mr Elliot came in—I shifted my seat to be near Sir George. Little said except jokes by Sir George on expected firing of guns at 8 which Sir George told Sophy would be done if we did not go. I ate nothing, but no notice taken—they seemed to wait for me & I for them to rise—rose simultaneously. They went together to fire—I approached also, & Sir George withdrew & left the room. I remarked to Lady Gipps she did not look well. She was not—feared it was her rising so soon—sorry she had done so—but she was determined to 'fill up measure of kindness to last'—I could not express my gratitude to her—she took my hand kindly—said scarcely anything, did not go, but Newport or Snachall being mentioned, I said I must go & see Newport to thank her for her kindness to Snachall—Lady Gipps sent for her now & I did so—Newport stood with unmoved countenance—would go to see Snachall when Dr thought it was safe. I hoped she would accompany Lady Gipps if she came to VDL & so shook hands with her—her hand is as small & well shaped as a high born lady, & her manner as cold.
   Went & found Lady Gipps & Sophy sitting in Drawing room—gents gone—here remained long, seeing nothing of them & talking—I began to be very tired myself & to fear she was, & said so—& at last went to look after gents—found Mr Elliot in his room—heard everything was ready, but Captain Wight not on board—thought this of no consequence & as soon as boat came back, we were to go. I suppose Sir George found out this signal when it occurred for he came into Drawing room, standing with back to fire & again saying Captain Wight sent his compliments &

would go within tomorrow or next day. Reggy came bouncing in saying 'Lady Franklin, I must wish you good bye & a very pleasant voyage.' 'Why, where are you going?'—going to walk down to boat—at same time our gents came in & I found we were in fact going—I then went up to Sir George, took his hand & said I was unable to thank him—he said nothing, but offered me his arm—I begged Lady Gipps to thank him for me saying I could not—she would. Walked with Sir George to boat—told him Captain Nyas had said he would bring him & Lady Gipps & the boy but would not bring the Bishop—he laughed, tho' perhaps he had heard it before—'Why?'—I did not follow this up with anything, but presently he said 'I should like very much indeed to visit VDL—have a great desire to do so—but fear it will not be in my power'. I said Sir John would be very happy to see him. He feared, he added, he should not be able to go till his time was over & that it would be too late—I thought he was going to say to find Sir John there, but he said too late to profit by it—'Oh,' I added, 'in that point of view, I don't think you could derive much advantage'—Yes he could, he replied. I thought all this shewed good taste & good feeling—he probably thought I should like to have my mind at rest on this subject—he probably knew I did not wish him to come & his expression of desire to come was introductory only to relieving my mind on this score, & enabled him, in accounting for his desire, to pay a compliment to the colony or its administration. Nothing could be more handsome than saying it would then be too late to profit by it. I added no more—we arrived at the boat—he shook me rather tenderly by the hand & I was in tears—the expression of his face was softened. Reggy looked at me with surprise.

I had nothing particular to say to Mr Parker tho' both he & Gilbert Elliot walked down also. Lady Gipps had told Sophy I must not expect her. Captain Wight was on board with Mr Braim & another young man, Mr Stenway, not known, who seemed attached to him & some steerage passengers. Wind fair from North East. We went slowly out of harbour & thro' heads, scarce moved. We were on board at about 11—South head of Botany Bay rose to view beyond steep narrow cliffs before we went to dinner at 3 or 4—only our own party, the 2 gents above named, Captain Wight in his stuffed arm chair & the 1st mate, Grant, succeeded by the 2nd. Captain talked much of South America—Sophy & I had the same cabin—3 slim windows on larboard side—she with a wide projecting berth with crimson curtains—I with my iron bedstead.

Louis Haghe (1806–1885)

[*PORTRAIT OF SIR JOHN FRANKLIN*]

[London?: s.n. 184–?]

lithograph; 34.6 x 25.4 cm

Rex Nan Kivell Collection NK1994

Voyage Home

JANE FRANKLIN HAD BEEN DELIGHTED to come to an arrangement with Captain Wight for their passages home on his 500-ton ship, the *Medway*. She had not cavilled at the single condition that he had insisted upon, 'that he would not go out of the Heads in a Southerly gale'. On the contrary, as she had written to Sir John:

> We of course did not differ with him in opinion on this matter. Our arrangement with the 'Medway' detains us longer than we wished, yet it is of such importance at this season in particular (as well as at all times) to sail in a safe and comfortable vessel that I feel assured that you will not be dissatisfied with it. However much you may wish me back, you can scarcely wish me back more than I do myself.[283]

But her cheerful prognostications for a 'safe and comfortable' voyage proved ill founded. Within 24 hours of the *Medway* putting to sea, the light north-easterly breeze that had sent them so slowly on their way on Tuesday 16 July was replaced by a south westerly gale. By Thursday, Lady Franklin had to spend the day in bed, 'it being impossible to stand'.[284] On Friday, though the wind had moderated slightly, she was imprisoned in her cabin by her 'inability to dress, broadsides that came in yesterday at window having drenched my clothes & particularly stays & were not yet dry'. The pattern continued: brief interludes of calm or moderate northerly winds, ever succeeded by wild winds from the west and south. For weeks the *Medway* was tossed in heavy seas, driven rapidly to the east even when she managed to make some headway to the south. Again and again Captain Wight, in growing gloom, talked of putting back into Sydney—always, in the prevailing conditions, an easier destination to reach than Hobart. Again and again Lady Franklin and her companions united to beg him to persist in his efforts to battle southward.

For five weary weeks the little ship lurched to and fro in storm after storm—once almost glimpsing the Tasmanian coast, only to be driven east again for another fortnight. Lady Franklin was confined to her cabin for 15 of the 35 days, sometimes miserable with seasickness, but more often contriving to read, and scribble her daily diary entries, by the light of a wildly swinging lantern. For many of those days she was otherwise in total darkness, with deadlights over the portholes to hold out the heavy seas that washed constantly across the deck. Sometimes she was held into her berth by chairs strapped to the side, sometimes she could stay in only by maintaining a tight grip on the bed itself, and was consequently unable to sleep. Sophy, always prone to seasickness, must have suffered even more. Within a day of leaving Sydney she had moved out of her aunt's cabin and into Captain Moriarty's, he having moved to a more forward berth. After three weeks of discomfort Lady Franklin too was persuaded to move from her cabin, in which her bed lay fore-and-aft along the ship, so that she was constantly being flung sideways out of it as the *Medway* heeled in the gale. She swapped with a fellow passenger, Mr Braim, whose berth lay across the ship. Here she managed at last some fitful sleep, but found herself, when she woke, all in a heap at the foot of her bed. Mr Braim suffered for his gallantry, and next day was driven from the dinner table by seasickness.

There were brief periods of respite, when the party could meet at the dinner table, to discuss their progress and colonial politics, and argue vociferously over the merits of Colonel Arthur. Lady Franklin struck up a strong camaraderie with the gallant Mr Braim, a schoolteacher from Hobart who had come to Sydney hoping to be ordained by the bishop, but had been disappointed. They swapped books and, when weather permitted, chatted in the main cabin, exchanging views on their reading and on church matters. Shared sufferings promoted a new level of intimacy and informality. On one memorable evening Sophy swung on a cot 'supported by Captain Moriarty & Mr Elliot holding it on each side to save her from motion' while Lady Franklin herself perched on one corner, keeping her position 'by grasping occasionally the knee of Captain Moriarty'.[285] Captain Moriarty from time to time visited Lady Franklin as she lay in her cabin, to keep her informed of the ship's progress and to soothe her alarms.

The death of one of the steerage passengers, Mrs Briggs, from an inflammation of the bowels, brought a new interest and occupation. Not much sympathy was expressed by the cabin party for the 'poor daft woman', but for a week or so afterwards Jane took an interest in her daughter Sarah, a girl of 11 or 12 years old. She sent for the child after the sea burial of her mother, and 'found her very interesting & as I thought clever'. But when she mentioned at tea her favourable impressions she found that 'all the gentlemen particularly Wight, Grant, Braim & Elliot agreed in thinking her a very bad child, & the Captain who was never mistaken—he said—in any one's countenance thought she had one of the worst he had ever met with'.[286] The storms that confined Lady Franklin so persistently to her cabin limited her opportunities of pursuing her interest, but a few days later she learned that Sarah Briggs 'had put on her other frock & the pinafore she had made herself & was very anxious to know if I should send for her'. Her conscience thus prompted, Jane summoned the girl to her cabin, where she lay in bed with a sick headache, and 'read to her, made her read &c'.[287] But a week later Lady Franklin was talking to Sarah of her 'ill conduct' and finding that she could answer no questions 'as to yesterday's chapter'. Disappointed, Lady Franklin 'dismissed her, apparently to her great satisfaction', and made no further reference to her in her diary.[288]

Amongst the adult passengers, tension gradually rose. By the fourth week, the ship's supplies were noticeably diminished. On 7 August the breakfasts and dinners served showed clearly that the stock was failing; by 10 August the salt beef for the hands was exhausted and they were placed on rations of rice, pudding, tea and sugar.[289] The cabin passengers were much better supplied: the potatoes were all gone but there were still 18 fowls, a ham and a case of pickled tripe. Captain Wight thought that with the remaining stores they might last 'a week or 10 days longer', and again talked longingly of Sydney. Mr Braim, and Lady Franklin in particular, became anxious about the state of provisions and the lavish quantities still served out in the cabin each day. Finding that their united remonstrances made no impression on the captain, Lady Franklin proposed that a letter should be written 'to which we should all subscribe our names'.[290] But she did not find equal support amongst her own party. A couple of days later as the two were conferring anxiously together, comparing notes on the loss of particular stores, including candles, and oil for the binnacle, Mr Braim remarked that he

had observed that Captain Moriarty always made very light of everything & said he could do with a crust. I said Captain Moriarty liked to shew off a little this way, as to his hardihood & Mr Elliot also—indeed as to latter, I believed the danger of starvation like that of any other danger only gave him a slight degree of pleasurable excitement.[291]

Lady Franklin had particular cause for bitterness. When her ration of tea was reduced to a single cup in the evening, she 'observed the gents had an ample jug of spirits & water'.[292] Two days later she 'took no water at dinner because no one else did, but could not, like them, drink porter & ale'. By then, too, the fowls were all gone, and dinner consisted of stewed beans and pickled salmon.[293] By the following day the rice and biscuit had failed, and the cabin passengers began to experience a faint shadow of the privation that the exhausted sailors had been enduring for over a week. On that day, 16 August, one of Jane's two silver sparrows, which had hitherto miraculously survived the journey, perished. Fortunately, by this time the wind had settled to a gentle but favourable breeze. Within two days, on Sunday 18

August, the *Medway* sailed 'calmly and slowly' past Cape Pillar. She was battered; her crew was emaciated; and she had lost a gig, which having filled with water in the heavy seas 'broke away from the grips, burst in two and drifted away towards New Zealand'.[294] But the ship was safe, and Captain Wight, in relief at having at last brought his voyage to a successful conclusion, resolved for the first time since leaving Sydney to have prayers after tea.

At about 10 am on the following morning—'hazy, nice breeze'—watchers on the deck of the *Medway* saw the government schooner *Eliza* standing out to meet them. The *Medway's* signal had been seen but not properly understood, and the first mate of the *Eliza* soon came aboard to make sure that Lady Franklin had indeed at last returned safe and sound. A flag was hoisted to the masthead to send the glad news to Sir John—who, wrote his wife, 'must have been very uneasy', since two ships that had left Sydney after them had arrived in Hobart in the meantime. Had they not returned that day, the *Eliza* would have been sent in search of them. And had the 'boat of the *Medway* been found and recognised, we should certainly have been thought to be lost'.[295]

And with those words, Lady Franklin's diary ends. There is no account of her return to Government House, or her reunion with her husband, no reflection on what she had gained, learned or suffered in the course of her journey. This quintessential travel diary ends on the last day of travel. Later letters and diaries show her plunged once more into the thick of Hobart politics and society, making little or no reference to her past adventure.

It was left to one of the colonial papers to sympathise with the 'anxious feelings which must oppress Sir John Franklin in the uncertainty as to the safety of Lady Franklin' and to hope he might find 'consolation' in the 'countless enquirers of all classes' who crowded the wharf when the arrival of the *Medway* was rumoured. *Murray's Austral-Asiatic Review* reported that 'as soon as [the *Medway*] was signalized, His Excellency went down the river in his barge, although the weather was extremely stormy, and returned with Lady Franklin in the evening to Government House'.[296] 'Welcome as was her presence wherever she bestowed it, during her late tour', the same paper declared the following week, 'no where was it so much so as in Van Diemen's Land. That to a powerful mind is added a clearness of judgement, and liberality of sentiment, a variety of circumstances has abundantly proved.'[297]

Other newspapers, less impressed, made light of the dangers and anxiety of her passage home. The *Hobart Courier* reported her safe arrival 'after a tedious voyage of three weeks', and while acknowledging that she had 'encountered no ordinary "perils by land and by sea"', was more interested in gleefully anticipating that she would soon publish her 'opinions' on New South Wales. 'We are induced to entertain this hope the more,' added the

Courier, 'from the very excellent answer delivered by her Ladyship to the Port Phillip address, distinguished alike for its correctness of style and vigour of thought.'[298] Lady Franklin had been right to think that the Van Diemen's Land papers would not let that address pass unnoticed. The *Sydney Monitor* assured its readers of Lady Franklin's safe arrival at Hobart, and added that there was 'no great alarm created in Hobart Town for her Ladyship's safety, as no vessel which left Sydney after the *Medway* had arrived in Hobart Town before her'.[299]

More interesting to the papers than the physical danger of her homeward journey was the moral and social danger she had courted by embarking on the trip at all. For six weeks they remained silent on the subject, but at the beginning of October they were galvanised into action by an article that appeared in *Murray's Austral-Asiatic Review*. The editor, Lathrop Murray, had decided to copy from 'that truly independent journal', the *Australian* in Sydney, the 'just tribute' it had paid 'to the high estimation in which LADY FRANKLIN is held, we may now say in both Colonies'.[300]

The *Australian*, which had once demanded with such bitterness who was to pay for her ladyship's 'freak', was now singing a different tune—and it is impossible to avoid the suspicion that it did so partly on purpose to rile its Van Diemen's Land counterparts by assuming a greater degree of enlightenment and chivalry.

> *During the stay of Lady Franklin amongst us, we abstained from speaking of her spirited and enterprising tour in so high a degree, as it deserves, lest such public notice of her proceedings might not have been agreeable to her Ladyship. From the simplicity of her habits, and the entire absence of anything like display, combined with the silent mode in which she prosecuted her inquiries, and extended her observations, it was clear that her Ladyship did not covet popularity. Now, however, that her tour is completed, we cannot forbear to offer our admiration of her Ladyship's attainments, and to express the high sense we entertain of the spirit in which so arduous a journey was undertaken. We feel, too, the more inclined to offer this just tribute of praise, as we happen to know that, in Van Diemen's Land, LADY FRANKLIN'S tour was spoken of as something quite unaccountable.*[301]

In the colony of New South Wales, by contrast, the paper asserted, her ladyship's 'spirited and enterprising tour was properly estimated by the respectable and thinking portion of the community she visited'. Instead of joining with the Hobart press in condemning Lady Franklin as an unladylike eccentric, the *Australian* presented her aims as both intelligible and praiseworthy, by emphasising her character as traveller rather than as woman.

> *Lady Franklin had in view those objects possessed in common by every enlightened traveler—to make herself thoroughly acquainted with the capabilities and resources of this colony. From the information thus obtained, the practical results aimed at are, the advancement of science and the increase*

of knowledge to the people, and the general amelioration of the state. Should Lady Franklin publish the notes she has taken on this occasion, we venture confidently to predict that each of these aims will, in some degree, have been attained. And from the activity she displayed in the pursuit of every object worthy of notice, we feel assured that her collection of them, and her general observations, will be not only valuable, but interesting.[302]

Here, once more, was the much-predicted 'book', focus of such dread and ridicule. But in contrast to the Hobart papers, the *Australian* avowed its pleasant anticipations of the event. 'So far as we are acquainted with her ladyship's views respecting this colony, they appear to us to indicate a clear perception, with an enlarged understanding.' The paper hoped soon to be able to report 'that her ladyship intends to publish the facts and observations connected with her late tour, as soon as she may have had time to collect them'.[303]

Murray's motives in bringing this lavish praise to the attention of the Hobart public can only be guessed at. Both the Franklins disliked and mistrusted him, but for the first couple of years of Franklin's administration, Murray had maintained a tone of restraint and moderation in his criticism of or advice to the governor. He was a friend and defender of the Colonial Secretary, John Montagu, and therefore at this time a defender of the government. Later, when Franklin and Montagu disagreed bitterly in 1841–1842, restraint vanished, and Murray allowed his dislike to appear in outbursts of 'reprehensible volubility [which] went even beyond the bounds set by the editorial codes of the time'.[304] For now, his purported motive was an implied rebuke to the 'semi-official' paper, the *Hobart Town Advertiser*, for failing to publish the *Australian's* tribute to the governor's wife. Though he presented himself at this time as filled with admiration for Lady Franklin's enterprise, other papers were skeptical of the sincerity of the compliment.

Whatever his intentions, the response was immediate. The *True Colonist* was swift to declare that the information contained in the article was 'no less interesting than it is new' to the Hobart colonists. The paper had 'no patience for this humbug-work, about her ladyship's eccentricities'. Amongst her many virtues the *Australian* had mentioned Lady Franklin's support of 'education on a liberal system' and her 'deep interest' in the discipline and reformation of convicts, and in the 'aboriginal natives [sic]'. When, demanded the *True Colonist*, had Lady Franklin ever given practical expression to these interests in Van Diemen's Land?

What a pity that her ladyship would not devote a little of her ardent support to the schools of this Colony: we are sorry that we are unable to record any manifestations, far less any good fruits, of this amiable propensity of her ladyship to be seen here, although the Female Orphan Schools afford a most tempting field for its gratification ...

We know nothing about Lady Franklin's interest in the reformation of the convicts, she has shewn no symptoms of it in the only instance where she could have done it with propriety, that is, in the case of the treatment and discipline of the Female Factory. If she has interfered in any other department of convict discipline, she has been travelling out of her place as a woman, and meddling with that she knows nothing about.[305]

She had taken no interest, declared the *True Colonist*, in the female lunatics in the New Norfolk asylum—an object that they would have deemed 'honorable to the feelings of a woman, and worthy of a Governor's wife'.

But they reserved their most vituperative abuse for her professed interest in Aboriginal people:

Strange, indeed, must be the interest and perversion of ordinary female qualities, that would tempt a decent woman to go scampering amongst hordes of native savages, leading a vagrant, gypsey life, voluntarily, and for no conceivable good purpose, for months, in the bush. Lady Franklin in her individual capacity, may indulge in all these vagaries at her pleasure, and the Press has no right to notice them, at least in the way of deliberate censure; but, when a female at the head of society, and holding a high and influential station amongst a young community, where her example must command great influence, engages in such exploits as are calculated to exert an unfavorable influence on the minds of young females, who fancy that everything the Governor's lady does must be right; and when we find a portion of the Press forcing her exploits on public attention, by ill-judged praise, we feel it our duty as Journalist of the People, to enter our protest.[306]

Lady Franklin's sphere of duties was thus narrowly prescribed. Her interest and efforts should be directed towards the wretched of her own sex and her own colony: the female orphans, prisoners and lunatics of Van Diemen's Land. But the papers were not yet finished with her. The *Colonial Times* next weighed in, its tone one of measured, balanced assessment. The *Colonial Times* deemed the publication of the initial article by the *Review* 'ill-judged', but condemned the *True Colonist's* editor for hurling 'his sledge-hammer blows at the whole of this article,—thereby … involving poor Lady Franklin in the fire-brands he has thus,—unconsciously, scattered about'. Lady Franklin's interests and intentions, the *Colonial Times* went on, 'were of the very best quality'—but '("oh! this but!")' she would have done better to stay at home and contribute to the relief of the poor and destitute. It printed, with apparent approval, a long contribution from an 'esteemed' correspondent which evinced a similar tone. Even if the initial praises were excessive, or their publication in bad taste, there was no justification for going to the other extreme of excess:

The object was a Lady: could the poison of a little adulation be so virulent, as to make it necessary to fly immediately to the rescue, and seek to neutralize it by another of incomparably worse character? For, surely, while the one could do no harm, and might, though we do not think that it did, bestow some gratification, the other can only have given unmitigated and, we will add, unmerited pain, excited irritated, or contemptuous feelings, indisposed towards the discharge even of duties so rudely pressed, and hardened against counsels which, had they been offered in a kindlier and more charitable spirit, might have been well taken, if not implicitly subscribed to.[307]

This correspondent went on to warn Lady Franklin against the very activities the *True Colonist* had laid down for her as fitting and womanly, and argued (not unconvincingly) that the dabblings of wealthy and benevolent ladies were the last things needed in the orphan school, the lunatic asylum or the Female Factory—all of which desperately needed reform in systems of management, 'consecutive thought and action', and professional expertise. A thorough overhaul of each, effecting changes in policy and structure, would be required to bring about lasting improvement. Meanwhile, the Female Factory was a far more dangerous place for a lady than the Australian bush.

It appears downright mawkish to us, to object to Lady Franklin's desire to witness the aspects of savage life, and the variety of enquiries and observations which the gratification of a laudable curiosity compels a traveller to make in order to complete the picture in his mind of a strange country. How, without these, are adequate impressions to be obtained in a short time at all? And if savages are a portion of the scenery, why are they to be excluded? Upon the same principle, we suppose, with that morbid delicacy which would forbid to females the inspection of the monuments of ancient art! This is too absurd. We have daughters ourselves, and are, we trust, as careful of their delicacy as any father ought to be; but, properly protected, they are welcome to follow Lady Franklin into the bush tomorrow; and we desire them even to imitate the suavity of mind and frame, which give her an interest in such expeditions, and reconcile her to their privations. But they should not, at present, go in any company to the Female Factory. They are welcome to see the infamy of our common nature; we deny that this can in any case prove injurious, though suggested objections to it may injure. But the maturity of vice can only be safely inspected when sought to be recovered from degradation, not when abandoned to it.[308]

× ⤢ ✗ ✘

What was Lady Franklin to do? If she made any meaningful intervention into local concerns she was meddling beyond her province. If she looked beyond the colonial boundaries for a broader field of activity, learning and general usefulness, she was betraying the needs of her own colony, revealing herself as wayward, eccentric and 'errant'—but was at least, in the kindest analysis, harmlessly out of the way. The contradictory, but universally baffled responses to Lady Franklin's enterprise, the failure of the Hobart newspapers to reach any agreement about how she could best direct her energies to the benefit of the colony, the ambivalence of praise and the plenitude of warnings—all reflect the fundamental problem that Jane Franklin faced in Van Diemen's Land. In a world defined on strictly, exclusively masculine terms, there was simply no room for a woman of her courage, energy, intellect and curiosity.

In New South Wales she had found some scope. Her courage and energy were demanded by the journey itself. And since her status as visitor guarded her from the charge of meddling, her intelligent interest in her surroundings was flattering and invigorating to the local inhabitants. Once separated from Van Diemen's Land, she assumed a new standing and legitimacy as a representative of both the colony and its governor. Throughout her time in New South Wales she thrilled to the lavish compliments bestowed equally upon herself and her colony, and was courteous in her turn about her hosts. Comparisons between the two, she wrote to Sir John, did not cause her to feel complacent. Rather, she felt inspired to 'strain every nerve' in the effort to ensure that Van Diemen's Land did not get left behind by the progress of the sister colony.[309]

For a brief time, Lady Franklin was recognised as a symbol and a leader of Van Diemen's Land. She was not always a comfortable presence, but she was invariably treated with the deference and respect due to an acknowledged position. She returned to Hobart refreshed, and charged with energy by all that she had learned and seen. The letters she had written to Sir John throughout her journey showed how eager she was to convert all her experiences and observations into lessons for future effort, conveniently forgetting how little such effort was valued in her own colony. It must have been disheartening to be greeted, within weeks of her arrival, by a press debate which so patently failed to agree upon any appropriate outlet for her longstanding energy and new found expertise, or to produce a single instance of her past beneficial endeavour on behalf of the colony.

But Jane Franklin was rarely disheartened. Despite ridicule of her 'errant' wanderings, she continued to travel in the following years: to South Australia, New Zealand and, most famously, overland to Macquarie Harbour—an intrepid adventure that almost ended in disaster. Despite the warnings of the *Colonial Times*, she began to take renewed interest in the conditions of women convicts, especially at the Female Factory, and suffered in consequence a new surge of abuse for her immodesty and indelicacy. Despite the distrust so clearly expressed of her 'masculine' intellect and her blue stocking tendencies, she happily extended her collection of fossils and natural history specimens, built her museum and played her part in fostering the Tasmanian Society and selling the

Tasmanian Journal when the first issue appeared in 1842. Despite the reiterated assertion that general questions of convict discipline or reform were beyond her sphere, she continued to take an active interest in all aspects of the penal system. And despite insistent and dangerous murmurs of 'petticoat government', she continued to assist Sir John in his administration, to help him with dispatches, negotiate with friends and enemies in Hobart and England, and to offer him lovingly and unstintingly her advice, sympathy, energy and support.

The consequences were predictable. Van Diemen's Land had no place for 'this errant lady', and little respect for a governor who tolerated her wanderings, accepted her assistance and openly valued her advice. The 'vagaries' of a confirmed traveller might have been tolerated, though deplored. But the meddling of a woman in political matters, and particularly in civic appointments, opened up nightmarish visions of a government guided by the unaccountable (in both senses of the word) whims of a woman who held no legitimate office, who would be swayed by personal likes and dislikes, and who, however 'clever' and well-read she might be, could never, under any circumstances, be right. Though Jane Franklin herself insisted repeatedly that she never stepped beyond the bounds of what any wife would do for her husband, that she was devoted 'soul and spirit to Sir John'[310] and did nothing save in his interests and in accordance with his desires, she underestimated her own power. A woman who so burned to be 'of use' to her husband, and who so profoundly equated his work with himself, could never recognise the nebulous, ideological boundary that lay between public and private interest. She trampled it, oblivious, beneath her feet, and was puzzled when others disapproved of her transgression.

When Sir John Franklin and his colonial secretary, John Montagu, came to open conflict in 1841, Lady Franklin's name was inevitably drawn into the dispute. Montagu clearly felt quite secure in referring to Lady Franklin's interference in matters of government as justification for his own disrespectful attitude to the governor. When Sir John dismissed him for insolence, Montagu sailed immediately for England, where he successfully persuaded the Secretary of State for the Colonies, Lord Stanley, that Franklin had allowed an improper degree of 'interference in Public matters' by his wife.[311] This suggestion of 'petticoat government' became one of the grounds on which Lord Stanley determined to overrule Montagu's suspension, and instead recall Sir John.

The later years of Franklin's administration in Van Diemen's Land thus passed for his wife in a welter of vexation, anxiety and self-justification. She could never understand the criticism heaped upon her. She did not challenge the rules that colonists laid down for the limits of wifely support. She held and worked to those rules herself—but understood and applied them in uniquely energetic ways. Her desire to help was like her desire to learn: both were driving forces in her life; both were, she believed, quite compatible with her sex; but both drove her to enterprises which were praised and condemned as 'masculine'. Perhaps what underlay and inspired those desires was her vibrant, passionate attachment to her nineteenth-century imperial world. It was a world that sparkled with the enticements of new discoveries and new knowledge, and offered boundless promise for future progress as the reward for enlightened and conscientious effort. But equally, and paradoxically, it was a world bounded by rules and conventions, hypocrisies and inequalities, which sought forcibly to delimit its participants and beneficiaries. Ultimately, Victorian society would explode under the pressure of these contradictions, into twentieth-century modernity. But Jane Franklin was both produced and constrained by the age she lived in. The intellectual curiosity that inspired both her Port Phillip journey and her diary of the excursion was fashioned in bourgeois, imperial terms, and harnessed implicitly to the purposes of colonisation and economic and social development. But that curiosity was separated from its objects and thus radically disempowered. It could not be converted into meaningful social activity or used to extend the social understanding of the wider world, simply because it was the curiosity of a woman.

Jane, Lady Franklin (1791–1875)
EXTRACT FROM MANUSCRIPT DIARY OF AN
OVERLAND TOUR TO SYDNEY 1839
Manuscript Collection MS114

Notes

'*Behold another Sheba comes*'

1 Letter, Jane Franklin to Mary Simpkinson, September 1841, Sir John Franklin, Diaries and Letters 1837–1859, Manuscript Collection, National Library of Australia (MS114). This quotation is cited in J. Gipps, *Every Inch a Governor: Sir George Gipps, Governor of New South Wales, 1838–46.* Port Melbourne: Hobson's Bay Publishing, 1996, p. 47. Mary Simpkinson was Jane Franklin's favourite sister, and Lady Franklin's long letters to her are an important source on the troubles of the Franklin administration.

2 The surviving archive at the Scott Polar Research Institute (SPRI, Cambridge, United Kingdom) amounts to 168 separate volumes of the diary, and includes over 2000 items of correspondence. The majority of Jane Franklin's papers are found at SPRI MS248. Microfilm copies of material of relevance to Australia from this collection are held at the State libraries of Tasmania and New South Wales. The numbers cited as catalogue references in this edition are those employed by the Scott Polar Research Institute, which are reproduced in the microfilm holdings.

3 A brief edition of her papers was published in 1923 by a descendant of the Franklin family, Willingham Rawnsley. Rawnsley justified the work by pointing to Jane Franklin's descriptions of early colonisation in Australia, and the insight she offered into her husband's character. He displayed little sense that her archive might equally be of interest for what it showed of herself. (W.F. Rawnsley, *The Life, Diaries and Correspondence of Jane, Lady Franklin.* London: Erskine Macdonald, 1923, Preface.) Consistent with this sense of her secondhand significance, he divided the archive, donating material on Tasmanian subjects to the Royal Society of Tasmania, and two diaries, including the account of her visit to Sydney in 1839, to the National Library of Australia. In 1939 Jessie Lefroy, into whose hands the rest of the collection had passed, bequeathed it to the Scott Polar Research Institute.

4 F.J. Woodward, *Portrait of Jane: A Life of Lady Franklin.* London: Hodder and Stoughton, 1951, p. 7. Woodward suggests that the Lefroys were influenced by Rawnsley's book in regarding Jane Franklin's records as 'of negligible merit'.

5 In the National Library of Australia, Jane Franklin's diaries and other private writings are catalogued under the heading 'Sir John Franklin, Diaries and Letters'. In Australia, Woodward's biography of her tends to be shelved in libraries under the heading of Tasmanian history; at the Scott Polar Research

Institute Library it must be sought among the biographies of polar explorers. Leigh Gilmore has pointed to the politics of shelving in relation to women's autobiography, noting that such decisions make clear the difficulty of finding a space for women's lives as lived and written on their own terms. The fate of Jane Franklin's archive is a classic example of this difficulty. L. Gilmore, *Autobiographics: A Feminist Theory of Women's Self-Representation*. Ithaca: Cornell University Press, 1994, pp. 7–8.

6   For an overview of traditional and revisionist histories of the self, *see* the introduction to *Rewriting the Self: Histories from the Renaissance to the Present*, ed. R. Porter. London and New York: Routledge, 1997, pp.1–14. On autobiography, see G. Gusdorf's classic article 'The Conditions and Limits of Autobiography', in *Autobiography: Essays Theoretical and Critical*, ed. J. Olney. Princeton: Princeton University Press, 1980; and for a range of feminist critiques of his understanding of autobiography *see*, among others, Gilmore, op. cit.; S. Bentock (ed.), *The Private Self: Theory and Practice of Women's Autobiographical Writings*. London: Routledge, 1988; S. Smith and J. Watson (eds), *De/Colonizing the Subject: The Politics of Gender in Women's Autobiography*. Minneapolis: University of Minnesota Press, 1992. On women's diaries specifically, *see* H. Blodgett, *Centuries of Female Days: Englishwomen's Private Diaries*. New Brunswick: Rutgers University Press, 1988; S. Gristwood, *Recording Angels: The Secret World of Women's Diaries*. London: Harrap, 1988; and K. Holmes, *Spaces in Her Day: Australian Women's Diaries of the 1920s and 1930s*. Sydney: Allen and Unwin, 1995.

7   John Giles Price was made civil commissioner of Norfolk Island in 1846. Noted for his harsh administration, he was the model for the evil 'Maurice Frere' in Marcus Clarke's *For the Term of His Natural Life* (London: Richard Bentley and Sons, 1885). In 1857 he was murdered in Melbourne by a group of convicts.

8   Letter, Sophy Cracroft to Jane Franklin, not dated (c.1844?), Papers of the Gell and Franklin Families, Mitchell Library, State Library of New South Wales (FM4/1550).

9   Letter, Jane Franklin to John Franklin, 1832, in Woodward, op. cit., p. 182.

10   For a more detailed discussion of the Franklin's marriage, and the significance it assumed in colonial politics, *see* 'Paradise Lost: Sir John and Lady Franklin', in *For Richer, For Poorer: Early Colonial Marriages*, ed. P. Russell. Melbourne: Melbourne University Press, 1994, pp. 50–72. *See also* K. Fitzpatrick's superb *Sir John Franklin in Tasmania, 1837–1843* (Melbourne: Melbourne University Press, 1949) and A. Alexander, *Obliged to Submit: Wives and Mistresses of Colonial Governors*. Hobart: Montpelier Press, 1999, pp. 133–167. A more critical assessment of Lady Franklin's character is offered by C.M.H. Clark in *A History of Australia*. Vol. 3. Melbourne: Melbourne University Press, 1973, pp. 199–225, *passim*.

11   On the Franklin administration and Lady Franklin's involvement in colonial affairs see P.W. Boyer, 'Leaders and Helpers: Jane Franklin's Plan for Van Diemen's Land', *Tasmanian Historical Research Papers and Proceedings*,

vol. 21, no. 2, June 1974; L.L. Robson, *A History of Tasmania*. Vol. 1. Melbourne: Oxford University Press, 1983, pp. 317–385; P. Russell, '"Her Excellency": Lady Franklin, Female Convicts and the Problem of Authority in Van Diemen's Land', *Journal of Australian Studies*, no. 53, 1997, pp. 40–50; and P. Russell, *Displaced Loyalties: Vice Regal Women in Colonial Australia*. London: Sir Robert Menzies Centre for Australian Studies, 1999.

[12] As Thomas Arnold, Headmaster of Rugby, wrote in a letter of congratulation to Sir John on his appointment. *See* Woodward, op. cit., p. 197.

[13] Three volumes of the *Tasmanian Journal* were published between 1842 and 1848, under the editorship of Robert C. Gunn. *See* A. Moyal, *A Bright and Savage Land*. Ringwood, New York: Penguin, 1993, p. 73.

[14] Letter, Jane Franklin to Mary Simpkinson, 23 February 1839, Scott Polar Research Institute (MS248/174/6).

[15] *See* Alexander, op. cit., pp. 137–139; Clark, op. cit, pp. 206–207.

[16] *True Colonist*, 4 October 1839.

[17] Ibid. *See also Colonist* (Sydney), 11 May 1839.

[18] Letter, Jane Franklin to John Franklin, 5 April 1839, Sir John Franklin, Diaries and Letters, Manuscript Collection, National Library of Australia (MS114). (Unless otherwise stated, all letters from Lady Franklin to Sir John Franklin cited in this volume may be found at this location.)

[19] *Australian* (Sydney), 16 May 1839.

[20] Letter, John Franklin to Mary Simpkinson, 14 April 1839, Sir John Franklin, Diaries and Letters, Manuscript Collection, National Library of Australia (MS114).

[21] *Australian*, 27 August 1839.

[22] Letter, John Franklin to Mary Simpkinson, 14 April 1839, Sir John Franklin, Diaries and Letters, Manuscript Collection, National Library of Australia (MS114).

[23] Jane Franklin, Manuscript Diary of an Overland Tour to Sydney 1839, *with* Sir John Franklin, Diaries and Letters 1837–1859, Manuscript Collection, National Library of Australia (MS114).

[24] In 1990 Roger Milliss was awarded a Harold White Fellowship by the National Library of Australia to work on Jane Franklin's diaries. This work included preparing a typescript of her manuscript diary.

[25] Roger Milliss, [Diary of Jane, Lady Franklin 1839 April 3 – August 19], Manuscript Collection, National Library of Australia (MS6642). Unless otherwise indicated, this typescript has been taken as the definitive version of Jane Franklin's manuscript diary.

[26] Jane Franklin, Diary, 29 June 1839 (see p. 171). Quotations that may be found within this volume are accompanied throughout by appropriate page references. Quotations from material omitted from this edition are indicated by the words 'original manuscript', and may be found in the Milliss typescript.

27 Jane Franklin, Diary, 18 and 24 May 1839 (see p. 111 and 119).

28 Letter, Jane Franklin to John Franklin, 15 June 1839.

29 Jane Franklin, Diary, 26 April 1839 (see p. 75).

30 Jane Franklin, Diary, 6 May 1839 (see p. 100).

31 Letter, Jane Franklin to John Franklin, 21 April 1839.

32 Edmund Charles Hobson, Diary of a Journey with Lady Franklin's Party, Overland from Melbourne to the Hume River, La Trobe Library Manuscript Collection, State Library of Victoria (Box 25/1, M383/09). Hereafter, Hobson, Diary.

33 D. Pike (ed.), *Australian Dictionary of Biography*. Vols 1–2, 4, 6. Melbourne: Melbourne University Press, vol. 1, 1966; vol. 2, 1967; vol. 4, 1972; vol. 6, 1976.

34 J. Kerr (ed.), *The Dictionary of Australian Artists*. Melbourne: Oxford University Press, 1992; G. Davison, J. Hirst and S. Macintyre (eds), *The Oxford Companion to Australian History*. Melbourne: Oxford University Press, 1998.

I: *Melbourne, 1–5 April 1839*

35 Fitzpatrick, op. cit., p. 44.

36 *Colonial Times*, 9 April 1839; Letter, John Franklin to Mary Simpkinson, 14 April 1839, Sir John Franklin, Diaries and Letters, Manuscript Collection, National Library of Australia (MS114).

37 Letter, Jane Franklin to John Franklin, 3 April 1839.

38 The You Yang Mountains.

39 Jane Franklin habitually referred to Aboriginal people as 'blacks', 'natives', and 'savages'. Her language has been retained for its reflection of contemporary attitudes, but I am conscious that her representation of Aborigines may offend many readers.

40 George Augustus Robinson had been recently appointed as Chief Protector of Aborigines in the Port Phillip district. He was famed for his earlier journeys around Van Diemen's Land, where he 'conciliated' the Aborigines and encouraged them to 'come in' to white settlement. In this he had received important assistance from Trukanini, who, as a young woman, was often represented by white colonists as the exotic princess Lalla Rookh, after the heroine of the popular Orientalist poem by Thomas Moore, published in 1817. Trukanini was of the party which agreed that the Aborigines would leave Van Diemen's Land in exchange for sanctuary on Flinders Island and fiduciary compensation, at a settlement under Robinson's charge. She soon, however, became a leading critic of the establishment, where many Aborigines died from disease and malnutrition. In 1839 she and 14 others accompanied Robinson to Port Phillip where

he hoped for their assistance in making contact with the Aborigines of the district. The rapid expansion of pastoralism doomed his work to failure, and most Port Phillip settlers regarded the protectorate as farcical. In 1841 Trukanini and four other Tasmanian Aborigines began a series of raids on white settlers, culminating in the shooting of two whalers. Acquitted of murder, Trukanini was returned to Flinders Island. She later returned to the Tasmanian mainland and at her death in 1876 was regarded by whites as the 'last' of her people. Her skeleton was held by the Tasmanian Government and displayed for many years at the Museum of the Royal Society of Tasmania, but in 1976 her ashes were returned to the Tasmanian Aboriginal community for burial. *See* L. Ryan, *The Aboriginal Tasmanians*. St Leonards: Allen and Unwin, 1996, pp. 197, 218–220; *see also* H. Reynolds, *Fate of a Free People*. Melbourne: Penguin, 1995.

41 Captain William Lonsdale (1800?–1864) arrived at the Yarra River settlement late in 1836 to assume duties as First Police Magistrate, following concerns about the growing numbers of unauthorised settlers there. He was required to superintend the new settlement, to submit reports and returns, take a census, and protect and conciliate the Aborigines of the district. The duties were straightforward but his powers were not precisely defined and led to frictions with other civil officials who would not recognise his authority. Lonsdale continued to act as police magistrate after La Trobe arrived as the new superintendent.

Of the Lonsdales, Lady Franklin wrote:

> Captain Lonsdale was of 4th regiment—sold out. She was Miss Smythe, once of Launceston—her father was an engineer, went out first to Swan River, where lost & injured himself, afterwards kept a school at Launceston—is now at Sydney—she met Captain Lonsdale at her sister's at Port Macquarie, is fair prettyish woman, talkative & rather intelligent— has 2 little girls oldest about 4. (Jane Franklin, Diary, undated note.)

42 In the *Port Phillip Patriot*, John Pascoe Fawkner invested the occasion of Lady Franklin's arrival with considerably more grandeur than did its heroine. On Thursday, the paper announced, Lady Franklin landed at the township of Melbourne and was 'honorably and respectfully attended by a select cortege of gentlemen to Fawkner's Hotel; at which her ladyship and suite sojourned whilst in Melbourne. At 3 pm Lady Franklin received the visits of persons desirous of paying their respects; and in the afternoon took a ride through the town and, accompanied by her suite and James Simpson, Esq. J.P., visited the commandant.' It went on:

> Short as the notice had been, numbers of Tasmanians had prepared for the occasion, and when night's sable wings enshrouded the earth, the blaze of their illuminations cast a splendour over this rising town. The office of this Journal, standing on the crest of a rising ground, and aided by its great height proudly towering over the lesser buildings, enabled it to diffuse its volume of light over the whole town—the four fronts of the building being equally lighted, rendered it a most imposing sight, on that

mirthful evening. The proprietor having purchased all the fireworks in the town, enlivened the sports of the evening by their aid; these together with a constant discharge of firearms, drew half the townsfolk to the spot. The firing requiring less preparation than the illumination, was in consequence more general, and was loudly reverberated from all parts of the town: In fact, Melbourne made a gay appearance on that memorable evening.

During the illumination, Lady Franklin paid a visit to the Aborigines, and saw their Arranmilly, or dance, in all its native force and vigor ... ACCIDENT.—During the firing on Thursday last, in honor of the arrival of Lady Franklin, A Blunderbus (no other gun would have made such a blunder) burst, and inflicted so dreadful a wound on the Hand an [sic] Arm of the mate of the Gem, as to require amputation. The man lost his Arm, which was amputated by Dr Cussen. He is likely to do well. (*Port Phillip Patriot*, 10 April 1839.)

43 Four assistants had been appointed to work under Robinson as Aboriginal Protectors: Lieutenant Charles Sievewright, Edward Parker, James Dredge and William Thomas. Though Robinson allotted them their districts in March, they took some time to go out—partly because they were not issued with effective instructions nor with the necessary equipment, staff and supplies. The establishment of a protectorate was controversial and Governor Gipps, though supportive of the principle, was concerned about the cost and reluctant to provide the necessary resources. Most early settlers resented any attempt to guard Aboriginal interests against their own hunger for land and pastoral wealth, and the protectors themselves were often misguided in their attempts to do so. For a summary of the difficulties and controversies surrounding the protectorate see A.G.L. Shaw, *A History of the Port Phillip District: Victoria Before Separation*. Melbourne: Miegunyah Press, 1996, pp. 115–127, and M.F. Christie, *Aborigines in Colonial Victoria 1835–86*. Sydney: Sydney University Press, 1979, pp. 81–106.

44 The ship on which the Franklins had made their passage to Van Diemen's Land.

45 The *Port Phillip Patriot* (3 April 1839) proclaimed that Fawkner's Hotel, with its 'spacious and lofty sitting rooms, bedrooms well aired and ventilated ... [and] choice and well assorted LIBRARY' was 'fully equal, if not superior to, any Hotel in this Town'. It is evident that J.P. Fawkner, proprietor of both the Hotel and the newspaper, saw no objection to self-advertising.

46 The *Port Phillip Patriot* first appeared in February 1838. The first few editions were prepared in handwriting, before a typesetting machine could be set up. Lady Franklin found the newspaper 'wretchedly printed—worse than Bent's news—Arden's better—he is bigoted—writes down whatever takes his fancy—has taken a great dislike to Captain Lonsdale—whom Cobb said was much disliked.' (Jane Franklin, Diary, undated note.)

47 George Augustus Robinson, *The Journals of George Augustus Robinson, Chief Protector, Port Phillip Aboriginal Protectorate*, vol. 1, 1 January 1839 – 30 September 1840, ed. Ian. D. Clark. Melbourne: Heritage Matters, 1998, p. 24.

[48] The Franklins had earlier visited Flinders Island during George Robinson's period of administration.

[49] The *Patriot* reported that on the second day of her visit, Lady Franklin 'again received visitors, and took an airing in the beautiful environs of Melbourne, and as we learn, felt delighted therewith'. (*Port Phillip Patriot*, 10 April 1839.)

[50] The address to Lady Franklin was printed in full in the *Port Phillip Patriot*, 10 April 1839:

> On Saturday morning an Address, numerously and respectably signed, was presented to Lady Franklin by Captain Lonsdale, P.M., James Simpson, Esq. J.P., and a numerous assemblage of gentlemen. The deputation was received by her Ladyship and suite in the large room of Fawkner's Hotel. The address was read to her Ladyship by Captain Lonsdale, and was received most graciously by Lady Franklin, who deputed the Hon. Mr Elliot to read her reply, which he did in a good, plain, nervous style. The deputation having made their congee, her Ladyship retired. Shortly after which a great concourse of persons assembled to honor her Ladyship, who on her stepping into the carriage to proceed on the way to Sydney, was most heartily cheered. Lady Franklin appeared highly delighted. The friendly and respectful feelings evinced by the Colonists towards her Ladyship, and by her reciprocated towards the Colonists, reflected honor upon both parties. Her Ladyship, in this Colony, is destitute of all political power—we therefore bow not in dependence, but to her Ladyship's eminent virtues, her philanthropy, her enterprize, and her moral energy: these bring down upon her, the admiration of all good people. Thus does her Ladyship concentrate around her, the wise, the good, and the brave.

> Lady Franklin was escorted some miles on her journey by two carriages and a cortege of horsemen. May her Ladyship complete her present difficult journey in peace and safety, is the earnest wish not only of the Editor of this Journal, but of the whole community.

> The following Address was presented previous to her Ladyship's departure:–

> THE UNDERSIGNED, CIVIL OFFICERS, MAGISTRATES, CLERGY, LANDOWNERS, MERCHANTS, STOCK PROPRIETORS, AND OTHER INHABITANTS, RESIDING IN MELBOURNE—

> Hasten to express their gratification on your Ladyship's safe arrival, and at the same time to allude to the pleasing circumstance of Melbourne having been selected for the honor of first welcoming your Ladyship to the shores of New Holland.

> They cannot allow the occasion of your Ladyship's arrival to pass, without referring to the amicable feeling entertained by them for the sister Colony of Van Diemen's Land, with which their intercourse is greater than with the Colony of New South Wales. They are well

acquainted with your Ladyship's character of kindness, benevolence, and charity, and they beg to express their admiration of the private and public virtues of your distinguished Consort, the intrepid and fearless explorer of the Northern Polar regions, whose name has become, by his fame, the property of the British nation.

They express their hope, that the appearance of Melbourne—the creation of only eighteen months, together with the fertility of their beautiful district—may impress your Ladyship with a favorable opinion of their enterprise and industry, and of the superior advantages of this Colony, for the promotion of colonization.

They cannot conclude without expressing their sincere and heartfelt regret, that the rapidity of your Ladyship's movement should deprive them thus early, not only of your presence, but also of the gratification they had looked forward to in being allowed the honor, to give on the occasion of your Ladyship's arrival, a public entertainment.

With their best wishes for your Ladyship's health, and with a conviction that your journey through the interior of New South Wales will be everywhere considered an honor by its inhabitants, they remain, with respect,

Your Ladyship's

Most obedient Servants,

W. LONSDALE, P.M., W.H. YALDWYN, J.P., JAMES SIMPSON, J.P., J.C. GRYLLS, (Clerk), Rev. JAMES FORBES, A.M., Rev. W. WATERFIELD— and 59 other gentlemen, whose names, for want of room, we are obliged to omit.

Lady Franklin replied: GENTLEMEN,—The unexpected and undeserved honor you have been pleased to confer upon me, in presenting me with an address, has taken me so much by surprise, that I feel considerable difficulty in expressing my sense of the honor thus conveyed.

I cannot but rejoice in the circumstances which have led me on my first visit to Australia, to land at Melbourne, since it has suggested to its inhabitants to remind me with such cordiality of the amicable feelings which exists between two countries so naturally and nearly related, and so capable of aiding each other's welfare. The creation of this substantial, well-built, and populous town, in a spot, where eighteen months ago, were to be seen only the few rude huts of the first settlers, is a remarkable instance of what industry, enterprise, and wealth can effect in circumstances favorable to their development, and must be a subject of congratulation also to those elder and almost parent Colonists, which see their own energies thus reflected in you.

I regret that it is not in my power to make a longer stay amongst you, and to visit every part of your beautiful environs.

Your kind and flattering allusion to my husband is very gratifying to me; I beg to thank you for it, and to assure you, that it will give him as well as myself the highest gratification to hear of the continued and increasing prosperity of Melbourne.

FAWKNER'S HOTEL,

Melbourne, 6 April 1839.

To the Civil Officers, Magistrates, Clergy, Landowners, Merchants, Stock Proprietors, and other Inhabitants residing in Melbourne.

51   Letter, Jane Franklin to John Franklin, 5 April 1839.

II: *Melbourne to the Goulburn River, 6-11 April 1839*

52   In 1839 the overland journey between Melbourne and Sydney was punctuated by river crossings. At these points the expedition would often halt for an additional day to rest and to water the horses. In wet weather the crossing itself could present difficulties and dangers. The Goulburn River crossing was near the present town of Seymour.

53   William Wedge Darke, Assistant Surveyor, formerly a private land agent and surveyor in Van Diemen's Land.

54   The cavalcade consisted of a heavy cart, or horse dray, for the baggage, and a light 'spring' cart for passengers. Two horses were harnessed to the spring cart, three in steep conditions, while the horse dray required three or four. In addition, there were mounts for the gentlemen and one pony, Kitty, which the ladies shared, having one side saddle between them. As the journey progressed, Jane gradually mentioned the names of most of the horses: Darke and Tulip, named after their previous owners, Hymagamas and Dandelion, Moriarty's mount, Jack Iodine, and Elliot's Belladonna. Hobson and Moriarty both preferred to walk—as indeed all members of the party did, from time to time.

55   Thomas Thornloe or Thorneloe had arrived in Van Diemen's Land as a steerage passenger in 1831, and by his work as clerk in the civil service soon recommended himself to the colonial secretary, John Montagu. When Governor Arthur left in 1836 he entrusted his Van Diemen's Land investments to Montagu. Montagu sent Thornloe to Port Phillip to investigate the prospects there and in 1838 Thornloe established a station near Craigieburn with Arthur and Montagu as joint owners. It is not known whether Thornloe had a share in the profits, or was paid by salary. *See* J.O. Randell, *Pastoral Settlement in Northern Victoria.* Vol 1: *The Coliban District.* Melbourne: Queensberry Hill Press, 1979, pp. 193–194.

56   Van Diemen's Land.

57   Probably Charles Sturt's *Two Expeditions into the Interior of Southern Australia, During the Years 1828, 1829, 1830 and 1831: With Observations of the Soil, Climate, and General Resources of the Colony of New South Wales.* (London: Smith and Elder, 1833.)

58   As both Elliot and Hobson were natural history enthusiasts, this carnage among the native bird-life would continue throughout the trip. Hobson's diary of the overland journey is said to be 'the first scientific natural history survey of the country between Melbourne and the Murray River'. See C.A. McCallum, 'Hobson, Edmund Charles', in Pike, vol. 1, op. cit., p. 544.

59   Hobson noted in his diary on this day that Lady Franklin had 'suffered a little from the jolting road'. (Hobson, Diary, 8 April 1839.)

60   Captain G.B. Smyth of the mounted police and his partner Mr Mundy held a pastoral run named Pyalong, which Lady Franklin visited on the following day.

61   When Smyth reported a theft of cattle by Aborigines to George Robinson, the latter was more sceptical than Lady Franklin. He told Smyth that he had received many reports of such outrages 'which when enquired into were found groundless complaints'. Robinson wrote in his journal that he believed that 'the story of the blacks was got up for the purpose of excusing himself from blame in leaving[,] Lady Franklin having arrived in his absence', an interpretation which is not fully borne out by Lady Franklin's account. (Robinson, op. cit., p. 25.)

62   Insecurity of tenure was a major source of grievance and vexation to the early squatters. The problem was settled in part, and on favourable terms to the squatters, by the Order-in-Council of 1847 which gave them 14-year leases, and more permanently but more expensively, by the opening of Crown lands for sale and closer settlement from the 1860s.

III: *Goulburn River to the Murray River, 12-20 April 1839*

63   For examples of alternative interpretations see Christie, op. cit., pp. 63–64; Shaw, op. cit., p. 114; Randell, op. cit., p. 29; J.M. McMillan, *The Two Lives of Joseph Docker*, Melbourne: Spectrum Publications, 1994, pp. 139–152; Roger Milliss, *Waterloo Creek: The Australia Day Massacre of 1838, George Gipps and the British Conquest of New South Wales*, Sydney: University of New South Wales Press, 1994, pp. 245–253.

64   *See* H. Reynolds, *Frontier: Aborigines, Settlers and Land*, Sydney: Allen and Unwin, 1987, especially chapters 1 and 7.

65   Joseph Hawdon (1813–1871) had overlanded cattle to Port Phillip in 1836 and remained in Victoria, taking up land near Dandenong. In 1838 he drove cattle to Adelaide along the course of the Murray River, and thereafter settled on his property, Banyule, at Heidelberg. In a letter to Sir John from the Murray, Jane names Mr Hawdon's men as 'Paddy' and 'Mick', from Ireland and Lancashire respectively, and the traveller to Sydney as a Mr Oak.

66   'Melbourne' in the typescript of the diary, but from the context she must have meant the police station at the Goulburn River.

67   Sam Sheldrake, a convict, had been coachman for the party since Melbourne.

68 Hobson wrote in his diary: 'This evening was spent in skinning the birds I had shot & in giving Lady Franklin lessons in the same art.' (Hobson, Diary, 13 April 1839.)

69 During his brief visit to his brother, Hobson had noted several times that the area provided a 'rich field for the naturalist', and lamented that he had too little time to make extensive observations. (Hobson, Diary, 4–6 April 1839.)

70 Never named in this diary, but much quoted hereafter, 'the Corporal' was one of the two mounted police who took over the escort of the party from Broken River to the Murray.

71 Hobson notes that the police hut was roofed only by an old tarpaulin 'in which there was not a foot without a hole. Under this shower bath our dinner table was laid. It rained in a perfect torrent all the time we were at dinner. The lightning danced among the trees with a rapidity and brightness that laughs at description. The claps of thunder were as if some huge mountain had been rent in twain and was vomiting its contents upon the plain below. The floor of our dining room was knee deep in water. After dinner it was a problem for solution how to convey the ladies to the tents. Moriarty and Elliott offered to support them on their shoulders. Moriarty started first with Lady F in his arms and was followed by Elliott with Miss Cracroft. They staggered along with their loads and after sundry and divers groans and puffs they landed safely and dry at their tents. I need not say this scene made me laugh.' (Hobson, Diary, 14 April 1839.)

72 Hawdon's men, Paddy and Mick, who had travelled with the party from the Goulburn River for fear of attack.

73 The image of the 'savage' implied in these stories gained legitimacy from contemporary theories of a Great Chain of Being. Elsewhere in her diary Jane Franklin recorded snippets of conversation on the subject with Dr Hobson, for example: 'The great toes of Savages, Dr Hobson says, are much separated from the others—as we descend in scale of animal creation they are more & more so, so as to become prehensile—witness monkeys.' (Jane Franklin, Diary, undated note.)

74 In an additional note revealing her continued interest in natural history, Jane Franklin wrote: 'A middle sized ant feeds on the large Moths—when latter is benumbed, or torpid, they attack it in strong bodies—at the Murray found their empty chrysalis of reddish yellow hue rising out of little holes in the ground like crocuses.' (Jane Franklin, Diary, undated note.)

75 Dr Hobson had been alarmed earlier that day by realising how far he had strayed along a 'native track' in search of duck. 'I now thought of the condition I was in and how easily I might be cut off by this worst of all the tribes of savages in New Holland. I was much relieved from this unpleasant feeling by seeing Mr Elliott advancing.' (Hobson, Diary, 16 April 1839.)

76 Joseph Docker, formerly Church of England chaplain at Windsor near Sydney, had not been 'defrocked' for drunkenness, despite the rumours that attended his resignation. It seems rather that he was forced to resign,

having been 'set up' by local magistrates. In 1838 he arrived at the Ovens River with his wife and five children, and took up the run formerly held by George Faithful, on the plains named Bontherambo by the Pangerang people. Though he never suffered the continued attacks which made the run untenable for George Faithful, it appears that one raid was made in April 1839, which the *Port Phillip Gazette* was swift to link with Lady Franklin's tour. On 24 April it reported that upon her arrival at Ovens River, 'the hitherto prosperous aspect of her route was suddenly altered and much serious alarm occasioned, by a depredation of the natives committed upon the station of the Rev. J. Docker':

> The attacks of these wild hordes have at first been confined to the destruction or abduction of the properties only of stockholders, [but] success without retaliation of injury has emboldened them to that degree that their love of plunder has carried them into committing acts of atrocious cruelty, and even murder, upon the unfortunate shepherds or masters that may have fallen into their hands. In the case we now recount, the well known tribe of the river made a descent upon the station and having laid hands upon the two overseers of the Rev. Mr Docker, stripped them of their clothes, and seizing them up, proceeded to attack the huts of the shepherds, whom they also succeeded in taking prisoners. The buildings were then indiscriminately rifled of every article that tempted either their cupidity or their innate sense of reckless destruction. They escaped without retribution, and we have not as yet learned anything further of their movements or the acts [sic] of their unfortunate victims.

Although an investigation by the assistant protector James Dredge later established that the incident had occurred much as it had been reported, neither Lady Franklin nor Dr Hobson made any reference to it in their diaries, and it is evident that it in fact did not at all disturb the 'prosperous aspect' of her excursion. *See* McMillan, op. cit., pp. 69–95 (on the circumstances of Docker's resignation from the church) and pp. 171–173 (on the raid on Bontherambo).

77 The Great Dividing Range, of which the Blue Mountains near Sydney form a part.

78 This letter to John Franklin from the Ovens River does not appear to have survived.

79 In a letter to her husband, Jane Franklin expanded on Captain Moriarty's disapproval of Dr Hobson's wanderings:

> The Doctor also trudges almost constantly on foot, gun in hand, shooting the birds and breaking the stones, sometimes wandering away from the track to the great discomfiture of Captain Moriarty, who considering him to be like all other naturalists he has ever seen, quite unfit to take care of himself, has a constant eye upon his aberrations and declares it to be his own firm belief that he would not be alive at

this hour if it were not for him. Captain Moriarty knew exactly one such person in the course of his naval life, they had him on board his ship in the Mediterranean—such a hammering of rocks and measuring of stones, and skinning and stuffing! his name was Twaddle, or Twiddle, or Twesdale. 'He was my second cousin,' said the Doctor, 'if it is the same who wrote a book on Greece.'—'Ah, to be sure,' replied Captain Moriarty, 'I knew two such fellows must belong to the same stock.' (Letter, Jane Franklin to John Franklin, 20 April 1839.)

80 Near this point in the diary, a number of undated and fragmentary notes seem to reflect the wide-ranging conversations that took place around the campfire, or as the expedition wound slowly along the track. In one, Lady Franklin observed:

> Dr Hobson says only one in 7 or 8 students is properly informed when he gets licence for studying medicine—till very lately could get no subjects [for dissection] but murderers—sometimes so gone, they did not hold together—a surgeon ought to have dissected 200 human bodies before he is qualified to understand thoroughly the anatomy of human body—requires repetition to recollect position &c. (Jane Franklin, Diary, undated note.)

81 The overland expedition of Hamilton Hume and William Hovell had discovered a river and named it the Hume. It was later established by Sturt that this was indeed part of the Murray. Lady Franklin herself used the name 'Murray' until informed later on in her journey that she should call it the 'Hume' until its junction with the Murrumbidgee. (Jane Franklin, Diary, 3 May 1839, p. 91).

82 Not the explorer Hamilton Hume, whom she would meet later at Yass.

83 'It' must refer here to Jane Franklin's scheme for ridding Van Diemen's Land of snakes by offering a bounty for each reptile killed.

84 Robert Brown, who had established his store at the Murray crossing a year earlier, was to become a noted figure in the town of Albury that grew up on the site.

85 Letter, Jane Franklin to John Franklin, 20 April 1839.

IV: *Murray River to the Murrumbidgee River, 20-27 April 1839*

86 The clover seed was not a completely original idea. Hamilton Hume had planted clover seed and peach stones at the base of a tree near the Murray River on which he carved his initials, during his expedition with William Hovell to the Port Phillip district in 1824–1825. A decade later, however, there was no sign of the seeds having grown. *See* Randell, op. cit., p. 103.

87   Quotations from Letter, Jane Franklin to John Franklin, 20 April 1839.

88   *Australian*, 18 May 1839.

89   Before leaving, the party enjoyed a luxurious breakfast: 'We breakfasted on mushrooms this morning—a contribution from a native. This people have a natural and unassuming manner that shames the lower order of Europeans ...' (Hobson, Diary, 21 April 1839.)

90   After this day, Hobson made no further entries in his diary.

91   This was a disappointment, as Lady Franklin had made clear in her letter to Sir John that she would be on the lookout for a postman: 'I shall close here my letter from the Murray to be ready for the first postman we meet or overtake on the road; indifferent whether it be for Sydney or Melbourne since I cannot guess in which direction it will have the best chance of arriving first at its destination.' (Letter, Jane Franklin to John Franklin, 20 April 1839.)

92   Father John Joseph Therry's Billabong run, now known as Yarra Yarra station, is situated a few miles north of the present town of Holbrook. *See* Randell, op. cit., p. 103.

93   'Unreasonable' in the Milliss typescript.

94   Native-born colonists.

95   Hundredweight (112 lbs).

96   A squatter of the region.

97   He later proved to be a brother of Mr Mates.

98   30¼ square yards.

99   A witness to Lady Franklin's arrival at this point at the Murrumbidgee sent an account of it to the *Sydney Herald*:

Lady Franklin arrived here today (April 26), on her way from Melbourne to Sydney. A long dray drawn by four strong horses, containing her paraphernalia, led the van; next, a cart well filled with domestics, two or three sportsmen, two mounted police troopers; and last though not least, Her Ladyship, on horseback, accompanied by a Gentleman on either side, safely—I should hope—though certainly not very speedily mounted, apparently; however, I should suppose the party would make twenty miles a day. It is a great undertaking; and I sincerely wish Lady Franklin success through the journey and a hearty reception in Sydney. (*Sydney Herald*, 6 May 1839.)

100   'Brodrip' in original manuscript diary. William Adams Brodribb, son of a 'political' convict, was a pioneer squatter. He made a number of overland expeditions to the Port Phillip district, and settled at Wanganella Station, near Deniliquin. He found there was 'nothing so interesting or exciting as travelling through an unexplored country'. *See* Shaw, op. cit., p. 98; Randell, op. cit., p. 283.

101 Jane Franklin inserted a separate section at this point in her diary, under this heading 'Brodribb's Account of Natives'. (Jane Franklin, Diary, undated note.)

V: *Murrumbidgee River to Yass, 28 April – 1 May 1839*

102 Now Jugiong.

103 Now Tumut River.

104 John Richard Hardy (1807–1858) migrated to Sydney in 1832, where for two years he edited William Charles Wentworth's paper, the *Australian*. In 1837 he married Clara, a daughter of John Stephen, Puisne Judge of the Supreme Court of New South Wales, and sister to Alfred Stephen. In the same year he became police magistrate for Yass, and acquired considerable property in the district. He is said to have significantly reduced the bushranging threat in the area, but to have quarrelled bitterly with a number of local settlers, in which disputes he was generally supported by Henry O'Brien's brother, Cornelius. In 1843 he was suspended 'after accusations of irregular magisterial procedures'. Soon after gold was discovered in 1851, he was appointed Chief Gold Commissioner of Crown Lands for the New South Wales goldfields. The position was abolished in 1852 following charges against him which he asserted were atrocious slanders, and Hardy retired to his property at Yass. *See* N. Keesing, 'Hardy, John Richard', in Pike, vol. 4, op. cit., pp. 343–344.

105 Alfred Stephen had arrived in Hobart Town in January 1825 and within a few months was appointed Solicitor-General and Crown Solicitor. In 1832, while on leave in England, he was appointed Attorney-General and returned in 1833 to a great backlog of work. Initially a favourite of Arthur's, he became estranged from him after a misunderstanding, and later fell out with the Colonial Secretary, John Montagu. When his first wife died in childbirth in 1837 Stephen resigned his position, sold his house and continued in Hobart in private practice. In 1838 he married Eleanor, née Bedford, and in the following year accepted a temporary judgeship in Sydney, at some pecuniary sacrifice. He left Hobart several weeks after Lady Franklin by the *Medway*, which would later take her home, landing in Sydney on 7 May. In 1841 he was made Puisne Judge and in 1845 Chief Justice of New South Wales, a position he retained until his death in 1894.

106 Jane later referred to this in a letter to Sir John as the occasion when 'we were entrapped by Mr Hardy ... into his house'. (Letter, Jane Franklin to John Franklin, 11 May 1839.)

107 Matthew Forster, Chief Police Magistrate in Van Diemen's Land since 1831, was currently acting as Colonial Secretary during John Montagu's extended absence in England. Though absenting herself from the scene, Jane Franklin could not leave the world of politics behind her entirely. Forster's letter was a reply to one of her own, written from Launceston before she embarked,

full of minute enquiries about matters he would undoubtedly have deemed beyond her provenance.

108 Lady Franklin reached Dr Gibson's house near Goulburn on 5 May. This remark is thus an indication that her diary was written up some days after the event.

109 George Frankland (1800–1838) was Surveyor-General in Van Diemen's Land from 1828. Jane Franklin found him 'more accomplished than efficient' but was drawn to him by his enthusiasm for science and exploration, his talent and his charm. He was on the point of leaving for England on leave, and perhaps never to return, having sold his house in Hobart, when he died suddenly in December 1838. Though she seemed fond of him, Jane Franklin did not take care of his cats.

110 Native-born colonists.

111 Henry O'Brien had married Isabella Macdonald in July 1836. She died in Sydney in July 1838, aged 27.

112 In May 1839 Hamilton Hume (1797–1873) was 41 years old. He had discovered the Yass Plains in company with two others in 1821–1822, and shortly afterwards penetrated the upper reaches of the Clyde River almost as far as the later site of Braidwood. Hume received a grant of 300 acres at Appin for these services. For his overland journey to Port Phillip with Captain William H. Hovell in 1824–1825 he was given a grant of 1200 acres, but was forced to sell this to pay outstanding expenses from the journey, which had not been backed by the government. Further exploration, in search of a new line of road across the Blue Mountains and attached to Sturt's expedition into the interior resulted in further grants, and in 1829 he took up land totalling more than 3000 acres on the Yass Plains. In the 1850s he clashed with Hovell over his role in the 1824 expedition, which he believed Hovell had not sufficiently acknowledged, and he died in the 1860s, obsessed with the idea that his place in that expedition had not been restored in the public's estimation. In 1839, as various remarks in Lady Franklin's diary suggest, a number of people felt he claimed rather too much of the credit for those expeditions in which he had taken part.

113 Robert Dixon had been appointed Assistant Surveyor in Sydney in 1826, and made a number of valuable surveys of the Illawarra district, the Blue Mountains, Goulburn, Molonglo River, Upper Hunter and New England districts, among others. In 1836 he took two years leave to go to England on urgent private business. In London he impudently published a map of the colony compiled from official surveys and documents, and on his return to Sydney in July 1838 the Surveyor-General, Major T.L. Mitchell, refused to reinstate him to his position. Mitchell's disapproval seems not to have been shared by other colonists, and clearly the map was a popular one. Lady Franklin ordered a copy of it while in Sydney but later cancelled the order after being presented with one as a gift by Bishop Broughton. Dixon went to Moreton Bay in 1839 and early in 1840 was made surveyor in charge of the district, but offended Sir George Gipps by again publishing a map on his own initiative, an act which Gipps regarded as 'calculated

defiance'. Dixon was suspended after an altercation with the commandant of the penal establishment there. *See* Louis L. Cranfield, 'Dixon, Robert', in Pike, vol. 1, op. cit., pp. 309–310.

114 T.L. Mitchell, *Three Expeditions into the Interior of Eastern Australia: With Descriptions of the Recently Explored Region of Australia Felix, and of the Present Colony of New South Wales.* London: T. and W. Boone, 1838.

115 William Bland (ed.), *Journey of Discovery to Port Phillip, New South Wales, in 1824 and 1825, by W.H. Hovell and H. Hume, Esquires.* Sydney: A. Hill, 1831.

116 This section of the original diary contains more detail of residents and housing in Yass, which might be of interest to local historians.

117 The appearance of friendship between the minister and the police magistrate as they accompanied Lady Franklin about Yass and its environs did not last many years. In 1841 a letter appeared in the *Sydney Herald,* charging the local police magistrate, Richard Hardy, with failing to observe the Sabbath as a day of rest and countenancing moral laxity. Rumour attributed the letter to Mr Brigstocke, who had been the itinerant minister of Yass since 1838, and in consequence he was suspended by the bishop in 1843, pending an investigation. A commission of inquiry found grounds for suspicion but insufficient evidence that he was the author and he was reinstated. He won an action against Hardy in the Supreme Court for malicious libel, but was awarded damages of only a farthing.

VI: *Yass to Goulburn, 3–6 May 1839*

118 Although Lady Franklin gives no reason for her sudden decision to dismiss the manservant Snachall, it seems that Yass, with its public houses and its drinking culture, had proved too great a temptation to a man who, at least in his mistress' eyes, had a problem with drink. Until this time she had been most strict, and almost successful, in keeping alcohol away from him. After she reached Sydney she would enlist the aid of temperance societies on his behalf, agreeing to retain him in her service only if he 'took the Pledge'. At the time, advocates of temperance showed much faith in the efficacy of individuals making a formal promise to drink no more.

119 William Hilton Hovell (1786–1875) had arrived in Sydney in 1813. Like Hamilton Hume he suffered from the expense of their expedition to Port Phillip, and the inadequate recompense offered by the government afterwards. He repeatedly thereafter sought more generous recompense from the governor or colonial office, with but limited success. Governor Bourke agreed to cancel his debts to government in 1837, at which time Hovell went to live on his property at Grabberdrack near Goulburn.

120 The original site of the town of Goulburn, on the banks of the Wollondilly River, was surveyed by Robert Dixon in 1828. The town was moved to its present site in 1833.

121 Jane Franklin gave Dr Hobson a draft on her bank for this purpose, but he later returned it, having found nothing that would interest her at the museum. *See* Jane Franklin, Diary, 18 May 1839 (p. 112).

122 William Pitt Faithful, who had shared with his brother George in the overland enterprise to Port Phillip in 1838, had earlier, in about 1827, established Springfield Station on the Goulburn Plains.

VII: *Goulburn to the Illawarra, 7–17 May 1839*

123 For reasons of space, this section of the diary has been omitted and is only summarised here. The diary is reproduced in *The Illawarra Diary of Lady Jane Franklin, 10–17 May 1839*, ed. Michael Organ. (Woonona, New South Wales: Illawarra Historical Publications, 1988.)

124 Letter, Jane Franklin to John Franklin, 11 May 1839.

125 Jane Franklin, Diary, original manuscript, 10 May 1839.

126 Jane Franklin, Diary, original manuscript, 11 May 1839.

127 Letter, Jane Franklin to John Franklin, 11 May 1839.

128 Jane Franklin, Diary, original manuscript, 12 May 1839.

129 Letter, Jane Franklin to John Franklin, 18 May 1839.

130 Jane Franklin, Diary, 29 June 1839 (see p. 173).

131 Letter, Jane Franklin to John Franklin, 18 May 1839.

132 *Colonist*, 15 May 1839; Jane Franklin, Diary, original manuscript, 17 May 1839.

133 Jane Franklin, Diary, original manuscript, 17 May 1839.

134 Jane Franklin, Diary, original manuscript, 18 May 1839.

VIII: *Sydney, 18–27 May 1839*

135 *Australian*, 16 May 1839.

136 Letter, Jane Franklin to John Franklin, 18 and 27 May 1839; *Sydney Gazette*, 21 May 1839; *Colonist*, 22 May 1839.

137 *Sydney Gazette*, 21 May 1839.

138 *Colonist*, 22 May 1839.

139 See J. Gipps, op. cit.

140 Henry Watson Parker (1808–1881), a cousin of Lady Gipps, had been unemployed and touring Europe for his health when Gipps took him to Sydney as his private secretary. Precise, methodical and shrewd, he retained his position for eight years and gave it up when he was appointed to the Legislative Council and given the salaried position of Chairman of

Committees in 1846. In 1856 he won the seat of Parramatta in the first general election, and in October of that year formed a ministry which lasted to 1857. In 1858 he was knighted and returned to England. *See* Gipps, op. cit., especially p. 40.

141 This probably refers to Sir George inviting Lady Franklin to take a glass of wine with him—an accustomed courtesy of the time, which she later reveals he was in the habit of offering her every night at dinner.

142 Dr (later Sir Robert) Officer, medical officer and landholder in Van Diemen's Land, was temporarily made Colonial Surgeon in 1839.

143 Lady Franklin had written to her husband from Yass that she was anxious to find an appointment for Dr Hobson:

> [Mr Forster, Acting Colonial Secretary] promises to use his influence at the Colonial Office for Dr Hobson, whenever you have found a situation as Naturalist or in any other department for him, saying it is of no use to ask for general assistance. It seems by this that Mr F. does not understand that what is wanted at the Colonial Office is the making of the office of Naturalist, or does Mr F. mean that if you and the Legislative Council created such an office, then would be the time to apply for the salary? Some public expression in the Council, perhaps, of the desirableness of such an appointment would be useful. The more I see of Dr Hobson the more anxious I am that the Colony should not lose the benefit of his services ... Private practice in Hobarton joined to the Naturalist situation is that which he prefers to all work. (Letter, Jane Franklin to John Franklin, 2 May 1839.)

Later she wrote from Sydney:

> I feel much pleased at your recollection of Dr Hobson. I am sorry he is gone so that I cannot give him your letter, upon which he might have reflected as he went along. The only thing which I think would prevent his accepting, is his health which he seems to think requires a warmer climate and therefore he thinks of Port Phillip, where I daresay he would establish himself to just advantage—I earnestly wish it were best for him to remain with us, we shall never get another ... (Letter, Jane Franklin to John Franklin, 21–22 May 1839.)

Sir John Franklin warmly supported Dr Hobson for appointment as Naturalist to the colony, but the suggestion was not taken further. Before Lady Franklin returned to Hobart, Sir John offered Dr Hobson a position as secretary to the Board of Education, of which to her delight he accepted. The *True Colonist,* somewhat overstating the real situation, declared that the appointment had been made 'on her Ladyship's recommendation', and added: 'Of his qualifications for that office, we know nothing.' In response to a complimentary article in Sydney's *Australian*, suggesting that Lady Franklin planned to contribute to 'the payment of a competent secretary to the Board of Education', the *True Colonist* offered what sounds like a subtle sexual slur. 'We have not heard that her Ladyship pays him any extra salary in this capacity, nor do we know whether or not he is her private medical attendant?' (*True Colonist*, 4 October 1839.)

Hobson remained for only a short time in Hobart, where he provided material assistance in the establishment of the Tasmanian Society for Natural History. In 1840 he suffered a severe attack of fever which weakened his already delicate constitution, and moved to Melbourne in the hope that a warmer climate would improve his health. There he resumed medical work and was appointed a physician to the new Melbourne Hospital in 1847. He died from a ruptured blood vessel in his lungs in February 1848, aged 33, and was survived by his wife Margaret and four children.

[144] This refers to the money she had given him on parting earlier in the journey to make purchases for her at the museum.

[145] The convict architect, Francis Greenway, had built a grand stable block for Macquarie to go with his grand design for a new government house in the form of a castle. The castle was later forbidden by the Secretary of State in London, but Governor Gipps was now watching with great anticipation the building of a new house of more modest design.

[146] Jane Franklin, Letter, 5 April 1839 (see p. 29), and footnote 51.

[147] In 1839 Anna Josepha King (née Coomb) would have been about 74 years old. But as Lady Franklin wrote to her husband: 'Old Mrs King ... can scarcely be called old. I don't know that I should take her to be more than 55.' (Letter, Jane Franklin to John Franklin, 21 May 1839.)

During Philip Gidley King's term as Lieutenant-Governor of New South Wales, Anna King had 'shared her husband's anxieties and labours; indeed, the influence she was thought to have over him earned her the nickname of "Queen Josepha"'. In 1806 she returned with him to England. His death in 1808 left her in financial need, which was partially relieved by income from land and cattle in New South Wales, to which she possessed dubious title. In 1832 she sailed with her son, Captain Phillip Parker King, to return, as she had long wished, to the colony, where two of her daughters also lived: Maria, wife of Hannibal Macarthur, and Mary, wife of Robert Copeland Lethbridge. She lived at her daughter Maria's home, The Vineyard, at Parramatta, until her death in 1844. *See* M. Bassett, 'King, Anna Josepha', in Pike, vol. 2, op. cit., pp. 52–54. *See also* M. Bassett, *The Governor's Lady Mrs Phillip Gidley King: An Australian Historical Narrative*. London: Oxford University Press, 1940.

[148] James Tegg was the son of a successful bookseller in Cheapside. In January 1835 he opened a business with his brother as 'wholesale and retail book merchants' in George Street, Sydney, and ran the business successfully until 1844, expanding his enterprise to include publishing and printing. Tegg's *New South Wales Pocket Almanac* appeared yearly from 1836 to 1844.

[149] Raphael Clint (1797–1849), engraver and map maker, began business in Sydney in 1835. He was an excellent craftsman, but his business declined

during the 1840s depression and he died insolvent in 1849. Of a later visit to the shop, Lady Franklin wrote: 'Went to Clint's—saw him—said he had been 3 years in VDL—was in Survey Office then set up engraving, but had no business & lost money—came here & succeeds well.' (Jane Franklin, Diary, original manuscript, 25 May 1839.)

150 The new court house on South Head Road (now Oxford Street) was still under construction, the old court house, which was more centrally located, having been deemed unsafe. *See* J. Maclehose, *Picture of Sydney and Strangers' Guide in New South Wales for 1839*. Sydney: J. Maclehose, 1839, p. 120.

151 Jane Franklin, Diary, 23 May 1839 (see p. 118), and footnote 168.

152 Cumberland was the first of the Nineteen Counties which purported to prescribe the limits of legitimate settlement in New South Wales in the 1830s. Bounded on the north and west by the Hawkesbury and Nepean Rivers, on the south west and south by the Nepean and Cataract Rivers and by a line bearing east to Bulli at latitude 20° South, it included all the principal towns of the colony: Sydney, Parramatta, Liverpool, Windsor, Richmond, Castlereagh and Penrith. It was consequently by far the most densely settled of the counties and in 1839 was said to have a population of almost 40 000 (white) inhabitants. *See* Maclehose, op. cit., p. 137.

153 William Grant Broughton (1788–1853) had arrived in the colony in 1829 as successor to Archdeacon Thomas Hobbes Scott. In 1836 he was consecrated Bishop of Australia for the Anglican Church. During the 1830s, the British Government, conscious of the advantages of religion for an orderly society, and of the growing numbers of Catholics and other denominations in New South Wales, was willing to limit the monopoly of power and State funding hitherto held by the Church of England. In 1835 John Bede Polding (1794–1877) arrived in Sydney as the first Catholic bishop in Australia. Governor Bourke's Church Act of 1836 provided for State aid to be shared equally between Anglicans, Catholics and Presbyterians. This Act greatly annoyed Broughton.

154 Francis Greenway (1777–1837), architect, was transported for forgery in 1814 but was allowed to begin private practice immediately. He was appointed Civil Architect in 1816, and the lighthouse on the South Head of Port Jackson was his first work for the government. Macquarie was so pleased with the stonework of the building, which was completed in December 1817, that he presented Greenway with conditional emancipation. The building was completed in 1818 but was later pulled down and the present replica (slightly enlarged from the original) built in 1880. For further detail *see* J. Broadbent and J. Hughes, *Francis Greenway, Architect*. Glebe NSW: Historic Houses Trust of New South Wales, 1997, pp. 52–53.

155 Hannibal Hawkins Macarthur (1788–1861) was a nephew of the celebrated merino sheep breeder John Macarthur. He spent three years in Sydney between 1805 and 1808, and returned to the colony again in 1812, when he married the former Governor King's daughter Anna Maria and assisted

Elizabeth Macarthur in the management of the Macarthurs' flocks. Increasingly he developed land and business interests in his own right and took some interest in politics. By 1839 he was one of the most prominent citizens of the colony, a member of the Legislative Council and chairman of the directors of the Bank of Australia. Following financial reverses in the depression of the 1840s he was declared bankrupt in 1844.

156 Letter, Jane Franklin to Mary Simpkinson, 21 June 1838, Franklin Papers, Royal Society of Tasmania (RS16/8/1).

157 Edward Deas Thomson (1800–1879) was appointed as clerk of the Executive and Legislative Councils of New South Wales in 1829, in which capacity he developed harmonious relationships with the governors Darling and Bourke. In September 1833 he married Bourke's daughter, Anne Maria. In 1836 Bourke recommended his promotion to colonial secretary in place of Alexander McLeay, and although the latter was reluctant to give up the position, Thomson was appointed in January 1837. When Gipps took over as governor, Thomson initially had doubts that he could work with him, privately criticising the governor's manner and abilities, but they soon established a close friendship. Thomson was conservative in his views, but efficient and fair minded.

158 Major George Barney (1792–1862) served as lieutenant and captain in the Royal Engineers in the Peninsular War and the West Indies. In Grenada, in about 1817, he married Portia Henrietta Peale. He arrived in Sydney in 1835 with his wife and three children, as captain of a detachment of Royal Engineers. He was soon placed in charge of superintending civil works in the colony, a task which presented formidable challenges, and his salary for this position was confirmed in 1837. The works for which he was responsible included the breakwater at Newcastle and the pier harbour at Wollongong, on the progress of both of which Jane Franklin commented. By 1839 he was a major. In 1839–1840, Governor Gipps, himself an officer of the Engineers, allotted a number of convicts to Barney to enable him to build the defence measures of the colony, after two US warships entered the harbour in darkness and undetected in December 1839, alerting colonists to the ease with which Sydney might be attacked from the sea. When he was succeeded in command of the Royal Engineers by Lieutenant-Colonel Gordon in 1843, Gipps retained Lieutenant-Colonel Barney in the position of Colonial Engineer. George Barney patronised artists in the colony and was elected President of the School of Arts in 1839. At least two of his daughters were taught painting by Conrad Martens. One daughter, Maria Jane, married David Scott and became a celebrated artist. See 'Barney, George', in Pike, vol. 1, op. cit., pp. 60–61.

159 In a later note Jane comments: 'Mrs William Cox said Mrs Broughton was more affable since she had become Bishop's wife than was before—used to be more reserved & shut up with her children.' (Jane Franklin, Diary: 'Gossip from the Hawkesbury', undated note.)

160 Franklin had recently responded to an urgent request from Gipps to send wheat to New South Wales, then suffering severely from drought.

161 In February 1843 Mrs James Snachall wrote to her 'dear brother' in Kent from Sydney:

> We have got little General Shop sell little of everything, and James as got situation in the Sheref Office his pay is the same as it was at Present but we are Every Day expecting somthing Better and I do not care how soon for we are trying hard to save few Pound to return to Poor Old England again. Please the Allmighty God to spare us this moment it is so Hot we can ardly Bare our own feelings it is now the 10 of Febaury it as been a veary Hot summer and I am sorry to say there is veary Grate Deal of Distress hear … Even in our small way we have lost Grate Deal in giving Creadet to People. But it as open our Eyes …

> The Governor Lady Lady Gibbs is veary good to us she send us good many things at times she sent us fine Pig Last Week. James goes to wait at all the Partys there and Balls wich come about twice a Week …

> I was sorry to see by the English Papers there is grate Distress so many hands out of Imploy and so many servants want places. (Letter, Mrs James Snashall to Mr T. Wise, Kent, 7 February 1843, Mitchell Library, State Library of New South Wales (MSS6067).)

The circumstantial evidence in this letter suggests either that the Snachalls settled in Sydney after they left the Franklins' service, and Sir George came to appreciate Mr Snachall's skills in waiting at table; or that this reference in Lady Franklin's diary is to a manservant of the Gipps's who bore a coincidentally similar name to her own servants.

162 Letters, John Franklin to Jane Franklin, 14 and 17 May 1839, in G. Mackaness (ed.), *Some Private Correspondence of Sir John and Lady Jane Franklin (Tasmania, 1837–1845)*. Part I. Sydney: D.S. Ford, 1947, pp. 80, 82.

163 Sir Edward Parry, a close friend of Sir John and a fellow Arctic explorer, had earlier spent several years as Commissioner for the Australian Agricultural Company, from 1829 to 1834, a position which had been offered first to Sir John himself.

164 Maconochie and Franklin, both erstwhile naval captains with an interest in geography and scientific exploration, had many friends in common. Most were in England, and able to be influenced only by letter, but Captain Phillip Parker King (1791–1856), son of the former governor, after spending many years in hydrography and exploration, had retired in ill health in 1832 to the estates he held by grant in his native Australia. A shareholder in the Australian Agricultural Company, he was appointed Resident Commissioner in 1839, and when Lady Franklin arrived in Sydney had only just departed to take up this position in Port Stephens. King could have no influence over Franklin's future, and Lady Franklin's apparent concern about his good opinion seems to be personal rather than political. That she was prepared to travel so far to speak with him may indicate how deeply troubled she still felt by the dismissal of Maconochie. Or perhaps she was simply trying justify her trip on grounds other than those of pure pleasure.

165 Lieutenant-Colonel Maurice O'Connell had arrived in Sydney in December 1809 in command of the 1st battalion of the 73rd Regiment, which accompanied Governor Macquarie when he replaced the deposed Governor William Bligh. In May 1810 O'Connell married Bligh's widowed daughter, Mary Putland—much to the distress of Bligh, who had planned to sail from Sydney with his family a few days later. The governor's daughter had shocked colonial society with her behaviour and attire, and Macquarie was soon embarrassed by her hostility to her father's enemies. By August 1813 he was urging the removal of O'Connell and the regiment from the colony, writing that 'Mrs O'Connell, naturally enough, has imbibed strong feelings of resentment and hatred against all those Persons and their Families, who were in the least inimical to her Father's Government ... tho' Lieut. Colonel O'Connell is naturally a very well disposed man, he allows himself to be a good deal influenced by his Wife's strong rooted Prejudices.' *See* 'O'Connell, Sir Maurice Charles Philip', in Pike, vol. 2, op. cit., p. 295.

O'Connell was transferred to Ceylon in 1814, but in December 1838 returned to the colony, where with his wife he held extensive land grants, in command of the forces in New South Wales. Later he claimed, on behalf of his wife and her sisters, Bligh's heiresses, 105 acres of very valuable land at Parramatta. The heiresses eventually surrendered this claim but were confirmed in their titles to a number of other grants.

166 The offending paragraph appeared also in the *Sydney Monitor*, as follows:

Yesterday afternoon [21 May], while Captain Innes and Mr Kerr were on the Bench disposing of summons cases in the prisoners Court, Lady Franklin, escorted by Colonel Wilson and followed by a young lady said to be her niece, Mr [Gilbert] Elliot (the Governor's aide-de-camp) and two other gentlemen, entered the police office. Having viewed the Court-room and taken a seat for a few minutes (during which the business was not suspended) her ladyship retired. Lady Franklin is a fine-looking woman, very intellectual countenance, vivacious and affable. She has a fine colour, with blue expressive eyes. (*Sydney Monitor*, 22 May 1839.)

Lady Franklin's concern about this item of 'news' did not lessen. In her next letter to Sir John she reverted to the subject, warning him: 'Don't believe a word about what the papers say about my hearing cases in the Police Office; it is a pure invention.' (Letter, Jane Franklin to John Franklin, 27 May 1839.)

The pushy Colonel Wilson had been a colonel in the army of one of the South American republics before coming to Australia. He was appointed Barrack Master at Sydney in 1832, and made First Police Magistrate in 1833. In this capacity he had escorted Lady Franklin up George Street to Government House upon her arrival in Sydney—a service on which she now felt he presumed too far. His irascible temperament had made him many enemies and during 1838 and 1839 he faced a number of charges of misconduct, for one of which he was formally removed from office in July 1840. But Maclehose's 1839 *Picture of Sydney* (perhaps from information Wilson himself supplied) observed that the interior of the police office, which he displayed to Lady Franklin with such pride, had been 'cleverly laid out by our worthy and much respected First Police Magistrate, Colonel Wilson'. (Maclehose, op. cit., p.136.)

167 Letters, Jane Franklin to John Franklin, 21 and 22 May 1839.

168 John Saunders (1806–1859) arrived in New South Wales in 1834 as pastor for the Baptists of Sydney. The first Baptist chapel was built in Bathurst Street in 1836, and Saunders was minister there for thirteen years. Known as 'the Apostle of Temperance' for his opposition to the rum traffic, he obtained thousands of signatures for total abstinence through his constant journeying over the colony. In the incident to which Jane refers here, Sir George Gipps had chaired one of his lectures in Sydney, and at the conclusion of the meeting led the way in the signing of a pledge. It would seem that Lady Franklin had resolved, or been persuaded, to give (Mr) Snachall one more chance in her employment on condition that he signed 'the Pledge'. As the manservant accompanied her on her return journey to Hobart, it can be assumed he consented to do so.

169 In other words, with her back to the horses—a less comfortable and less honourable seat than those facing forward. In this passage Lady Franklin observes a small drama of marital politics, and judges the patriarch unfavourably.

170 The Female School of Industry was established by a group of elite women of Sydney in 1826, under the leadership of the governor's wife, Eliza Darling. Through her example, writes Elizabeth Windschuttle, 'Sydney charity work became respectable and fashionable'. The aim of the Female School of Industry was to 'rescue' destitute girls from the danger of ruin and the influence of their parents, and provide them with instruction and training in religion and domestic labour, while encouraging 'habits of obedience and submission'. Lady Gipps was less noted for her interest in such philanthropic ventures—not surprisingly, perhaps, in view of her husband's attitude, expressed here. See E. Windschuttle, 'Feeding the Poor and Sapping their Strength', in E. Windschuttle (ed.), *Women, Class and History*. Sydney: Fontana/Collins, 1980, pp. 53–80. Quotations are from pp. 64 and 72.

171 This is not Mary King, who married Copeland Lethbridge, but the wife of a cousin of his.

172 Macquarie had intended to build a magnificent cathedral in George Street, designed by Francis Greenway, but was prohibited by the Colonial Office after Commissioner J.T. Bigge visited Sydney and deplored the expenditure on public buildings. An alternative design, by James Hume, was approved and St Andrew's Cathedral was built between 1837 and 1841. The building was later incorporated into the present cathedral. The old burial ground to the north was the site of the present Town Hall. See P. Cox and C. Lucas, *Australian Colonial Architecture*. Melbourne: Lansdowne Editions, 1978, p. 206.

173 Alexander McLeay (1767–1848) arrived in Sydney with his wife Elizabeth and six daughters in January 1826, to assume his appointment as Colonial Secretary, which he held until Bourke put Edward Deas Thomson in his place in 1837. In 1838, after Bourke's recall, McLeay sought compensation for this 'injurious' incident, and Gipps recommended that he should receive £1750 from the colonial office in recompense for his lost salary of £2000 a year. McLeay was unable to reduce his expenses after the loss of his salary—largely because he poured so much money into the building of Elizabeth Bay House—and was soon in debt. The arrival of his eldest son, William Sharp Macleay, who took over his father's liabilities and forced a number of economies including the subdivision and sale of most of the Elizabeth Bay property, saved Alexander McLeay from insolvency. He was an entomologist of distinction and his scientific collection, augmented by his son and nephew, was transferred to the Macleay Museum at the University of Sydney in 1890. The inconsistent spelling of McLeay/Macleay evident in Jane Franklin's diary was common in colonial society. The *Australian Dictionary of Biography* gives the spelling 'McLeay' for Alexander, but 'Macleay' for his sons William and (Sir) George. Other works standardise the spelling as 'Macleay'.

174 Captain Maurice O'Connell, son of Sir Maurice and Lady O'Connell, settled in Australia after an 'eventful military career'.

175 The *Sydney Gazette* described the fair in detail:

The Fancy Fair wore a pretty effect from the variety of the articles exposed to view, comprising many neat specimens of drawing needlework, fancy baskets made of shells and such like; the only draw-back being want of room, a defect which was very evident. The attendance or company from the time of opening continued numerous; the back of the lawn was covered with carriages, while the front was occupied by the band of the 50th Regt., which continued to play several favorite airs during the afternoon; this, added to the groups of beautiful and elegantly dressed females, gave to the whole a pleasing effect. The attendance of the company, we hope, was of substantial advantage to the funds of the Society, as the wares began perceptibly to diminish, and by some, large purchases were made. Sir George Gipps and Lady Franklin visited the place in the course of the afternoon and remained some time. Sir Maurice O'Connell likewise paid a visit; the fair was, in fact, attended by most of the principal inhabitants of Sydney. (*Sydney Gazette*, 28 May 1839.)

176 William McPherson, Esq., was clerk for both the Executive and Legislative Councils, the position formerly occupied by Edward Deas Thomson.

177 Mr Peck's exhibition of his model of Hobart Town, set up in the saloon of the Royal Hotel in George Street, had opened to the public on the day of Lady Franklin's arrival in Sydney. The *Sydney Monitor*, more impressed than she, heaped praise upon the exhibition, and described it in minute detail:

The *coup d'oeuil* it presents to the beholder on entering the saloon is captivating. In the foreground you have Sullivan's Cove, the Old Jetty, and the new Circular Wharf and Warehouses, with views up Macquarie-street, and the leading streets running parallel to it, flanked by Mount Wellington and the seven umbrageous hills, upon which the town is built. The undulations of the ground, the buildings (even to weather-boarded cottages with their enclosures, fences and shrubberies) are all minutely and accurately laid down and coloured to imitate the things they represent. To those who have visited Hobart Town this model will be very interesting, as it will to some recall places forgotten, and enable others to behold in miniature the houses of their relatives and friends, and the scenes of, perhaps, many happy days; while to those who are desirous of seeing the capital of the sister colony, it will be found a treat, well calculated at once to gratify curiosity and excite admiration. (*Sydney Monitor*, 20 May 1839.)

No hint of Lady Franklin's disapproval reached the press. The *Colonist* reported that on the day of her visit, which coincided with that of 'many of the grandees of the town', all expressed 'their unqualified admiration of this truly ingenious and beautiful work of art'. (*Colonist*, 29 May 1839.)

[178] Jane herself had voyaged up the Nile to the Second Cataract in 1834. *See* P. Russell, 'The Allure of the Nile: Jane Franklin's Voyage to the Second Cataract, 1834', *Gender and History*, vol. 9, no. 2, August, 1997.

[179] Curiously it was the brief visit to St Philip's Parochial School that got notice in the press, while the visit to St James' was ignored. Clearly Mr Barton resembled Colonel Wilson in his desire to generate publicity for himself and his concerns via Lady Franklin. The mocking tone sustained in the *Colonist's* report throughout suggest the editor was aware of his transparent desire for reflected glory:

LADY FRANKLIN.—The Sydney newspapers have had some notice or other respecting Lady Franklin in almost every publication ever since, and indeed long before, her arrival amongst us. Our contemporaries have been so engrossed with the Sailors' Home, that they have left her Ladyship out for one number. But Lady F. is too good a subject for a par, not to be recurred to as often as they can contrive to say anything about her. We ourselves feel somewhat at a loss this publication, from a peculiar dearth of news either in town or country; and so here comes our friend Mr Barton, of St Phillip's Parochial School, to inform us that Lady F. did him the honour of visiting his school on Church Hill, on Sunday last, accompanied by the Bishop of Australia. This will make a very good paragraph; and what a picture it contains! There was Lady F. quite delighted to see so many smart little boys and tidy little girls, in their Sunday array, with their Bibles and Catechisms, all undergoing a process of religious instruction. There again was his Lordship the Bishop, seeming highly pleased with Mr Barton's exhibition. There also was Mr B. himself, never more gratified in his life, than by the flattering terms in which both her Ladyship and his Lordship were graciously pleased to express the satisfaction which this examination afforded them. And last of all, the little scholars that underwent this honourable inspection; their little countenances exhibited the mingled emotions of bashfulness and joy at the interest and attention of which they were the objects from such distinguished guests. (*Colonist*, 1 June 1839.)

180 'Ly F' (Lady Franklin) in original manuscript.

181 The Government House in which Sir George lived in 1839 was the original building, much extended and altered since early days, situated at the hub of the town of Sydney and overlooking the cove. Successive governors had long considered it inconvenient and inadequate, and complained about its state of repair. In 1837 building commenced of a large, highly picturesque, castellated mansion further into the Domain. The new Government House, designed by Edward Blore, the 'special architect' to William IV and Queen Victoria, was completed in 1845. Oriented away from the town and with tall gates excluding the general public, the new building represented a withdrawal on the part of the governor 'from the hurly-burly of colonial life'. The timing of this withdrawal was significant, since it coincided with moves towards representative government which would make the role of the governor increasingly a symbolic one in the later part of the century. In 1836 a 'Government House Committee' recommended that the first Government House should be demolished once the new building was completed, to allow for the extension of Macquarie and Phillip Streets. Demolition began soon after Gipps fulfilled his ambition and moved into the new house in 1845. *See* H. Proudfoot et al., *Australia's First Government House,* North Sydney: Allen and Unwin, 1991, pp. 124–127; also Cox and Lucas, op cit., p. 206.

182 James Armstrong Wilson (1804–1852), portrait painter, emigrated to Australia with his family in 1836, travelling on the *Fairlie*, which at the same time brought the Franklins to Van Diemen's Land. He hoped to improve his prospects, but found pioneering life near Braidwood so severe that he returned to portrait painting in Sydney from October 1838. Arriving with four shillings to his name, he soon established himself, being introduced to Sydney society by Major Barney. He was a close friend of the landscape painter Conrad Martens (1801–1878), who had arrived in Sydney in 1835 with the *Beagle* and was instantly entranced by the harbour. Martens remained in Sydney for the rest of his life, rapidly building up 'a clientele of leading citizens', for whom he painted landscapes and views including large oils and watercolours of their own houses and estates. The depression of the 1840s which ruined many of Martens' patrons had a disastrous effect on his own fortunes, but his work remained popular and highly regarded. As a colonial artist he 'stood alone in his period'. *See* S. Jones, 'Martens, Conrad', and N. Parbury, 'Wilson, James Armstrong', in J. Kerr (ed.), op. cit., pp. 513–516 and pp. 846–866.

Jane Franklin misspelled Conrad Martens' name as 'Martin' throughout her diary.

[183] Gipps later gave Maconochie the chance to implement his 'marks scheme' at Norfolk Island, but the experiment failed, largely from lack of support and resources.

IX: *Excursion to the Hunter River and Port Stephens, 27 May – 4 June 1839*

[184] Letter, Jane Franklin to John Franklin, 27 May 1839.

[185] *Colonist*, 29 May 1839.

[186] J. Kociumbas, *The Oxford History of Australia*. Vol. 2: *1770–1860*. Melbourne: Oxford University Press, 1992, pp. 202–203. *See also Historical Records of Australia*, ed. Frederick Watson, series 1, vol. 20. Sydney: Library Committee of the Commonwealth Parliament, 1924, pp. 247–256, 280.

[187] In a later entry, Lady Franklin calmly announces that Mr Christie of the mounted police had gone 'raving mad'. *See* Jane Franklin, Diary, 13 July 1839 (p. 192).

[188] Lancelot Edward Threlkeld (1788–1859), a Congregational minister, was appointed as a missionary to the Aborigines on Lake Macquarie in 1825. The mission was abandoned, largely due to its expense, in 1828. Threlkeld then acquired land by grant from Governor Darling and was confirmed as missionary by the Executive Council in 1831 with a salary of £200. He learned the local dialect and acted as interpreter for Aborigines on trial in Sydney. Threlkeld's *An Australian Grammar: Comprehending the Principles and Natural Rules of the Language, as Spoken by the Aborigines in the Vicinity of Hunter's River, Lake Macquarie, &c. New South Wales* was published by the Society for Promoting Christian Knowledge in Sydney in 1834. Though his mission had some success and was highly regarded by individual humanitarians, it came under savage criticism, and Threlkeld himself 'regarded it as a failure because he made no apparent converts'. In 1840 he reported that few Aborigines were left at the station—many having died of European disease and malnutrition—and Gipps terminated government support. The mission officially closed in December 1841. Threlkeld had supplemented his stipend by grazing stock and by developing the coal seams on his property 'in defiance of the monopoly of the Australian Agricultural Company'. Although Jane Franklin described him as 'elderly', he was only three years older than she was herself, and was at this time 50 years old. *See* N. Gunson, 'Threlkeld, Lancelot Edward', in Pike, vol. 2, op. cit., pp. 528–530 (quotations from p. 529).

[189] Captain Richard Tasker Furlong was commandant at the stockade at Newcastle. The 80th (Staffordshire Volunteers) Regiment was stationed in New South Wales from 1837 to 1844.

[190] Charles Pleydell Neale Wilton (1795–1859), a Church of England chaplain, arrived in Sydney in April 1827 as Chaplain for New South Wales, and was appointed to Newcastle in 1831, his parish at that time including the whole

Hunter River district. The formation of new parishes at Maitland, Hexham and Raymond Terrace in 1839 eased his duties. A keen naturalist, he lectured and published on many topics, including agriculture, education, Aborigines and natural history.

191 The Scott brothers, Robert and Helenus, had arrived in Sydney to seek their fortunes in 1821 and acquired extensive land on the Hunter River— their combined estate, Glendon, reaching 10 000 acres. They bred blood horses and by 1832 had over 300. Their brother Alexander Walker Scott made a series of financially disastrous voyages to the colony with his ship *Australia* before settling in 1831 on a grant of land which he had previously obtained on Ash Island. The Scotts' widowed mother and only sister accompanied him to Sydney. Robert Scott 'entered fully into the social and political life of the colony's exclusivists'. An active supporter and initiator of 'attempts to reduce the depredations of Aborigines and bushrangers', he arrogantly defended the Myall Creek murderers in 1838. Gipps marked the government's disapprobation by removing him from the magistracy. Glendon was a 'cultural centre' in its time but Robert was extravagant and at the time of his death, unmarried, in 1844, his brother Helenus was left almost penniless by the depression and the failure of the Bank of Australia. Walker Scott built Newcastle House on the harbour front in 1837 and established a forge and foundry, as well as the salt works on Mosquito or Moscheto Island, described by Lady Franklin. *See* Jane Franklin, Diary, 3 June 1839 (p. 141). Another brother, David, arrived in the colony in 1835 and married Maria Jane, daughter of Major Barney, who became a celebrated artist. *See* N. Gray, 'Scott, Robert and Helenus', in Pike, vol. 2, op. cit., pp. 428–429; N. Gray, 'Scott, Alexander Walker', in Pike, vol. 6, op. cit., pp. 93–94.

192 Alexander Brodie Spark (1792–1856), merchant.

193 The Rev. George Keylock Rusden arrived in Sydney in 1834 with his wife Anne and 11 children, and became the rector at Maitland. His family became well known and highly respected in the district. He died in 1859. His daughter Sarah later married Helenus Scott and their daughter Rose became a prominent feminist.

194 Charles Grant (1778–1866) was appointed Secretary of State for the Colonies in April 1835 and created Baron Glenelg in May. Unpopular in the colonies for his refusal to allow constitutional reform, he had resigned in February 1839. News of his resignation did not reach Sydney till early June.

195 'I wish,' wrote a correspondent from Maitland to the *Colonist*, regarding Mr Grant, 'you would send us some one in the shape of a Police Magistrate, Mr Grant having absconded for the last three weeks, and no one to act regularly in his stead; in fact the public interests are sadly neglected for want of an efficient Police Magistrate at Maitland.' (*Colonist*, 1 June 1839.)

196 The name of Edward Charles Close (1790–1866) is 'indissolubly linked with the foundation of the Church of England in the Hunter Valley'. As a lieutenant in the army in the Peninsular War, Close vowed that if his life

were spared he would build a church as a thank-offering. In 1817 he arrived in Sydney with a detachment of his regiment and a few years later he was transferred to Newcastle. In 1822 he resigned from the army to settle on his 2560 acre grant at Morpeth at the head of navigation of the Hunter River. He was a magistrate until he was removed for his uncooperative attitude in the affair of Lieutenant Lowe, but in 1829 he was appointed to the Legislative Council. He assumed the position reluctantly and resigned in 1838. In 1836 he built a local school, and in 1837, in fulfilment of his vow, his son laid the foundation stone of St James' Church of England, for which Close gave the site and met all construction costs. The church was consecrated by Bishop Broughton in December 1840. *See* N. Gray, 'Close, Edward Charles', in Pike, vol. 1, op. cit., pp. 231–232.

197 James Backhouse and George Washington Walker, both Quaker missionaries, visited penal settlements, missions and houses in most of the scattered Australian settlements between 1832 and 1838. From 1835 to 1837 they produced three reports for Governor Bourke on the penal settlements of New South Wales. Throughout the settlements they held large public meetings and distributed tracts, promoting temperance and Aboriginal protection committees. They approved Threlkeld's missionary work.

198 Kenneth Snodgrass (1784–1853), a veteran of the Peninsular War, was appointed as Major of Brigade in Sydney, arriving with his wife and six children in 1828. As a serving military officer he was not entitled to any grants of land, and this he bitterly resented, both for the contrast with the generous town allotments made to civil officers and because he had repeatedly assumed extra duties without payment. He was selected to act as Lieutenant Governor of Van Diemen's Land between the departure of Colonel Arthur and the arrival of Sir John Franklin (October 1836 – January 1837) and again to act as Governor of New South Wales between the departure of Sir Richard Bourke and the arrival of Sir George Gipps (December 1837 – February 1838). Soon after his arrival, Gipps realised that Snodgrass had on both of these occasions drawn the full salary allowed for the positions, although the Colonial Office ruled that he was entitled only to half. Snodgrass refused to repay anything, claiming instead that he should be paid for earlier duties for which he had received nothing. The controversy lasted over two years and was settled when the government allowed him a grant of £755 for his extra duties, retaining the funds in satisfaction of its own claims. In 1839, with this dispute still in full swing, Snodgrass sold his commission and retired to his estate, Eagleton, near Raymond Terrace.

199 Sophia Susannah Close née Palmer (1803–1856) was 36 years old when the 47-year-old Jane Franklin passed these unkind remarks. She was the daughter of John Palmer (1760–1833) who had arrived in Sydney with the first fleet as purser of the *Sirius* and was appointed Commissary in June 1791. A loyal supporter of Governor Bligh's cause, he was among those dining with him at Government House on the night of the Rum Rebellion. His fortunes thereafter were shaky until during the 1820s he acquired considerable estates.

200 Carmichael's neighbour James King had planted vines in 1832 and made his first wine in 1836. King's great success inspired imitation and experiment by other Hunter Valley settlers and marked the early development of this as a notable wine-growing region. *See* Jane Franklin, Diary, 1 June 1839 (p. 138), and footnote 212.

201 The Rev. Henry Carmichael (died 1862), schoolmaster and educational theorist, was engaged as a tutor by the Presbyterian clergyman, J.D. Lang, for the Australian College in Sydney. Lang, who had earlier considered and rejected the alternatives of cooperating with the exclusivist Anglican Bishop Broughton in promoting secondary education, or supporting the nondenominational Sydney College, had resolved, upon coming into some property, to establish his own Presbyterian secondary school. On a visit to England in 1830–1831 he engaged three schoolmasters, Carmichael among them. The Australian College opened soon after they all reached the colony in October 1831. Carmichael broke with Lang at the expiry of his contract, and set up his own school, the Normal Institution. Lang had previously intended Carmichael to be editor of the *Colonist* and he was also offered, but rejected, the editorship of the *Sydney Monitor*. In 1833 he founded the Sydney Mechanics' School of Arts, 'the first of its kind in the colony'. He left Sydney to become assistant surveyor in the Hunter River district and, like King, became a pioneer in viticulture on his property at Porphyry Point. He was a strong advocate and disseminator of advanced educational ideas, distilling his views from the writings of Jeremy Bentham (whose name he gave to one of his sons), George Combe and Johann Pestalozzi— whose school in Switzerland Jane Franklin had herself visited with much interest in 1814. Strongly anti-clerical, he believed that education, rather than doctrine, would help man to develop moral and religious feeling, and in 1836 denounced Lang for sowing 'the seeds of Sectarianism and hateful bigotry' into the national character. The Australian College survived with ups and downs until 1854; the Normal Institution continued after Carmichael left Sydney under the superintendence of Mr Gordon. *See* G. Nadel, 'Carmichael, Henry', in Pike, vol. 1, op. cit., pp. 210–211; *see also* D.W.A. Baker, 'Lang, John Dunmore', in Pike, vol. 2, op. cit., pp. 76–83.

202 Adam Smith's *An Inquiry into the Nature and Causes of the Wealth of Nations* (London: W. Strahan and T. Cadell, 1776), is probably the most celebrated work of political economy ever written.

203 'Government men' refers to Carmichael's convict labourers; George Combe's, *The Constitution of Man Considered in Relation to External Objects* (Edinburgh: John Anderson, 1828), provoked violent opposition upon its publication because it was seen as inimical to revealed religion.

204 Carmichael's *Hints Relating to Emigrants and Emigration* was published in London in 1834 and ran to three editions.

205 Tahlee House was the residence of the successive commissioners of the Australian Agricultural Company, established in the early 1820s to take up one million acres of land. The company was managed in New South Wales

by a local committee dominated by the Macarthur family. Robert Dawson, engaged as chief agent for the company in 1824, had reached Sydney with stock in November 1825 and, under pressure from the local committee, hastily took up his million acres at Port Stephen. The humid coastal pasturage proved unsuitable for stock, and his attempts to build his flocks were foiled by the committee, which persistently foisted on him old and diseased sheep at high prices. When he refused to continue to accept this stock the Macarthurs accused him of extravagance and incompetence and suspended his appointment in 1828. He published a rebuttal of these charges and returned to England to press for justice, but was never granted a full hearing. His place was taken in 1829 by Sir William Edward Parry, an Arctic explorer and good friend of Sir John Franklin. Parry found the land poor and morale low, but during his four years in Australia secured fertile land on the Liverpool Plains, made good the losses of the company and restored the confidence of servants and proprietors. Parry was in turn replaced in 1833 by Henry Dumaresq, the brother of Governor Darling's wife Eliza, who had come to Sydney as Darling's private secretary in 1825. Dumaresq died at Tahlee House in March 1838 and his widow, Elizabeth née Butler-Danvers, returned to England a few years later with her children. Though she had remained at Tahlee House for some time after his death, Captain and Mrs King were now facing the challenge of making a vacant house habitable. The Australian Company (as Lady Franklin consistently calls it) was unpopular not only for its vast acreage but also for the monopoly it claimed on all mining in the colony. Only a few individuals—among them Captain Westmacott and the Rev. Threlkeld—had managed to make an income from mining on their properties in defiance of the company's claim.

206 Intermarriage knit close webs in colonial society. Captain King's sister Mary had married his wife Harriet's brother, Robert Copeland Lethbridge, and now lived near Penrith. Lady Franklin had previously met the wife of a Lethbridge cousin in Sydney. King's sister, Maria, had married Hannibal Macarthur, one of the directors of the Australian Agricultural Company, and to this connection King owed his place as shareholder and commissioner in the company. Macarthur's daughter, Anna or Annie, was now visiting her uncle at Port Stephens. Captain John Clements Wickham, to whom she was engaged, had previously served under King during a survey expedition off the coast of South America. He was now in command of the *Beagle*, charting the north-western coasts of Australia.

After her return to Sydney, Lady Franklin wrote to her husband: 'The "Beagle" I think I told you, after being driven far to the Southward, went into Port Stephens for shelter, much to the amusement of Sir George and all the world; Miss Annie Macarthur (Captain Wickham's love) being on a visit there to her uncle Captain King. She is a very charming person indeed.' (Letter, Jane Franklin to John Franklin, 15 June 1839.)

Their marriage did not take place until 1842, after Wickham had retired in ill health from the navy and settled in New South Wales.

207 Captain King was in fact just 47 years old, nine days younger than Jane Franklin herself.

208 Now Karuah.

209 'At Port Stephens, the whole of the coal beds have been thrown off, and a beautiful rosy porphyry rises to the surface.' *See Bailliere's New South Wales Gazetteer and Road Guide: Containing the Most Recent and Accurate Information as to Every Place in the Colony: With Map,* comp. R.P. Whitworth. Sydney: F.F. Bailliere, 1866.

210 Captain King was appointed to the Legislative Council in February 1839 and was appointed Resident Commissioner to the Australian Agricultural Company soon afterwards. Gipps induced him to retain his seat in council until October 1839 but was then advised to accept King's resignation.

211 William Macquarie Cowper, born at Sydney in 1810, was the son of William Cowper, the strongly evangelical minister of St Philip's Church from the time of its completion in 1809, and his second wife Ann née Barrell. After completing his education at Oxford, and spending some years in Dartmouth as a curate, he returned to New South Wales as chaplain to the Australian Agricultural Company, and remained in the Port Stephens district until after his wife's death in 1854. Within a few years he moved to Sydney, and after his father's death was made Dean and Archdeacon of Sydney. He died, still in office, in 1902.

212 James King (1800–1857), no relation to Captain King, set up as a merchant in Sydney in 1827. Soon after his arrival he obtained a grant on the Williams River near Raymond Terrace, which he called Irrawang. In 1831 he drew the attention of the authorities to the value of the white sand in dunes along the South Head Road, for glass manufacture, and although it proved not to be commercially viable to export the sand he was awarded a silver medal by the London Society of Arts and Manufactures in 1837 for his discovery. Around 1835 he settled at Irrawang, where he manufactured pottery. But King's main interest was in his vines, which he planted in 1832. In 1836 he made his first wine, and with the help of expert workmen, whom he imported from Europe in the 1840s, he gradually improved the quality of his wines. By the 1850s these received recognition in Europe. King is credited as a pioneer in viticulture, one of the first to achieve significant success, whose example 'encouraged experiment by many of his neighbours'. *See* D.S. Macmillan, 'King, James', in Pike, vol. 2, op. cit., pp. 54–55.

The Australian Agricultural Company was not the only neighbour to be annoyed by his fences. During 1839 he was also involved in a dispute with Colonel Snodgrass, who broke a boundary fence which King had erected. An exchange of correspondence ended in Snodgrass writing an angry letter, on the basis of which he was charged with attempting to provoke a duel and fined in the Supreme Court. The disputes continued throughout at least the next decade, with Snodgrass persistently attempting to gain right-of-way through Irrawang.

213 *Bailliere's New South Wales Gazetteer and Road Guide* (op. cit., p. 408, issued in the 1860s) notes that by that time the breakwater connected Nobby's Island to the mainland. It adds that 'a few years ago' the island was partly demolished for the erection of a lighthouse—before which it was a 'picturesque feature' of Newcastle, and a 'geological … frontispiece' for the district.

214 Jane Franklin, Diary, 28 May 1839 (see p. 130), and footnote 190.

215 Wilton accepted this invitation and became a correspondent of the Tasmanian Society.

216 Coming down the river from Raymond Terrace after dark the previous evening, Lady Franklin had taken the large wooden building of the salt works, with a tall brick chimney rising from its roof, for an isolated island with a tower on it. The works supplied Sydney with salt.

217 Wilton's *Australian Quarterly Journal of Theology, Literature and Science,* a journal he founded and edited in 1828, ran to four issues.

X: *Interlude: Sydney, 4–13 June 1839*

218 Publicly, Gipps praised King for his 'ingenuity, enterprise and perseverance'. *See* Pike, vol. 2, op. cit., p. 54.

219 In a letter home Lady Franklin wrote of this too-hasty return:

> After a hurried and somewhat unsatisfactory visit [to the Hunter], during which we took a hasty peep of Captain King at Port Stephen, without having time to see the Company's establishments, we returned to Sydney in time to be ready for the Bishop, who, we understood was to be ready for us on the 6th—but in the mean time, the papers proved to us that he had made engagements beyond that date at home, and we soon concluded that he could not leave till after the first day of the meeting of the Legislative Council on the 11th. Had we known this before hand we should not have left the Hunter so soon and should have spared Sir George the trouble of entertaining us alone while his wife was still ill and keeping her room. (Letter, Jane Franklin to John Franklin, 15 June 1839.)

220 'Reading' in Milliss typescript.

221 George William Evans (1780–1852) surveyor, arrived at Port Jackson in 1802. He was appointed Deputy Surveyor in Van Diemen's Land in 1812, but Macquarie's need for his services in New South Wales continually drew him away until the end of 1818. By this time land surveys were in serious arrears and the administration of the department remained lax. When Arthur became Governor in 1824 he alleged that Evans was involved in bribery and illegal sale of Crown lands and endeavoured to force him from office. The accusations seem to have been baseless, but Evans retired from office on grounds of ill health before an enquiry could be instituted, and

left for England in 1826. In 1832 he returned to Sydney, set up as bookseller and stationer, and became drawing master at The King's School in Parramatta, but the old scandal continued to haunt him. In 1844 he returned to Hobart, where he died in 1852.

222 Frances Trollope, *The Vicar of Wrexhill*. London: Richard Bentley, 1837.

223 This is a reference to Gipps whose father was the Rev. George Gipps, a clergyman at Ringwold, Kent, in England.

224 Several of the people Lady Franklin met or heard of in Sydney made their way in time to Hobart. In a letter home she warned her husband of some impending visits:

> I suppose the French musicians are at Hobarton. Sir George told me they were horrible. They contrived to get up one concert at Sydney, but their after attempt was a total failure, as well as their French plays ...

> We shall also have visits soon from Count Strzelecki, a most agreeable Pole, and from Mr Clark from China, a person Sir George seems to hold in particular consideration. Lady Gipps said she heard we kept a great deal of company. I assure you we do keep twice as much as they do. (Letter, Jane Franklin to John Franklin, 15 June 1839.)

225 This page of the diary has been badly torn making some sentences hard to decipher.

226 This painting has been tentatively identified with one signed by the artist which was found by a London dealer around 1975 and acquired by the Australian National Gallery in 1979. Inscribed on the back as 'Gunbal (alias Judy), third Gin of Moravanu, Chief of the Wig Wigley tribe, County St Vincent NSW Sept 1 1838', it presents, despite the ethnological title, 'a romantic vision of the Aboriginal woman as a lady of fashion—silk turban, hair dressed in bangs, lips and cheeks rouged, gold necklace & *décolleté* possum-skin cloak—and as such is unique in Australian art'. N. Parbury, 'Wilson, James Armstrong', in Kerr, op. cit., pp. 864–846.

227 As the younger son of an earl.

228 Captain Harding, a friend of Sir John's, was in command of the *Pelorus*, then visiting Sydney.

229 Presumably the new Government House under construction.

230 The management of convict labour and particularly the issue of convict discipline were matters of recurring interest to Lady Franklin.

231 The Australian Museum owed its existence to the efforts of Alexander McLeay, who, as Colonial Secretary, was the 'driving force' behind the annual grant of £200 made by the British Government to the colony in 1827 to found a colonial museum. McLeay administered the small museum until a governing committee of superintendents was appointed in 1836 and the enterprise was renamed the Australian Museum. In 1837 Dr George Bennett, a Sydney naturalist, was appointed as secretary and executor. *See* Moyal, op. cit., p. 76.

232 At this point the diary disintegrates into minute and random jottings for several days. In a letter home, Lady Franklin described her visit to Alfred Stephen in more detail:

> We have at the express invitation of Mrs Alfred Stephen, crossed the water to the north shore of the bay where they live in great seclusion and where a breakfast or luncheon was prepared for us. They were entirely alone and seemed extremely happy ... He seemed exceedingly amused in telling us of the extraordinary curiosity and interest I and my achievements excited in Sydney on his arrival. He believes people called on purpose at his hotel to ask questions about me; and they were exceedingly surprised to hear of and see such a different sort of person from what they expected. They evidently expected (though Mr Stephen did not distinctly tell me so) a stout, sturdy and perhaps masculine person. Of course he assured me they found me a most 'delightful' creature. (Letter, Jane Franklin to John Franklin, 15 June 1839.)

233 James Dunlop (1793–1848) arrived in Sydney in November 1821, with Carl Rümker, as an assistant for the observatory established by the Governor, Sir Thomas Brisbane, at Parramatta. During the 1820s, Dunlop made numerous detailed observations, published in W. Richardson, *A Catalogue of 7385 Stars: Chiefly in the Southern Hemisphere, Prepared from Observations Made in the Years 1822, 1823, 1824, 1825, and 1826, at the Observatory at Parramatta, New South Wales, Founded by Lieutenant-General Sir Thomas Makdougall Brisbane.* London: Wm Clowes and Sons, 1835. In 1831 he was made Superintendent of the Parramatta Observatory, which had been taken over by the government. By 1837 he was suffering from ill health and his activity had notably declined. He was not recalled, but retired to his farm at Brisbane Water in 1847, where he died the following year.

234 Robert Wardell (1793–1834) spent ten years in the colony, where he was for some time editor of the *Australian*, established a lucrative legal practice, and speculated profitably. In September 1834 while inspecting his estate at Petersham he was shot by a party of convict escapees. His body was found the following day. Two convicts were later hanged for his murder.

235 Edward Deas Thomson, Colonial Secretary and Bourke's son-in-law.

XI: *Excursion to the Hawkesbury, 14–29 June 1839*

236 Quotations from Letter, Jane Franklin to John Franklin, 15–16 June 1839.

237 Thomas Cooper Makinson (1809–1893) arrived in Sydney in 1838 in response to an appeal for more clergy for Australia, and soon took up parish duties at Mulgoa. He established a boarding school of 12 pupils at his parsonage, and was highly respected as a parish priest. In 1848, critical of the apostolic nature of the Church of England, he converted to Catholicism, later becoming Archbishop Polding's secretary and confidant. Of his twelve children three died in infancy, and the six who were born at Mulgoa were baptised Anglicans by their father but became Catholics, with their parents, in 1848.

238 William Cox (1764–1837) had arrived in Sydney as a lieutenant and paymaster in the New South Wales Corps in 1799. He acquired land first at Dundas and then on the Hawkesbury (on the estates of Clarendon and Fernhill) where he was a popular magistrate. He supervised the building of the first road across the Blue Mountains, and received the first grant of land west of the mountains in recognition of this work. He died in 1837. Three of his sons lived for many years in the Mulgoa Valley; his second son, James, took up a grant of 6000 acres in Van Diemen's Land at Morven, which he named Clarendon after his father's home, and became a prominent Van Diemen's Land pastoralist and member of the Legislative Council from 1829 to 1834.

239 A despatch from Sir George Gipps to Lord Stanley, dated 19 July 1842, may explain some of this appearance of ill feeling. Gipps reported to the Secretary of State for the Colonies that on his arrival in Sydney he had learned that the bench of magistrates at Penrith had long been pressing for the appointment of a paid police magistrate for the district. In 1838, in response to their application, he appointed to the position David Dunlop, formerly of Coleraine, who came highly recommended by the Irish Government. Later he discovered that what the magistrates had really wanted was that one of their own number, Robert Copeland Lethbridge, should be appointed to the position. This, wrote Gipps, 'would in reality have been nothing more or less than what is commonly called a JOB', as it would simply have been paying Lethbridge to maintain order in his local community, which, as a justice of the peace, was already his duty without payment. After such a beginning, it was perhaps not surprising that Dunlop should find himself in frequent disagreement with the bench of magistrates in Penrith, and Gipps was relieved when later in 1839 a committee of the Legislative Council determined that there was no need for a paid magistrate at Penrith. He transferred Dunlop to Wollombi and persisted in his principled stand against Lethbridge's appointment. *See Historical Records of Australia*, vol. 22, op. cit., pp. 158–159.

240 Sir John Jamison (1776–1844) arrived in Sydney in 1814 to look after estates he had inherited from his father, a surgeon's mate on the first fleet. By the 1820s he was one of the largest landholders in the colony, with extensive property in the Penrith region. Regentville was his principal estate. He had seven children by his housekeeper, Mary Griffiths, whom he married in 1844, several months before his death.

241 Lieutenant William Cox, after emigrating to Sydney in 1804, had returned to England and served in the Peninsular War. In 1813 he married Elizabeth, the daughter of Captain John Piper, and returned to Australia in 1814. By 1816 he had purchased the estate to which he gave the name of Hobartville, and the new house was finished in about 1828. He died at Hobartville in 1850. *See* H.C. Baker, *Historic Buildings: Windsor and Richmond*. Sydney: State Planning Authority of New South Wales, 1967, pp. 56–59.

242 In the original manuscript detail follows here of William Cox's children and their marriages.

243 Samuel Marsden, Anglican chaplain and magistrate at Parramatta, had died in 1838, survived by one son and five daughters.

244 In a note Lady Franklin pursued genealogy with enthusiasm:

> Mrs Blatchford, mother of Mrs Berwick whom we saw at Hobartville & who is wife of a lawyer at Windsor, & of Mrs Comack, married second time to surgeon at Windsor, but whose first husband was the old paymaster Cox father of all the present ones—the younger half brothers of the Cox family have their home with her at Windsor. (Jane Franklin, Diary: 'Gossip from the Hawkesbury', undated note.)

245 For more detail on Archibald Bell, see Jane Franklin, Diary, 27 June 1839 (p. 167), and footnote 257. His wife was one of Mr North's daughters, and his sister was married to George Cox.

246 A diary note may explain Lady Franklin's refusal of this invitation:

> The present portion of 80th Regiment at Windsor are not visited by married families in neighbourhood, owing to the officers living improperly, unmarried—Colonel Baker is here. Major Christie on account of his wife requested to be sent elsewhere than to Windsor. These new officers have lately arrived from England—former portion of 80th were better. (Jane Franklin, Diary: 'Gossip from the Hawkesbury', undated note.)

247 St Matthew's Anglican church at Windsor is one of Francis Greenway's most admired works of architecture. For further detail see Broadbent and Hughes, op. cit., pp. 57–58; and for a discussion of the rectory (built 1822)—the design of which is also sometimes attributed to Greenway, though he never claimed authorship—see pp. 82–83. Cox and Lucas, op. cit., p. 146, suggest the rectory may have been designed by Henry Kitchen.

248 Some family papers of Rev. H.J. Stiles of Windsor are held at the Mitchell Library, State Library of New South Wales.

249 'Father' in Milliss typescript.

250 In a note, Lady Franklin commented on Snachall's view of the colony: 'Snachall has been asked 20 times if VDL is not a much finer place than this—she answers, she likes it a great deal better.' (Jane Franklin, Diary, undated note.)

251 In a letter commenced on this day Lady Franklin wrote candidly to her husband of her conversations with Bishop Broughton concerning various colonial governors:

> I remarked to the Bishop that I thought Sir George had always great confidence in himself. He said he had and that it was the most valuable element of character. He did not allow that Sir Richard Bourke possessed the same high quality; he leant much upon the opinion of others and those were all on one side. On my comparing Bourke and Arthur, he said Col. Arthur was cunning and mysterious in a much worse way than Bourke; indeed he seems to regard him as a much

inferior man. Sir Richard was a good scholar. Col. Arthur was very ignorant—ignorant he believes even of the history of England ... The Bishop, who certainly has a strong predilection for this Colony in preference to ours (which is natural and even proper as he lives in it) says Sydney is free from the petty feeling which exists in Van Diemen's Land as respects this country. 'In fact,' he says, 'except when they want grain, I do not believe they ever think of Van Diemen's Land.' This was not very complimentary. I told him that certainly many people arrived from Sydney giving greatly the credit to our Colony, at least they told us so. 'They think it will be acceptable,' he said. 'Colonel Arthur laid himself out for such compliments, for the praises of Van Diemen's Land, and was angry with every one who did not prefer it. Consequently people paid their court to him in this way.'

Don't let us subject ourselves to the same weakness. I do assure you that Sir Geo. Gipps is above any feeling of the kind, though his sensitiveness on the subject has been a little tried,—not by me however. It would be unhandsome indeed, if enjoying his hospitality and treated with such distinguished honor, I were to seek any occasion of crowing over some real or fancied superiority. I am much more disposed to strain every nerve that our colony may keep pace with this in its rapid march of improvement.

Sir George, it is evident, is very desirous to render his reign illustrious by noble and useful works. He said the other day in shewing me the Bath house at Parramatta, that that was the only thing Sir Thomas Brisbane had ever done during his Government ... 'I never allow of any difficulties,' he says. 'The great secret of being useful and successful is to admit of no difficulties.' (Letter, Jane Franklin to John Franklin, 20–21 June 1839.)

252 Cyrus Matthew Doyle came to Sydney as a boy in 1803 after his father, Andrew Doyle, was exiled for life for his part in the Irish uprisings in 1798 and 1801. Andrew Doyle acquired extensive land on the Hawkesbury, near Lower Portland. His four sons also held property on the Hawkesbury and eventually throughout northern New South Wales and southern Queensland. Cyrus had five children by his first wife, Frances née Bigger, and three children by his second wife, Elizabeth née McDougall, whom he married in 1828. Until 1839 they lived on their farm, Ulinbawn, at Sackville Reach—later that year they moved to Doyle's estates near Maitland, though as Jane's diary entry here indicates, they retained the property at Sackville Reach, leasing it to tenants.

253 Now Gronos Point.

254 Kurrajong.

255 Robert Forrest (1802–1854) arrived in Sydney in January 1832, having been appointed to a colonial chaplaincy and the headmastership of The King's School, Parramatta, founded by Broughton in 1830. Forrest opened the school in temporary quarters in 1832 with 12 pupils and by November had 41 boarders and 12 day scholars. He resigned in June 1839 because of

ill health and in July assumed duties as minister in Campbelltown. The King's School fell on hard times in the 1840s. Forrest returned to it in 1848 and had a hard struggle to revive it.

256 It was probably on this day that the bishop took leave, having invited Lady Franklin and Sophy to stay with them on their return to Sydney the following Tuesday.

257 Archibald Bell (1804–1883) 'discovered' a new route across the Blue Mountains in 1823 (by following the directions of an Aboriginal woman), via Richmond and Mt Tomah into Hartley Valley. 'Bell's Line of Road' (the name it still bears today) proved too arduous for general use until several deviations from the original line were made. Bell later established an estate, Corinda, near Singleton, and in 1849 moved to estates at Milgarra in the Hunter Valley.

258 'Mrs William Cox' in original manuscript.

259 The letter Lady Franklin here summarises was one she did not receive until some days later. In writing up her diary (obviously retrospectively) she may have included it here partly to show how misjudged had been her decision to return with speed to Sydney—and partly to show how many of the bishop's recommendations they accomplished in Parramatta, without the benefit of his advice.

260 The bishop's judgment is repeated by J.V. Byrnes who states that Thompson's life and work 'illuminate many aspects of life in early Australian history'. Thompson (1773?–1810) was transported for theft, arriving in Sydney in 1792. He joined the police force in 1793, and was appointed to Green Hills (later Windsor) in 1796. Pardoned in 1798, he rose quickly to the position of Chief Constable which he held until 1808. Meanwhile he gradually accumulated land in the district by purchase and grant, established a store, an inn, a toll bridge, a brewery, a ferry and a tannery, and built or acquired five ships. By 1806 he was the wealthiest settler in the colony. Governor Bligh appointed him to develop his two model farms in the Hawkesbury region; their success and prosperity led to accusations of corruption on the part of the governor and were a factor in Bligh's arrest. Under the rebel regime, Thompson was dismissed from his position as Chief Constable but continued to prosper, and was restored to favour by Macquarie, who appointed him magistrate at Green Hills and trustee, with fellow emancipist Simeon Lord and the chaplain Samuel Marsden, of the new turnpike road between Parramatta and the Hawkesbury. Marsden, a bitter opponent of Macquarie's emancipist policy, refused to act with Lord and Thompson on the grounds that they were immoral. Thompson died a bachelor in October 1810, possessed of an estate worth around £20 000. J.V. Byrnes, 'Thompson, Andrew', in Pike, vol. 2, op. cit., pp. 519–521, quotation p. 520.

261 James Druitt (1775?–1842) formerly a major in the 48th regiment and civil engineer on Macquarie's public works program, held extensive land grants between Penrith and Parramatta.

262 Lady Franklin had mentioned Mr Forrest's imminent retirement in her diary. *See* Jane Franklin, Diary, 26 June, 1839 (p. 164).

263 In contrast, K.J. Cable suggests that he had 'a reputation for sternness'. *See* 'Forrest, Robert', in Pike, vol. 1, op. cit., p. 402.

XII: *Sydney Again, 30 June –16 July 1839*

264 *Sydney Gazette*, 11 and 18 July 1839.

265 Between 1817 and 1822 King had made four surveys of northern and north-west Australia in the cutter *Mermaid*, with Allan Cunningham as botanist. Cunningham (1791–1839) had arrived in Sydney in 1816. His efforts as botanist and explorer in New South Wales from this time until 1831, when he returned to England, resulted in significant discoveries. In 1837 he returned to Sydney as Colonial Botanist, but 'found the duties … uncongenial, objected to superintending "the Government Cabbage Garden" where among other things he was expected to grow vegetables for the governor's table, and resigned after a few months' to resume his botanical collecting. In October 1838 he returned from a visit to New Zealand dangerously ill, and died of consumption on 27 June 1839. Soon after her arrival in Sydney, Jane Franklin noted in her diary some reports of Cunningham and his illness, and added, 'He was described as a delightful person'. (Jane Franklin, Diary, original manuscript, 20 May 1839.) *See* T.M. Perry, 'Cunningham, Allan', in Pike, vol. 1, op. cit., pp. 265–267 (quotation p. 267).

266 John Gould (1804–1881) is thought to have begun life as a gardener, through which occupation he was drawn to the study of birds and plants. He joined the staff of the Zoological Society of London at the age of 23, and became a noted ornithologist and zoologist. In the 1830s he produced a series of books on birds and mammals, illustrated by his wife Elizabeth, née Coxen, a talented natural history artist. In 1838 the Goulds made an expedition to Australia, arriving in Hobart in September. John Gould then spent some months visiting New South Wales and South Australia while Elizabeth remained in Hobart, staying at Government House, where she gave birth to a son who was named Franklin, after the governor. She and Lady Franklin were on terms of warm friendship.

267 Alexander Berry (1781–1873), merchant and landowner, possessed extensive property at Shoalhaven. He had developed business interests in the colony in partnership with Edward Wollstonecraft, whose sister, Elizabeth, he married in 1827. Edward Wollstonecraft died unmarried in 1832, and left his property, including his north shore cottage, Crows Nest, to Elizabeth. The Wollstonecrafts were niece and nephew to the feminist Mary Wollstonecraft, and sought to escape her notoriety through travel. Alexander Berry has been described as conservative in his social views but a man of intelligence and wide reading, with an interest in the geology and geography of the country. He was 'interested' too in Aboriginal society, but expressed this interest by making a collection of Aboriginal skulls.

268 John Edye Manning (1783–1870) had been Registrar of the Supreme Court since 1829. He was also Curator of Intestate Estates but by the time Lady Franklin met him was experiencing financial difficulties which would later cause him to default on the payment of trust money.

269 Alexander Brodie Spark (1792–1856) arrived in Sydney in 1823 and quickly established himself as a successful merchant, also acquiring extensive land on the Hunter River and a number of houses in Sydney. Tempe, at Cook's River, containing a farm, orchard and vineyard, was his favourite 'country residence' and he managed to retain it even after his prosperity was destroyed in the 1840s depression. He died there in 1856. *See* 'Spark, Alexander Brodie', in Pike, vol. 2, op. cit., pp. 461–463.

After seeing Lady Franklin at the Queen's Birthday Ball, Spark had written in his diary that she was 'by no means the Amazon proposed, but a gentle affable woman'.

270 Miss Williamson had accompanied the Franklins from England as governess to John's daughter, Eleanor.

271 The *Religious Establishment Act 1836* was introduced on purpose to finance the building of churches in the rapidly expanding settled areas of the colony. St Peter's Church at Cook's River was 'among the most interesting churches' erected as a result. Designed by Thomas Bird, it was one of the first serious attempts at archaeological Gothic style in Australia. See Cox and Lucas, op. cit., pp. 172 and 174. The building of this church was actively supported by Alexander Spark. It was consecrated in 1839.

272 Mr Steele, in addition to his clerical duties, was tutor to Sir George's son Reginald.

273 William Cowper took up duties as minister of St Philip's Church in 1809. His second wife Ann, née Barrell, was the mother of William Macquarie Cowper, whom Jane had met at Port Stephen. After her death in 1831 William Cowper married for a third time. Noted for his extreme evangelicalism, in 1848 he became Broughton's first archdeacon.

274 Jane Franklin was indeed a firm believer in the cutting of women's hair as a punishment, and she seems here to be moderating her views out of courtesy. In August 1841 she wrote indignantly to the Quaker prison reformer, Elizabeth Fry, about the insufficient punishment of women who became pregnant out of wedlock. After being cared for throughout their pregnancies, she wrote, they were returned to the Female Factory:

> You will ask what is the nature of this punishment with which she is now to be visited, and may perhaps suppose that on re-entering the prison where, in compassion to her situation she was before treated with tenderness, instead of severity some signal mark of the reprobation in which her offence is held, will be inflicted on her. You might conclude perhaps that she is subjected to that most harmless yet most efficacious of female punishment, the being deprived of the ornament of her hair … Oh! no! (Letter, Jane Franklin to Elizabeth Fry, 3 August 1841, in Mackaness, Part II, op. cit., p. 24.)

275 In 1838 Jane Franklin had purchased 640 acres of land on the banks of the Huon River and spent an additional £300 building a vessel to service the needs of the little colony she planned to establish. Her aim was to encourage free immigration by enabling farmers of modest means to buy land upon easy terms. The land was valued at 10s 6d per acre and the occupant had seven years to pay off the debt. Lady Franklin interviewed all applicants herself, assessing morals as well as (or perhaps more than) suitability for the hard life of pioneer farming. In August 1839 she noted contentedly in her diary the good reports she was receiving from her manager of the 'progress and prosperous condition of the settlement'. Settlers did not, however, have an easy time, and as with all of her projects, Lady Franklin received a mixture of praise and blame. Every inch of the heavily timbered land needed to be cleared, and some found the terms and conditions too gruelling.

The outcome, for James Wilson, was not happy. He accepted Lady Franklin's offer of land and moved with his family to the Huon River, but in the backbreaking conditions the Wilsons suffered further hardship and for a second time returned broke to Sydney. In 1844 Wilson returned to London with his family but his hopes for the patronage of the Franklins were disappointed, presumably because they were occupied with Sir John's final and fatal Arctic expedition. Wilson soon returned to New South Wales where in 1852 he drowned in a shipwreck with his wife, all but two of his children and all his possessions and paintings. See Kerr, op. cit., pp. 864–866; Fitzpatrick, op. cit., pp. 239–240.

276 J.H. Plunkett's *The Australian Magistrate* (Sydney: Gazette Office, 1835), was the first Australian legal practice book, and encouraged uniformity of procedure in the inferior courts. Presumably Lady Franklin wanted copies of her husband's narratives of his Arctic voyages to the shores of the Polar Sea to distribute as mementoes to her new friends. J. Franklin, *Journey to the Shores of the Polar Sea: In 1819, 1820, 1821, 1822, with a Brief Account of the Second Journey in 1825, 1826, 1827.* London: John Murray, 1829.

277 The gardener at the botanical gardens—already referred to as a beneficiary of Cunningham's will. See Jane Franklin, Diary, 2 July 1839 (p. 176).

278 Sir James Gordon Bremer had recently returned to Sydney from Port Essington where he had been in charge of an expedition to promote the revival of a northern trading station. In October 1838 he had established a post named Port Victoria but though this flourished for several years it was abandoned in 1849 because of hurricanes and tropical illness. Jane Franklin's diary for these early weeks of July contains considerable commentary on Sir Gordon Bremer's impressions of Port Essington, as Gipps deputed her to read Bremer's journal of his expedition. But since her comments consist of summary and hearsay, and do not relate to her own experience, they have been omitted from the present edition.

279 This refers to an earlier short-lived attempt by Bremer to establish a trading post in the same area, which lasted from 1824 to 1829.

280 During the late 1840s and the 1850s Lady Franklin and Lady Gipps, by then both widowed, maintained a friendly relationship in London.

281 William Horatio Walsh (1812–1882) had been appointed in London in 1838 as Colonial Chaplain to Van Diemen's Land. There was some confusion about his official destination, however, and when he landed in Sydney in December he was retained as minister to the penal establishments, and in April 1839 licensed to the new parish of St Laurence. He was ordained as a priest by Bishop Broughton at St James' Church on 22 September. He would later become noted for his constructive efforts on behalf of the poor and underprivileged.

282 Sir James Dowling (1787–1844) was Chief Justice of the Supreme Court of New South Wales and had been knighted in 1838. Overworked and underpaid, he collapsed while on the bench in June 1844 and died the following September when on the point of embarking on a passage home for his health. Of his second wife Harriet, Lady Franklin picked up the following gossip at Windsor:

> Lady Dowling is a daughter of Mr Blaxland, Member of the Legislative Council. She was the widow of Mr Ritchie of the mercantile house of [illegible] & Ritchie which failed in India—he died of drinking after first being separated from her—She had 3 children by him, 2 sons of whom one is gone to England to prepare for bar & a daughter married to Mr Boydell. She is in 40th year & a grandmother—has a sister of about 35, unmarried, one married to Mr Walker of Rhodes (plain & a great talker) one in ill health gone with her mother also a great talker to Rhodes—Sir James Dowling by his first wife had a daughter married to Mr Blaxland brother of Lady Dowling who was thus sister & mother in law together—2 unmarried daughters are not yet come out. (Jane Franklin, Diary: 'Gossip from the Hawkesbury', undated note.)

Voyage Home

283 Letter, Jane Franklin to John Franklin, 15 June 1839.

284 Jane Franklin, Diary, original manuscript, 18 July 1839. This and all the quotations on the following pages are from the original manuscript.

285 Jane Franklin, Diary, 21 July 1839.

286 Jane Franklin, Diary, 1 August 1839.

287 Jane Franklin, Diary, 6 August 1839.

288 Jane Franklin, Diary, 13 August 1839.

289 Jane Franklin, Diary, 7 August 1839.

290 Jane Franklin, Diary, 11 August 1839.

291 Jane Franklin, Diary, 13 August 1839.

292 Jane Franklin, Diary, 13 August 1839.

293 Jane Franklin, Diary, 15 August 1839.

294 Jane Franklin, Diary, 9 August 1839.

295 Jane Franklin, Diary, 19 August 1839.

296 *Murray's Austral-Asiatic Review*, 20 August 1839.

297 Ibid., 27 August 1839.

298 *Hobart Courier*, 23 August 1839.

299 *Sydney Monitor*, 6 September 1839.

300 *Murray's Austral-Asiatic Review*, 1 October 1839.

301 *Australian*, 27 August 1839; reprinted in *Murray's Austral-Asiatic Review*, 1 October 1839.

302 Ibid.

303 Ibid.

304 E.M. Miller, *Pressmen and Governors: Australian Editors and Writers in Early Tasmania*. Sydney: Sydney University Press, 1973 (facsimile of 1952 edition), p. 34.

305 *True Colonist* (Hobart), 4 October 1839.

306 Ibid.

307 *Colonial Times*, 8 October 1839

308 Ibid.

309 Letter, Jane Franklin to John Franklin, 20–21 June 1839.

310 Letter, Jane Franklin to Mary Simpkinson, 13 February 1839, Scott Polar Research Institute (MS248/175/5).

311 Fitzpatrick, op. cit., p. 357.

Select Bibliography

Primary Sources

Bailliere's New South Wales Gazetteer and Road Guide: Containing the Most Recent and Accurate Information as to Every Place in the Colony: With Map, comp. R.P. Whitworth. Sydney: F.F. Bailliere, 1866.

Jane Franklin, Manuscript Diary of an Overland Tour to Sydney 1839, *with* Sir John Franklin, Diaries and Letters 1837–1859. Manuscript Collection, National Library of Australia (MS114).

Jane Franklin, *The Illawarra Diary of Lady Jane Franklin, 10–17 May 1839,* ed. Michael Organ. Woonona, New South Wales: Illawarra Historical Publications, 1988.

Jane Franklin, [Diary of Jane, Lady Franklin 1839 April 3 – August 19]. Typescript prepared by Roger Milliss [1990]. Manuscript Collection, National Library of Australia (MS6642).

Sir John Franklin, Diaries and Letters 1837–1859. Manuscript Collection, National Library of Australia (MS114).

Papers of the Gell and Franklin Families, Mitchell Library, State Library of New South Wales (FM4/1550).

Edmund Charles Hobson, Diary of a Journey with Lady Franklin's Party, Overland from Melbourne to the Hume River. La Trobe Library Manuscript Collection, State Library of Victoria (Box 25/1, M383/09).

G. Mackaness (ed.), *Some Private Correspondence of Sir John and Lady Jane Franklin (Tasmania, 1837–1845).* Part I and II. Sydney: D.S. Ford, 1947.

J. Maclehose, *Picture of Sydney and Stranger's Guide in New South Wales for 1839.* Sydney: J. Maclehose, 1839.

George Augustus Robinson, *The Journals of George Augustus Robinson, Chief Protector, Port Phillip Aboriginal Protectorate.* Vol. 1. 1 January 1839 – 30 September 1840, ed. Ian. D. Clark. Melbourne: Heritage Matters, 1998.

Frederick Watson (ed.), *Historical Records of Australia.* Series 1, vol. 20. Sydney: Library Committee of the Commonwealth Parliament, 1924.

Secondary Sources

A. Alexander, *Obliged to Submit: Wives and Mistresses of Colonial Governors*. Hobart: Montpelier Press, 1999.

H.C. Baker, *Historic Buildings: Windsor and Richmond*. Sydney: State Planning Authority of New South Wales, 1967.

M. Bassett, *The Governor's Lady, Mrs Phillip Gidley King: An Australian Historical Narrative*. London: Oxford University Press, 1940.

P.W. Boyer, 'Leaders and Helpers: Jane Franklin's Plan for Van Diemen's Land', *Tasmanian Historical Research Papers and Proceedings*, vol. 21, no. 2, June 1974.

J. Broadbent and J. Hughes, *Francis Greenway, Architect*. Glebe: Historic Houses Trust of New South Wales, 1997.

M.F. Christie, *Aborigines in Colonial Victoria 1835–86*. Sydney: Sydney University Press, 1979.

C.M.H. Clark, *A History of Australia*. Vol. 3. Melbourne: Melbourne University Press, 1973.

P. Cox and C. Lucas, *Australian Colonial Architecture*. Melbourne: Lansdowne Editions, 1978.

G. Davison, J. Hirst and S. Macintyre (eds), *The Oxford Companion to Australian History*. Melbourne: Oxford University Press, 1998.

K. Fitzpatrick, *Sir John Franklin in Tasmania, 1837–1843*. Melbourne: Melbourne University Press, 1949.

J. Gipps, *Every Inch a Governor: Sir George Gipps, Governor of New South Wales, 1838–46*. Port Melbourne: Hobson's Bay Publishing, 1996.

J. Kerr (ed.), *The Dictionary of Australian Artists*. Melbourne: Oxford University Press, 1992.

J. Kociumbas, *The Oxford History of Australia*, Vol. 2: *1770–1860*. Melbourne: Oxford University Press, 1992.

J.M. McMillan, *The Two Lives of Joseph Docker*. Melbourne: Spectrum Publications, 1994.

E.M. Miller, *Pressmen and Governors: Australian Editors and Writers in Early Tasmania*. Sydney: Sydney University Press, 1952, 1973.

R. Milliss, *Waterloo Creek: The Australia Day Massacre of 1838, George Gipps and the British Conquest of New South Wales*. Sydney: University of New South Wales Press, 1994.

A. Moyal, *A Bright and Savage Land*. Sydney, New York: Penguin, 1993.

D. Pike (ed.), *Australian Dictionary of Biography*. Vols 1–2, 4, 6. Melbourne: Melbourne University Press, vol. 1, 1966; vol. 2, 1967; vol. 4, 1972; vol. 6, 1976.

R. Porter (ed.), *Rewriting the Self: Histories from the Renaissance to the Present*. London and New York: Routledge, 1997.

H. Proudfoot et al., *Australia's First Government House*. North Sydney: Allen and Unwin, 1991.

J.O. Randell, *Pastoral Settlement in Northern Victoria*. Vol 1: *The Coliban District*. Melbourne: Queensberry Hill Press, 1979.

W.F. Rawnsley, *The Life, Diaries and Correspondence of Jane, Lady Franklin*. London: Erskine Macdonald, 1923.

H. Reynolds, *Frontier: Aborigines, Settlers and Land*. Sydney, Allen and Unwin, 1987.

H. Reynolds, *Fate of a Free People*. Melbourne: Penguin, 1995.

L.L. Robson, *A History of Tasmania*. Vol. 1. Melbourne: Oxford University Press, 1983.

P. Russell (ed.), *For Richer, For Poorer: Early Colonial Marriages*. Melbourne: Melbourne University Press, 1994.

P. Russell, '"Her Excellency": Lady Franklin, Female Convicts and the Problem of Authority in Van Diemen's Land', *Journal of Australian Studies*, no. 53, 1997.

P. Russell, 'The Allure of the Nile: Jane Franklin's Voyage to the Second Cataract, 1834', *Gender and History*, vol. 9, no. 2, August, 1997.

P. Russell, *Displaced Loyalties: Vice Regal Women in Colonial Australia*. London: Sir Robert Menzies Centre for Australian Studies, 1999.

L. Ryan, *The Aboriginal Tasmanians*. St Leonards: Allen and Unwin, 1996.

A.G.L. Shaw, *A History of the Port Phillip District: Victoria Before Separation*. Melbourne: Miegunyah Press, 1996.

E. Windschuttle (ed.), *Women, Class and History*. Sydney: Fontana/Collins, 1980.

F.J. Woodward, *Portrait of Jane: A Life of Lady Franklin*. London: Hodder and Stoughton, 1951.

Index

Aaron, _Dr_ 135,140

Aboriginal Australians _see_ Aborigines

Aboriginal Protectors 26,28,212,214,239 _see also_ Chief Protector of Aborigines 'vulgar illiterate men' 28

Aborigines 61,203,212 _see also_ Baldinilla; Ball, John; 'blacks'; Jem; Joe; natives; Pangerang people; Trukanini; amusement with 62; and the police 54; cannibalism 53; 'civilisation' for 19,48; cruelty to 19,128; defence of their land 18; dispossession of 16,48; drinking blood 53; fear of 47,48,68,219; feast for 28; girl raised by settlers 54; grieving 78; languages 21,101,153; massacre of 128,238; Melbourne corroboree 28,214; mission to 237; on pastoral stations 11,14,58; sexual abuse of 47; shepherds killed by 11,220; skills of 19,63; treat snake bite 58; women and children 61–62,63,74,75,78

accidents 55,63

Adams, _Captain_ 131

Addison, _Captain_ 110

address presented in Melbourne 32,33,112,201,215–217

Adelaide 86

agricultural settlement in Huon Valley 9,252

alcohol _see_ drunkenness

Alligator, _ship_ 188

Allman, _Captain_ Francis 104,107

Alps, European 4

Anderson the Gardener 177,188

Andrews 76

Anglican church 15,106,114 _see also_ English church; Episcopal church Diocesan meeting 146

Antigua 6

Appin, _NSW_ 104,107

Arctic expedition, 1845 3

Argyll district 42

Argyll Stores 99

art purchases 178

Arthur, _Colonel_ George 6,25,155–156,198

'Arthur faction' 8

Arthur's Seat, _Victoria_ 27,35,37

assigned servants _see_ convicts—assigned

Auburn Street, _Goulburn_ 99

Augustus Caesar, _ship_ 111,179

Australian, _newspaper_ 12,88,109,201,202

Australian Agricultural Company 133,137,140,231,240–241,242

Australian Auction Company 80

Australian College 135,240

Australian Museum 244

Australian Research Council _vii_

Australian Stores 99

axes 82

Ayrcough, _Mr_ 163

Bacchus, _Captain_ 33

bacon 51,85

Baggebury, _NSW_ 76

Baldinilla 163

Ball, John 35

bananas 138,186

Banks, _Sir_ Joseph 119

bark hut 84,89

bark roofing 40–41,52

Barney, _Major_ George 110,115,192,230

Barney, Portia Henrietta née Peale 115,192,230

to Menaroo [Monaro] 123; washing 39,59; with catarrh 42,123

sheep stations 86

Sheldrake (Sam) 44,49,58,70,218

Shelley, *Mr* 84

shepherds 36,43,57,70,161; attacked by natives 47

Shoalhaven district 105,109

Sievwright, *Lieutenant* Charles 28,314

signal station, *Sydney* 113

Simpkinson, Mary 12,114,209

Simpson, *Mr* 29,32,33,35

Slack, Joe 58,59

Sloane St, *Goulburn* 99

small cart 50

Smith, *Major* 180

Smith, *Mr* 74

Smith, *Mr* James 35

Smith, *Mrs* 68,72

Smith's hut 72

Smyth, *Captain* G.B. 39,41,52,218

Smyth, *Major* 116

Snachall [servants] 11,26,51

Snachall, James 97,115,119,189,193,233 driving cart 39; tipsy 69,96,118,225

Snachall, *Mrs* [maid] 52,85,92,115,129,140,165,247 *see also* indifference of Lady Franklin 18; moved to hospital 192,194; taken ill 176,183,189,190,191; thrown off carriage 15,161; to be in tent 50

snake bite treated by natives 38

snakes 58,59,68,105; eradication scheme 9–10,13,59; Dr Hobson's dread of them 58,59; Dr Hobson shoots one 41

Snodgrass, *Colonel* Kenneth 134,135,139,239

Snodgrass, *Mr* 60

Snowy Alps 55

Snowy Mountains 63

spur winged plover 69

social inferiors 18

social vignettes 17,110

soil in Sydney 113; on the Illawarra 104; on Murrumbidgee 76

soldier bird 69

soldiers 52

Solomon, *King* 1,122

Somerset, *Mrs* 122

Sons of St Andrew 153

Sophia Jane, *steamer* 141

Sophy *see* Cracroft, Sophia

South Australia 86,205

South Creek, *NSW* 156,165

South Head, *Sydney* 114,175

South Head lighthouse 15,113,179

South Yarra 31

Sowerby, *Chaplain* 97,98,99

Spark, Alexander Brodie 175,179,181,238,251

specimens 142,172 *see also* birds, botanical specimens, fossils

spellings 21

spring cart 32

Squatter's Clock [kookaburra] 58

squatters 74,86

stage-coaches 131

Stanley, *Mr* 188

Stapleton, *Lieutenant* 70

station life 8

steam mill, *Goulburn* 98,101

Steele, *Mr* 180,181,182,186

Stephen, *Judge* Alfred 87,111,112,115,147,148,149,151,180, 183,185,223,245

Stephen, Eleanor née Bedford 112,223,275

Stewart, George 47,48

Stewart, *Mr* 100

Stiles, *Rev* 159,160

stockade, *Maitland* 131

stockman 84,93

stockyards 57,70,74

Stone Quarry, *NSW* 63

Stony Creek, *Victoria* 43

DR PENNY RUSSELL has been researching the life and life-writing of Jane, Lady Franklin for almost a decade. She is a senior lecturer at the University of Sydney, where she teaches Australian history, autobiography and scandal, and researches and writes on aspects of the figure of the 'lady' in the British empire in the nineteenth century. She is the author of *A Wish of Distinction: Colonial Gentility and Femininity* (Melbourne: University Press, 1994) and has published a number of articles on Jane Franklin. A full scale biographical study is nearing completion.